BEING ARAB

MCGILL-QUEEN'S STUDIES IN ETHNIC HISTORY
SERIES ONE: DONALD HARMAN AKENSON, EDITOR

MCGILL-QUEEN'S STUDIES IN ETHNIC HISTORY
SERIES TWO: JOHN ZUCCHI, EDITOR

Being Arab

Ethnic and Religious Identity Building
Among Second Generation Youth
in Montreal

PAUL EID

McGill-Queen's University Press
Montreal & Kingston • London • Ithaca

© McGill-Queen's University Press 2007

ISBN 978-0-7735-3221-2 (cloth)
ISBN 978-0-7735-3222-9 (paper)

Legal deposit third quarter 2007
Bibliothèque nationale du Québec

Printed in Canada on acid-free paper that is 100% ancient forest free (100% post-consumer recycled), processed chlorine free

This book has been published with the help of a grant from the Canadian Federation for the Humanities and Social Sciences, through the Aid to Scholarly Publications Programme, using funds provided by the Social Sciences and Humanities Research Council of Canada.

McGill-Queen's University Press acknowledges the support of the Canada Council for the Arts for our publishing program. We also acknowledge the financial support of the Government of Canada through the Book Publishing Industry Development Program (BPIDP) for our publishing activities.

Library and Archives Canada Cataloguing in Publication

Eid, Paul, 1971–
Being Arab: ethnic and religious identity building among second generation youth in Montreal / Paul Eid.

(McGill-Queen's studies in ethnic history. Series 2 ; 22)
Includes bibliographical references and index.
ISBN 978-0-7735-3221-2 (cloth)
ISBN 978-0-7735-3222-9 (paper)

1. Arab Canadian youth – Québec (Province) – Montréal – Social conditions. 2. Arab Canadian youth – Religious life – Québec (Province) – Montréal. 3. Arab Canadians – Québec (Province) – Montréal – Ethnic identity. I. Title. II. Series.

FC2947.9.A65E33 2007 305.892'7071428 C2007-900522-5

Typeset by Jay Tee Graphics Ltd. in Sabon 10.5/13

Contents

Introduction

Arab communities have been studied less than most ethnic groups in Canada. Since the first thorough sociological and historical mapping of these communities, Baha Abu-Laban's *An Olive Branch on the Family Tree* (1980), studies of Arab Canadians have been scarce. Even less attention has been paid to the second generation in Arab communities, which is hardly surprising given that, before the end of the 1980s, there was very little research at all, in Canada, on ethnic or religious identity building among children of immigrants. During the last two decades, however, research on ethnoreligious identity building among the second generation has burgeoned, though it still lags behind work conducted on the first generation. Drawing on a sample of Christian and Muslim youth of Arab origin attending cegep in Montreal, this book makes a contribution to the growing body of literature on ethnoreligious identity (re)construction processes among the second generation.

One common shortcoming of research in ethnic studies is that it fails to conceptualize the multilayered foundations of ethnicity. In postmodern fashion, recent research has tended to approach ethnicity primarily from a subjectivist standpoint in which subjects can freely "imagine" their ethnic bonds and self-definitions. In this volume, the ethnicity of Arab-origin youth is understood not only in terms of self-identification but also in terms of the subjects' integration into ethnically based sociocultural structures and networks. The underlying premise is that identity can, to varying degrees, be driven by socialization agencies that transmit shared patterns of collective meanings to individuals. In the case of second-generation Arab Canadians it is interesting to examine whether their ethnic self-concepts are sustained through ethnically based socialization processes, thus contributing to their incorporation into a shared ethnic culture, and integrated ethnic community.

It must be acknowledged that children of immigrants never mechanically replicate the cultural models and patterns to which they have been exposed. Rather, they draw on them to make contextual and multifaceted identity choices. As a result, Arab-origin youths are bound to revisit, even reinvent, the cultural scripts they are expected to pursue as actors enmeshed in ethnic groups and networks.

But which ethnic cultures and communities are at issue here? Indeed, the Arab world, far from being monolithic, comprises several subgroups divided along various national, religious, and denominational lines. Moreover, within each Arab nation-state, there are further ethnically based divisions leading to different group subcultures, allegiances, and solidarities. Many Moroccans and Algerians, for instance, give precedence to their Berber identity over national membership. In certain Arab countries, Kurdish and Armenian identities compete fiercely against national allegiances as a source of collective identification. Because of the plurality of subcultures and allegiances in the Arab world, my inquiry into the maintenance of ethnic identity is not about Arab identity per se but rather about what Arab-origin youth perceive to be "ethnic," or culturally different, in their self-identification patterns and sociocultural practices.

Nevertheless, focussing on the Arabs as a group can be justified for several reasons. One is the relative "sociological unity" of the Arab world, a unity that has been maintained, according to Abu-Laban (1980, 49, 1995, 203), in spite of cultural diversity and the fragmentation of the region into a score of politically independent Arab states. Most importantly, as heterogeneous as Arab communities may be, Arabs living in the West are confronted with the majority group's tendency to impose on them a one-size-fits-all label. This form of outside categorization forces the Arab diaspora to engage the notion of Arabness (critically) when negotiating their ethnic identity in a Western context.

I am also concerned with the significance of religion in the building of ethnic identity. More specifically, I examine whether religion operates as an "ethnic-like" identity marker, or group binder, among both Christian and Muslim youth of Arab origin in Montreal. The interplay between religion and ethnicity constitutes a largely neglected issue within ethnic studies (with perhaps the notable exception of Jewish studies). As Bramadat pertinently noted (2005, 18–19), although many people may have decided views about the respective parts played by religion and tradition in their beliefs, attitudes, and behaviours, a closer look into their narratives reveals that there is a considerable amount of intragroup disagreement (and at times contradiction) over which practices and norms are derived from religion and which from "traditions." For example, in many societies, the emphasis placed on the prematrimonial virginity of women is presented by some as a religious obligation, whereas others a deeply entrenched cultural tradition. These delineations between ethnicity and religion are drawn differently across social class and gender lines. What tends to remain invisible are the ideological struggles and power dynamics whereby certain norms and behaviours come to be socially construed as symbols of religious or cultural authenticity. I pay special attention to these concerns in the course of my investigation.

To what extent, in multicultural Canada, do religion and ethnicity overlap in the self-definitions that individuals and groups construct for themselves? The place occupied by religion in Canada, as in most other Western countries, is not what it used to be. Today, the various Christian churches that make up Canada's religious landscape are completely disengaged from state structures. In Quebec, however, up until the Quiet Revolution of the 1960s, the Catholic church exerted a profound influence over most institutions, both in the private and public spheres. Then, within less than twenty years, the close ties between Quebec's Roman Catholic church and the state had largely, if not completely, been severed, as the state was turned by francophone elites into a key lever for socioeconomic development and national assertion.

This secularization of state structures was not restricted to Quebec or to Canada. It occurred in varying degrees and at different times throughout the twentieth century in most Western and industrialized countries. This is not to say that the Church has entirely ceased to intervene in public affairs, quite the contrary. As Jose Casanova pointed out (1994, 2001), in many societies where religion and politics were disentangled as part of a modernization process, the Church, both through its most progressive and its most conservative elements, has recently made a comeback in the public arena, but this time as a civil society actor promoting its normative agenda, thus reinstating notions of morality and the "common good" into public debate. But as Casanova stressed, the main difference between now and the presecular era is that, today, religious rhetoric in the public sphere competes on an equal footing with various secular discourses (e.g., feminism, environmentalism, humanism) originating from civil society in an open struggle for social and political legitimacy. As a result, the Church, in most Western countries including Canada, has lost the prominent role it once played in the ideological making of the nation (Dobbelaere 1999; Lambert 1999).

Correlatively, the majority of Canadians of European ancestry do not consider religious membership to be intertwined with ethnic or national identity.[1] The same cannot be said, however, about many non-Western ethnic groups that became established in Canada during the post-1967 immigration period. Many of these groups migrated from formerly colonized countries where religion had just recently started to operate as a binding force that gave meaning to the postcolonial brand of nationhood. These migrants were coming from countries where religion had recently been reinstalled in state institutions as a reaction against Western secularism and liberalism, which were rejected as symbols of the colonial legacy. Most postcolonial Arab migrants to Canada fit this picture – though they are not the only ones.[2] Indeed in the post-1970s Arab world, Islam has come to play an increasingly crucial role in the redefinition of postcolonial national narratives, and in the making of public policies (Shukrallah 1994; Eid 2002; Esposito and Burgat 2003). The fact that, in most Arab countries, national narratives and Islam are now so closely interwoven makes it increasingly difficult for members of Arab Christian minorities to identify fully with the national communities to which they belong. Perhaps partly in reaction to this symbolic exclusion, religious minorities in the Arab world have tended even more to view *their* religion as an essential part of their own ethnic boundaries. Moreover, both the Ottoman Empire, which ruled the Arab world from the sixteenth century to the First World War, and later the European colonial powers greatly contributed to strengthening Arab Christian's denominational identities.

In Canada, the role played by religion in the construction of ethnic identity is likely to be different for Christian Arab Canadians than for their Muslim peers, especially in the context of September 11 and its aftermath. Because prejudicial representations of Islam often fuel Western perceptions of Arabs, it becomes harder for Canadian Muslims of Arab origin to dissociate their religious from their ethnic identity. Many of them may even mobilize religion as a structuring force to help in the building of a group identity. Christian Arab Canadians, on the other hand, share with their host society a wide range of religious beliefs and symbols. Nonetheless, they often strive to remain resolutely distinct from Western Christian denominations and communities. Moreover, within Middle Eastern Christianity there are several separate denominations (Maronite, Coptic, Melkite, Greek Orthodox, etc.), each giving rise to different group allegiances and solidarities. As a result, Christian Arabs often maintain their specific denominational identities and institutions upon migration to North America.

Whatever their religious affiliation, Arab immigrants living in the West often regard religion as a moral safeguard against Western mores and values, which are perceived as potential threats to the community's ethnocultural heritage. However, it can be expected that, as they become familiar with and develop a sense of allegiance to both their host society and their ethnoreligious groups, second-generation Arab Canadians will occupy a far more ambiguous position in the realm of competing identity discourses and models. This book, then, attempts to shed light not only on the intersections of ethnicity and religion among Arab-Canadian youth but also on the creative transformations performed by this group in the process of ethnoreligious identity building. There are two broader questions at issue: how do socially inherited ethnoreligious identities come to be "transplanted" in a migratory context; and, above all, how are they adapted by second-generation youth so as to make them fit the largely secularized cultural and identity models prevailing in Canadian society? As demonstrated by Reginald Bibby (2002), young Canadians today are overwhelmingly disengaged from religious structures and organizations. To what extent, then, are the children of Arab immigrants equally inclined to cultivate their religious identity outside of formally organized structures, or even to confine their religious beliefs to the realm of personal consciousness, as so many young Canadians do?

Gender traditions have become a key component in the merging of ethnicity and religion that took place in the post-1970s Arab world. As a result, within Arab communities settled in the West, traditional models of gender relations often serve as a cultural buffer that contributes to the retention of ethnoreligious identity and helps to maintain hermetic frontiers between "us" and "them." The relationship between religion, ethnicity, and gender has been overlooked by researchers in the realm of ethnic studies. Such a gap in the literature is problematic not only for studies of the Arab diaspora but also for those focussing on other non-Western ethnic groups that, for various premigratory reasons, draw as well on religion and gender as primary catalysts for the maintenance of ethnic identity (see for example Monisha Das Gupta's excellent 1997 study of religion, gender, and ethnicity among the East Indian community in New York City).

My inquiry, therefore, aims at determining the extent to which gender traditions act as ethnic or religious identity markers for young Canadians of Arab descent. It illuminates the discrepancies between the gender relation models internalized by Arab-Canadian youth and those prevailing among their parents. It should be kept in mind that the efforts of Arab parents to maintain gender traditions target daughters far more than sons, especially with regard to sexuality issues. It is thus important to take into consideration sex-based variations when examining how youth of Arab origin relate, and respond, to the recycling of gendered traditions into symbols of ethnic or religious authenticity.

Finally, this book pays close attention to perceived stereotyping, prejudice, and discrimination. As mentioned, in Western popular representations, individuals living in, or originating from, an Arab country are frequently construed as "Arabs." Needless to say, in the Arab world, individuals and groups can define themselves by making use of less globalizing categories, allowing for more complex and multidimensional identity constructions. They can play up and combine multiple identity labels, whether national, ethnic, or religious, that often prevail over the Arab label as a source of self-designation.

However, in the Western world in general and in North America in particular, the importance of the "Arab" category in the formation of Arab minorities' ethnic identity tends to be magnified. Arab-origin minorities are ascribed a prefabricated "Arabness" that they can hardly disregard since the notion lies at the centre of the system of representations through which the majority group conceives of its ethnicity. In other words, in a Western context, groups and individuals of Arab origin are often perceived by the majority group as Arabs, irrespective of national variations, let alone subnational ones. As a result, in order to be acknowledged by the host society, the individuals and groups so labelled are often forced to mobilize and identify as Arabs in order to present a self-definition compatible with the majority group's frame of reference.

In addition, in the West, the Arab and Muslim categories convey a series of negative stereotypes that are integrated into a coherent and self-referential system of representations. Thus, in Western popular imagery, Arab/Muslim and Western "civilizations" are often perceived as being informed by two antithetical cultural systems, the former leading ineluctably to bigotry, tribalism, religious fanaticism, and cultural backwardness, and the latter to democracy, liberal ideas, and freedom (see Said 1979).[3]

Furthermore, levels of anti-Arab and anti-Muslim prejudice, at any given time, fluctuate considerably according to national and international politics. In this respect, my study takes on particular relevance in the wake of the attacks on the World Trade Centre on 11 September 2001.[4] Since then, Arab and Muslim diasporas in the West have become even more exposed to ethnic and racial profiling, prejudice, and discrimination. In the aftermath of the attacks on US soil and the ensuing wars in Afghanistan and Iraq, Arab and Muslim minorities everywhere have received much unwanted attention, as the Arab or Muslim components of their ethnocultural background became suspect in the eyes of a great many Westerners. This upsurge in anti-Arab and anti-Muslim sentiment in the West resulting from international politics is by no means unprecedented: the Arab-Israeli conflicts, Iranian revolution, Gulf War, and terrorism committed by Arabs or Muslims (whether religiously or politically motivated) are all events that, once filtered through media lenses, have helped to generate and reinforce derogative generalizations about Arabs and Muslims as inherently violent and fanatical peoples. For all these reasons, in a Western context, Arab identity tends to be socially compromised and compromising for its holders.

The Arab label, however, also carries its own self-produced symbolism rooted in a rich history and language that can be traced back to the seventh century. As a result, and despite various subgroup allegiances and intergroup conflicts, a pan-national Arab identity and culture can be activated or discarded, made more or less salient, by those belonging to the Arab world and the diaspora, depending on the political, historical, and economic conjuncture, as well as subgroup and individual predispositions. Thus, although Arab identity can be activated or deactivated in reaction to prejudice and discrimination, it can also, quite self-sufficiently, provide individuals with the symbolic materials needed to construct their minority identity. Similarly, Muslims can also identify as members of the *Umma* (the universal community of Muslims), a self-ascription that, like Arabness, can act for some individuals as an overarching form of identity sustained by a common history and a shared system of meanings.

It is out of the interaction between self-produced and externally produced images of themselves that minority groups come to shape their group identity in a migration context. The last section of this book thus examines strategies among young Arab Canadians of reappropriation, reinvention, or rejection of the Arab label in relation to perceived prejudice and discrimination. I pay far less attention to the issue of perceived anti-Islam bias, not because I deemed it an unwarranted concern but because, for comparative purposes, I gave priority to the contrast between Christian and Muslim reactions to racialized images and exclusionary practices targeting them indiscriminately as Arabs. In any case, Arab and Muslim categories often overlap in popular representations, to the point where they sometimes become interchangeable. Therefore, Islam can hardly be left out of an analysis aimed at teasing out the social symbolism of Arabness; for it constitutes one of the most potent signifiers of Arabness in the Western mind.

BEING ARAB

The Arab Presence and Identity in Canada

HISTORICAL BACKGROUND OF ARAB IMMIGRATION TO CANADA

The Pioneer Cohort, 1882–1945

The pioneer cohort of migrants who came to Canada from what is known today as the Arab world arrived in the late 1880s with Turkish passports. Almost all of these first migrants came from the Greater Syria region, and more specifically from the mountainous regions of Mount Lebanon, which at the time were still under Ottoman domination (Suleiman 1999). The overwhelming majority of them were Christians affiliated either with the Maronite church, the Melkite church, or the Greek Orthodox church (Kayal 1983). The Muslim minority among these migrants established the first organized Muslim community in Canada, at Lac La Biche, Alberta, around the end of the nineteenth century (McDonough, Hoodfar 2005, 136).

The growth of the Arab-Canadian population was fairly rapid in the formative period of the community; by 1911 there were an estimated seven thousand individuals of Arab origin in Canada, both foreign-born and Canadian-born. From 1911 to 1941, however, the growth rate of the Arab-Canadian community slowed dramatically as Arab immigration dropped to negligible proportions. The decline in immigration resulted from two restrictive Orders-in-Council enacted in 1908 by the Canadian government. The declared objective of these laws was to reduce "Asiatic" immigration in general, and Hindi immigration more specifically. But Syrian-Lebanese immigration, which was included in the "Asiatic" category, was also greatly reduced as a result. The population of Syrian-born Arab Canadians grew only from 2,907 to 3,577 individuals in thirty years (B. Abu-Laban 1980).

Most of the early immigrants wanted to accumulate capital and return to their home countries and villages as soon as possible. They typically had little or no education, were often illiterate, and knew neither English nor French. Some of them worked as unskilled industrial labourers, but the large majority became peddlers or shopkeepers. They had nomadic pattern of settlement in the early years due to the business activities of the numerous peddlers among them. While many among the second and third generations of Syrian Christians followed in their father's footstep by becoming peddlers, many others turned to new and diverse occupations, thus undergoing rapid upward mobility.

Various factors contributed to the large predominance of Syrian-Lebanese Christians among the pioneer cohort of Arab immigrants to Canada. First, Syria was geographically very close to Istanbul and was thus subject to firmer control than other dominions of the Ottoman Empire. This led many Syrian-Lebanese to migrate for political reasons. Secondly, whereas the oppression endured by Muslim Syrians was toned down thanks to their religious affinity with the Ottoman administration, there was no such mitigating circumstances for Christian Syrians. Thirdly, denominational divisions between Christian minorities were deliberately exacerbated by the Ottomans, who played one church against another by designating each rite, both politically and socially, as a separate nation (called "Millet") endowed with relative autonomy over matters pertaining to personal status, such as divorce, marriage, and inheritance (B. Abu-Laban 1980). The Millet system set up institutional walls that hermetically divided the different Christian denominations one from another, fostering jealousy, rivalry, and suspicion. These tensions degenerated into interchurch conflicts that turned out to be a major contributor to Christian migration from Syria to North America. Another important push factor is the deplorable and harsh economic conditions faced by the inhabitants of the mountainous regions of Greater Syria (especially the region known today as Lebanon). These mountain peasants – many of whom were Christians – were driven to emigrate because of low agricultural productivity and the downfall of the silk industry in a context of high population growth (B. Abu-Laban 1980; Kayal 1983; Naff, 1983).

Finally, one of the most fundamental factors behind the large predominance of Christians among Syrian-Lebanese migrants to the New World is European colonial penetration into the region, which goes back to the nineteenth century. Even prior to the dismemberment of the Ottoman Empire, several European missionaries and traders were sent to the Greater Syria region under agreements between the Sublime Porte and certain European countries. Through their emissaries in the region, colonial powers such as France and England set up schools that drew large numbers of Christian locals who, in the course of their education, were strongly influenced by Western ideas and culture. On a more political level, European powers competed for influence throughout the tottering Ottoman Empire by exploiting the loyalties and interests of various Christian churches. Alexa Naff provides a partial overview of the nature of these politically motivated alliances: "In Syria, the French supported the Maronites and the Melkites; the Russians supported the Eastern Orthodox; and England vacillated between the Christians and the semi-Islamic Druze as its interests dictated. France encouraged a Maronite dream of political dominance and alienated Muslims, Druze, and the Orthodox Christians who tended then as now to support the Muslims in politics. In Egypt, England's support of the Copts antagonized the Muslim majority" (Naff 1983, 13).

European imperialists thus found fertile ground in which to cultivate denominational antagonisms between Christian minorities, which each hoped to benefit from these alliances in order to secure for themselves greater economic and political power. The Maronites of Lebanon are paradigmatic. As Naff suggested, their rapprochement with France was strongly dictated by their dream of securing a homeland for themselves in Lebanon. These strong nationalist sentiments are still at work today: the Maronites of Lebanon tend to identify strongly with the land they inhabit and harbour a distinct ethnoreligious identity that is inextricably tied to the history of the Lebanese state. Thus, in Lebanon and Syria as in other regions of the Arab world, denominational allegiances and loyalties (and even nationalism in the case of Lebanese Maronites) were largely fostered by European imperialist powers.

Furthermore, the higher socioeconomic status enjoyed by the Western-backed Christian minorities led them to behave arrogantly towards Muslim populations, which were already embittered by their subjugation to colonial powers. This situation antagonized Muslim majorities, whose own emerging nationalist discourses and identities were cutting across denominational interests. Consequently, Christian minorities often became natural targets for the Muslim majorities' growing anti-imperialist sentiments. Thus, not only did European interference accentuate rivalries and factionalism among the various Christian churches but it also begat hostility between Muslims and Christians (Naff 1983). The end result is that, by the end of the nineteenth century, the tradition of accommodation between Muslim majorities and Christian minorities had been seriously eroded, which accounts in large part for the first wave of Christian Syrian-Lebanese who migrated to Canada from the early 1880s up to 1945.

It is dubious, however, to speak of a Syrian or a Lebanese identity in North America toward the end of the nineteenth century since the early migrants' concept of nation was still rather weak. Although some thought of themselves as Syrians, the majority found a stronger source of collective identity in their ancestral village, their family, and, above all, their denominational affiliation (Naff 1983; Kayal 1983).[1] As a result, the ethnic consciousness of the newcomers was extremely feeble and fragmented since it was not rooted in the history of a nation-state that provided a unifying frame of reference. This disinclination to maintain ethnic identity was compounded by the immigrants' strong religious and cultural affinities with Western culture. The end result is that, according to most authors, pre-World War II Syrian communities in Canada and the US underwent high rates of acculturation from one generation to the next such that, following the first migratory wave, subsequent generations of Arab Canadians and Arab Americans rapidly lost their ethnic language (Suleiman 1999, 9), generally contracted interethnic marriages (Kayal 1983, 53), and became one of the least residentially segregated ethnic groups (B. Abu-Laban 1980, 63).

The only ethnocultural buffer on which early Syrian-Lebanese communities in Canada relied to ward off assimilationist pressures was denominational identity. But because of their sojourner mentality, high geographical mobility (thanks to peddling), and dramatic lack of priests, it was a while before the early migrants were able to institutionalize their faith, which they eventually did in Montreal and Toronto at different periods depending on each church.

The first Syrian Orthodox church, St-Nicholas, was founded in Montreal in 1905. The first Maronite church was established in the early 1920s, and the first Melkite church, Saint-Sauveur, came into being in Montreal in 1924.[2] The early Syrian-Lebanese migrants, however, had problems securing an institutionally viable community outside of the religious sphere. What's more, the maintenance of a viable ethnoreligious identity across generations was severely impeded by Syrian-Lebanese migrants' emphasis on economic prosperity and material wealth, which further increased their desire to be assimilated. Finally, Middle Eastern Christian churches were considerably weakened as a result of a sharp decline in their membership, which was trickling away to non-Arab churches that had been established for a longer time. While the Russian Orthodox church attracted the Syrian Orthodox, for example, the Latin churches recruited large segments of the Melkite and Maronite populations. Hoping to win back younger generations, several Syrian Eastern Rite and Latin Rite churches responded to disaffection and defection of the faithful by Westernizing and North Americanizing their services and rites. By doing so, ironically, they accelerated their own decline (Kayal 1983; Naff 1983). Furthermore, although collective identity among early Syrian migrants was for a while more or less successfully sustained through church-based solidarities and networks, this model soon became obsolete as the ethnoreligious culture it fostered became too superficial to require institutional support (Kayal 1983). Thus, by World War II, second, third, and fourth generations of Canadians and Americans of Syrian origin had turned into an ethnocultural group almost completely indistinguishable from the mainstream (Suleiman 1999).

Postwar Migrants: From 1945 to Now

While the overwhelming majority of the pioneer cohort came in relatively small numbers from Syria and Lebanon, Arab immigration to Canada increased dramatically after World War II. Of the 324,160 Arab migrants who came to Canada between 1882 and 1997, as many as 313,478, or ninety-seven percent, came after 1950; 273,535 came between 1970 and 1997 alone.[3] The postwar cohort was much more diverse in terms of national origins and migrated not just for economic reasons, as the earlier cohort had, but for political motives as well. The large number of Christian

Egyptians who migrated to Canada, along with a much smaller number of Egyptian Muslims, from the late 1950s through the 1960s, felt politically and religiously alienated by the socialist revolution undertaken by Gamal Abdel Nasser in 1952 (Hayani 1999, 286). In particular, many Coptic and Syro-Lebanese Christians emigrated from Egypt because they feared increasing discrimination. These latter groups, who had sometimes been associated with foreigners, were also affected by a series of nationalization laws passed in the 1950s and the1960s under the Nasser government (Assad 1995).

Lebanon can also claim a large share of the political refugees fleeing to Canada because of the civil war that was being fought from the mid-1970s through the 1980s. Thus, says Hayani (1999, 286–7): "The precarious balance that had kept in check volatile and explosive religious forces in Lebanon came apart with horrendous consequences for the Lebanese people in the mid-1970s. Ten of thousands of Lebanese came to Canada, where most already had relatives who could sponsor or nominate them. Some came under the new immigration category of business investors, and others came as refugees. Many of the latter category were probably of Palestinian origin."

While a large percentage of the postwar Lebanese immigrants to Canada were educated professionals, the civil war brought refugees of all educational levels and occupations. As a result, migrant and non-migrant Lebanese Canadians can now be found in managerial, professional, clerical, sales, and service occupations. Today Lebanese communities in large cities such as Montreal, Toronto, Ottawa, Edmonton, Calgary, and Halifax have attained a significant level of institutional self-sufficiency by means of ethnic clubs, schools, churches, organizations, and associations (Jabbra and Jabbra 1995).

The creation of the State of Israel in 1948 and the subsequent Arab-Israeli conflicts in the region (most notably the Six Day War in June 1967) produced overall around three million Palestinian refugees, of which significant numbers migrated to the US and Canada. Also, immigration from Arab Gulf countries, which was insignificant before 1945, grew substantially during the postwar period as eighteen thousand migrants came from that part of the world. Finally, immigration from Jordan, Syria, and North Africa also helped considerably to swell the ranks of postwar Arab migrants to Canada.

As mentioned earlier, one important characteristic of the postwar migratory wave is that it has been split more equally between Muslims and Christians, although Christians still formed the majority of immigrants of Arab origin during the 1945–67 period. Also, and this is fundamental, there are important class differences between pre-war and postwar cohorts. While most early Arab migrants arrived in Canada as unskilled and illiterate peasants, the postwar cohort comprised a large proportion of university students and university-educated professionals such as lawyers, professors, teachers, engineers, and doctors (B. Abu-Laban 1980; Naff 1983; Suleiman 1999). The Arab migrants, both Christian and Muslim, who came to North America between 1945 and 1976 were typically secular, largely Westernized, and had often been schooled in either Western or Western-type institutions. Contrary to the earlier cohort, their ethnic identity tended to be structured along national rather than religious lines. Moreover, large segments of the postwar cohort were under the influence of Nasser's Pan-Arabist ideology and were thus prone to identify themselves as Arabs, even as Arab nationalists (Abraham 1983; Suleiman and Abu-Laban 1989). According to most authors, Pan-Arab sentiments and identities were exacerbated by the creation of the State of Israel, by subsequent Arab-Israeli wars, and, above all, by the common thread running through these latter events: the Palestinian cause.[4]

In North America the formation of Arab-based ethnic bonds was fostered by the biases and hostility directed at individuals of Arab origin, irrespective of national, religious, congregational or other such differences. Indeed, Arab Canadians of various national origins and religious allegiances often found themselves lumped together in the media as one undifferentiated ethnocultural entity. According to Suleiman and Abu-Laban, the Six Day War marked the height of this cross-national Arab consciousness, both in the Arab world and within the Arab diaspora. This growing consciousness was informed by a desire to keep in check the disparaging stereotypes of the Arabs conveyed by most North American media in their treatment of Arab-Israeli conflicts and, later, the first Gulf War (1991). Among the unexpected consequences of the Six Day War and the subsequent blossoming of pan-Arab sentiments was a rapprochement between older and newer Arab-Canadian communities (Suleiman and Abu-Laban 1989; Haddad 1994; Suleiman 1999).

On the eve of the Six Day War, Christian Syrians and Lebanese of the second, third, and fourth generations were on the verge of "dissolving" as a distinct ethnic group into North America's mainstream ethnocultural fabric. But because the Palestinian issue was construed and presented in North American media as a question of Arab versus Jew, Christian Syrians and Lebanese were led to probe their history and ethnic identity in relation to other Arab groups (Kayal 1983, 55). As a result, several Canadians and Americans of Syrian and Lebanese origin who were largely incorporated into the cultural mainstream suddenly started to identify themselves as Arabs in order to be heard by a society that was continually confronting them as such. Other North American Arabs, however, preferred to de-emphasize their Arab origins, and to identify themselves in less socially compromised ways, by nationality, for example, Egyptian, Lebanese, Algerian, etc.), or religion (Coptic, Syrian Orthodox, etc.).

The Muslim Differentialists: From the 1970s On

By the mid-1970s a new cohort had begun to enter Canada and the US in increasing numbers, at a time when the flow of secular and Westernized Christian Arab migrants was declining. This new cohort of migrants comprised Muslim Arabs who were striving to "transplant" in their new Western environment a strong religious identity, either coexisting with, or in some cases prevailing over, national and Arab identities. This ethnic identity with strong religious overtones is largely a by-product of the post-1970s Islamic revival in the Arab world, a movement that grew stronger after the 1967 Arab military defeat by Israel. Whereas most Arab migrants coming to Canada between 1945 and the early 1970s were secular and highly educated, this new migratory wave included many semi-educated and religious migrants who felt the need to institutionalize their faith through the establishment of mosques and religious organizations. Furthermore, being strongly committed to maintaining an ethnoreligious identity rooted in an Islamized notion of culture, this cohort of migrants often rejected secularism and Westernization.

According to Yvonne Haddad (1983), the new Muslim Arab religious migrants tended to assign a strictly devotional function to mosques and religious organizations, compared to their secular American-born ethnoreligious peers of the second and third generations, whose participation in religious networks and mosques, if any, was often geared toward community binding. Further, the Muslim Differentialists' strong emphasis on gender segregation and traditional gender roles (both inside and outside of religious institutions) was off-putting to most second- and third-generation Muslim Arabs in Canada (Haddad 1983, 1994; S.M. Abu-Laban 1989). However, there are strong indications that Islam in Canada fails to take the prescribed universal form, as mosques in Toronto and Montreal tend to be divided along broad ethnocultural lines. For example, the Indo-Pakistanis and the Arabs each attend separate institutions (B. Abu-Laban 1983).

Finally, it should be mentioned that, since the 1970s, many mosques and Islamic organizations in Canada have been targeted by Saudi Arabia's transnational efforts at converting Muslims to their orthodox reading of Islam. The Saudi state embraces the puritanical Wahhabi doctrine, which is based on Hanbalism, the most conservative school of religious law within Sunni Islam. Outside Saudi Arabia, Wahhabism has been a minority movement and tradition, but it became influential in the 1970s after the oil revenues were used massively by the Saudi monarchy to finance the building of mosques throughout the world and organize the training of imams in the rigorous Wahhabi version of Islamic thought. Although not all Canadian Muslims support the Wahhabi orthodox religious doctrine – indeed, many are categorically opposed to it – the brand of Islam proffered within many Canadian mosques became increasingly political as a result of Saudi Arabia's funding and proselytizing activities (McDonough and Hoodfar 2005, 141).

Canadian-Born Arab Youth Today: Which Ethnic and Religious Identities?

The different brands of ethnic and religious identities carried on in Canada by previous migratory cohorts are likely to continue to colour the ethnoreligious self-concepts developed by today's Arab-Canadian youth. At present, the majority of second-generation Arab Canadians are children of immigrants who arrived in Canada in the late 1970s and in the 1980s, so the Muslims among them are likely to have an ethnic self-concept with significant religious underpinnings. In the Arab world, the Islamized brand of national identity flourishing among Muslim Arabs certainly helped to reactivate, among Christian minorities, a deeply entrenched tendency to retreat into their own ethnoreligious identities, which can always easily resurface depending on the conjuncture. Therefore at present, Christian Arab-Canadian youths also tend to hold on to an ethnic identity with marked religious undertones. However, the acute Westernization and Americanization undergone by Muslim and Christian second-generation Arabs is hardly consistent with a rigid conservative religious framework such as the one imported from the home country by their more traditional parents (Haddad 1994). In the following chapters, I shall explore how these youths reinvent the ethnoreligious traditions and identities of their parents in order to reappropriate them in a Western and more liberal context.

At the same time, certain external factors foster the (re)production of a transnational Arab ethnicity among the second generation. Some persistent aspects of the West's largely undifferentiated postwar view of Arabs and Muslims still help today to transcend subgroup differences among Arab Canadians and Arab Americans. Since the first Palestinian intifada (1988–91), for example, and especially since the Gulf War (1990–91), Arab villains have increasingly supplanted communist bad guys in Hollywood movies. In his compendium of all Western films with Arab or Muslim characters (2001, 2003), Jack Shaheen found that in Hollywood films, the traditional Arab stereotype of the rich, evil, and lecherous sheikh was gradually superseded, from the 1970s onwards, by that of the violent, fanatical Arab or Muslim terrorist who is often expressing hatred against Christians or Jews. Movies such as *Black Sunday* (1977), *Terror Squad* (1988), *True Lies* (1994), *Executive Decision* (1996), *The Siege* (1998), and *Rules of Engagement* (2000) all portray this type of Arab character (Shaheen 2003). Such prejudicial stereotypes – reinforced and fuelled by the media coverage of Middle Eastern politics – bolster transnational solidarities among Arab-Canadian youths of various national and religious backgrounds, who all find themselves confronted by negative biases directed against the "Arabs" construed as one monolithic and undifferentiated cultural entity. Again, though, others are likely to respond to derogatory ethnic prejudice and stereotypes by downplaying the Arab component of their identity.

NATIONAL IDENTITY IN THE POSTCOLONIAL ARAB WORLD: THE ROLE OF RELIGION

I argued above that the Arabs who have migrated to Canada since the 1970s are more likely, compared to previous cohorts, to hold on to an ethnicity saturated with religious references and meanings. Because the Arab-origin youth investigated here were born in Canada or arrived here before the age of twelve, most of them have parents who belong to the post-1970s migratory cohort and, as such, are more likely to have attempted to instil in their children an ethnoreligious identity. These second-generation Arabs could be inclined, in turn, to negotiate their ethnic identity by drawing on religion as well. It is thus useful to examine the sociohistorical conditions that contributed to the rise, in the postcolonial Arab world, of movements and discourses that have refashioned national and metanational narratives along religious lines. I will then discuss the implications of this revamped postcolonial Arab-Islamic identity for the Arab diaspora.

The colonial powers were driven out of Arab countries during the second half of the twentieth century, following wars of independence (as in Algeria and Morocco) or military coups that overthrew centuries-old monarchies (as in Egypt and Iraq). The pervasive influence of Western cultural models remained, however, exacerbating an identity crisis that permeated the Arab world. One of the most important catalysts of this identity crisis was the disruptive impact of modernization during the postcolonial era. At a time when national narratives were being revisited and purged of references to Western norms and culture, modernization, although certainly not a novelty in the region, became increasingly associated with a form of rampant neo-colonialism (Loomba 1998; Eid 2002). The movement toward modernization, which was initiated by the new ruling elites in order to emulate the technological and economic advances of the West, was coupled with the importation of non-indigenous behavioural norms and values. The process of "cultural colonization" was most noticeable within the small circle of the elite, who often indulged blindly in the mimicry of Western modes of dress and behaviour, which were considered by many to be contrary to traditional Arab-Islamic values and practices. This situation sharpened the gap between rulers and ruled, exacerbated the pronounced class differences related to the unequal distribution of economic wealth, and fed the social discontentment with the generalized corruption prevailing in state institutions. For all these reasons, the national self-narratives offered by postcolonial regimes and elites became unappealing to large segments of the increasingly pauperized and uneducated masses (Farah 1987; Dekmejian 1995; Loomba 1998).

From 1952 to the late seventies, the only ideology that almost succeeded in gaining social consensus as the framework defining a collective postcolonial Arab identity was the pan-Arabism of Egypt's General Abdel Nasser.[5] Secular and socialist, this ideology was aimed at preserving Arab culture and identity from Western influences. According to such authors as Raouf (1984), Mellah (1985), and Ajami (1987), Nasser's personal charisma was the main pillar on which the popularity of Nasserism was based, which explains in part why, despite the tremendous impact of this ideology throughout the Arab world, it never really outlived its founding father, who died in 1970. Furthermore, the Arab military defeat at the hands of Israel in 1967 was experienced by Arab masses and intellectuals as a humiliation that largely discredited the ruling elites of the time, including Nasser himself (Ajami 1987; Farah 1987; Karim 2003). While the Six Day War helped in the short term to set up Arab consciousness as an effective safeguard against anti-Arab sentiment, it was not enough to turn the notion of Arabness into a unifying and durable force.

The failure of pan-Arabism and Western-type liberalism to provide the principles needed to shape a postcolonial identity triggered a search for new normative grounds that might give meaning to the idea of "Arabness." Toward the end of the 1960s, a new religious nationalism emerged within this ideological vacuum, a nationalism asserting a collective identity freed from the remnants of the former "colonized" identity imposed by the West. Islamist discourses and movements became increasingly politicized and militant, advocating for the Islamization of social structures in both public and private domains. Furthermore, over the past three decades, and despite certain national variations, this religious nationalism led to the embodiment of orthodox Islam-based values in state institutions and in the family. Islam as a means of national assertion expressed the need of many natives throughout most of the Arab world to re-emphasize the value of their own ancestral traditions

TUNISIA

and customs that, under colonial domination, were systematically disparaged. Thus, with one notable exception,[6] one can contend that religion became interwoven with national selfhood in the post-1970s Arab world (Dekmejian 1995; Gelvin 1999; Baali 2004, 40).

This intersecting of religion with ethnicity is not limited exclusively to Muslim Arabs. The strong emphasis placed on Islam by dominant national self-narratives in the Arab world has helped, ironically, to make religion central to group identity building among religious minorities as well. The religious material shaping the self-narratives of Christian Arabs is drawn from their own reservoir of symbols and references, but the language in which they assert their identity tends to echo the language in which the majority group's own identity struggles and debates are encoded. This explains in part why, in postcolonial Arab societies, Christian minorities have not been immune to the ever-growing influence of religion on collective, as well as individual, identity building. Moreover, Christian Arabs tend to be excluded, and to exclude themselves, from these (postcolonial) national "great narratives" that are structured along Islamic lines. As a result, the Islamization of Arab societies' symbolic and institutional structures have alienated religious minorities from Muslim majority groups. This, in turn, has led to the increasing salience of religion within the identity structure of religious minorities.

To the extent that this recreation of a postcolonial identity in the Arab world should indeed be seen as a movement of symbolic emancipation from the West, the same dynamic is even more likely to be at work within Arab minorities striving to maintain a distinct identity and culture in a Western context. Thus, from the 1970s onwards, one can observe a shift in the type of ethnic identity cultivated by the average Arab migrant to the United States and Canada. Whereas Arab-origin migrants who came to North America in the 1950s and 1960s tended to be secular, Western educated, and inclined to assimilate into the host society, the post-1970s cohort actively attempted to retain an Arab or national identity that was solidly anchored in religion and tradition, or in "re-invented tradition" (Haddad 1994). It might therefore be argued that, among the post-1970s cohort of Arab migrants, especially when compared to the earlier cohort, religion can hardly be dissociated from national and metanational (Arab) group membership (Cesari 1998).

A SOCIODEMOGRAPHIC PROFILE OF
ARAB CANADIANS TODAY

As mentioned earlier, the Arab community in Canada is one of the least-studied ethnic groups. The paucity of literature on this group is hardly consistent with the important size of the Arab-Canadian population. Thus, according to the 2001 Statistics Canada census data, 370,975 Canadians claimed one or more ethnic ancestry related to what is considered geographically as the Arab world (e.g., "Arab", Lebanese, Palestinian, Moroccan, Maghrebi, etc.). Of these, 159,020 (42.9 percent) lived in Ontario and 145,810 (39.3 percent) in Quebec.[7] The third largest Arab community is located in Alberta, with 29,625 residents (eight percent) of Arab origin. British Columbia and Nova Scotia occupy the fourth and fifth places, with Arab populations of 15,695 (4.2 percent) and 2,035 (0.6 percent) respectively. Thus the bulk of the Arab population in Canada, 82.2 percent, is concentrated in Ontario and Quebec. In Quebec, as many as 91.1 percent of the residents of Arab origin are located in Montreal. This accords with the marked tendency of other ethnic minorities in the province to congregate in the Greater Montreal area (by contrast, only 48.2 percent of Arab Ontarians are Toronto residents). Therefore, by focusing exclusively on the Greater Montreal area, my research will yield results applicable to the overwhelming majority of Arab-origin individuals in Quebec.

According to 2001 census data, most Arab Canadians reported themselves to be of Lebanese (38.7 percent), Arab (19.3 percent), Egyptian (11.1 percent), Syrian (6.0 percent), Moroccan (5.8 percent), or Iraqi (5.2 percent) origin. Of this subset 51.2 percent were Christian and 40.0 percent Muslim, while 8.7 percent reported another, or no religion. Whereas historically Arab migrants have always been predominantly Christian, during the past two decades the Muslim-to-Christian ratio has slowly but steadily increased. The majority (58.9 percent) of Canadians claiming ethnic ties to the Arab world are immigrants, of which half arrived in Canada before 1991. The picture is not very different in Quebec's Arab community, where the six most commonly reported ethnic origins are Lebanese (33.6 percent), Arab (16.3 percent), Moroccan (12.0 percent), Egyptian (10.3 percent), Algerian (9.3 percent) and Syrian (7.2 percent) (Statistics Canada, *Census Data*, 2001).

If we look at recent Arab-origin migrants only – that is, those who arrived in Canada between 1996 and 2001 – it appears that, both in Canada (31.8 percent) and Quebec (28.4 percent), the "Arab" label constitutes the most commonly reported descriptor of ethnic ancestry.[8] At the national level, the second most commonly reported descriptor among recent immigrants is "Lebanese" (15.7 percent), followed by "Algerian" (12.4 percent) and Iraqi (11.2 percent). In Quebec, because of the provincial government's increasing preference for French-speaking migrants, "Algerian" (26.1 percent) and "Moroccan" (18.9 percent) now rank second and third. There are surely many reasons why the "Arab" designation has come to supplant nationality as the most common descriptor of ethnic origin among recent Arab migrants. One reason is that, within this cohort of Arab immigrants Muslims have come to outnumber Christians. Thus, during the 1981–91 period there was about one Muslim for every Christian among migrants from the Middle East and Western central Asia; the ratio jumped to 2.5 for the 1991–2001 period (Statistics Canada, *Census Data*, 2001). This factor alone, however, cannot account for the dramatic upsurge in popularity of the Arab label among recent migrants. It would be interesting to gather further information on the profile (nationality, religion, sex, class, etc.) of migrants who claim to be partly or solely of Arab origin. Certain context-related factors that may also come into play will be examined later in the book.

The Arab population in Canada is highly educated compared to the rest of the population:[9] in 2001, 24.5 percent of Arab-Canadian females and 33.0 percent of Arab-Canadian males aged fifteen years and older (the active population) held university degrees, compared to the national average of 14.9 percent for women and 16.0 percent for men. Similarly, while the proportion of Canada's active population that holds no more than a high school degree is 46.1 percent for females and 44.6 percent for males, the figures are only 40.0 percent for Arab-Canadian females and 31.3 percent for Arab-Canadian males. In 2001 the average income of Arab-Canadian males aged fifteen and over was $32,996, as opposed to $36,865 for Canadian males' active population, a difference of $3,865. Such discrepancies are very similar to those prevailing among women: the average income of Arab-origin females aged fifteen and older was almost $4,000 lower than the national average income of Canadian women: $18,970 as opposed to $22,885. It should be noted, however, that these figures do not take into account much-needed control variables such as Canadian job experience, knowledge of Charter languages, and education, all of which have considerable impact on income. Finally, in 2001 there were more males of Arab origin in Canada than females. In Quebec, for instance, the female-to-male ratio was 0.88 (Statistics Canada, *Census Data*, 2001).

2

Building Ethnic and Religious Identity

In this chapter, I expound on the theoretical foundations of my research, beginning with a discussion of the most recent theoretical debates on ethnic and religious identity construction and their contribution to our understanding of the "second generation".

DECONSTRUCTING ETHNIC IDENTITY

Ethnicity Revisited by Poststructuralism

Over recent years, theories of ethnic identity have been torn between two epistemological camps with very different views about the relative importance of the concepts of agency and structure. The first approach embraces the poststructuralist notion that ethnic identity formation results from a series of choices, decisions, creative transformations, and adaptations, leading to a largely negotiated and always moving identity. The second, more orthodox, approach posits a top-to-bottom relation between culture and agents. According to this perspective, certain external cultural frameworks supply actors with the normative, cognitive, and behavioural knowledge they need to form what comes to be seen as a largely ready made ethnic self. Of course, this debate is by no means restricted to the issue of ethnicity but takes place in the broader framework of group identity theories in general.

The poststructuralist perspective challenges classical theories of culture and identity on the ground that they regard notions of culture and identity as reified monolithic blocks. This traditional approach to ethnicity, argue the post-structuralists, rests on a fallacious assump-

tion that ethnic identities are derived from an all-encompassing ethnic culture, which is itself produced by a unified ethnic community.
For Gerd Baumann (1996), this discourse reduces sociocultural groups
to homogeneous and stable communities, which in turn delineate the
boundaries of stable and quasi-naturalized identity structures. In
contrast to the view that culture and identity are natural and fixed
entities, the anti-essentialist camp defines them as contextual and
dialogical processes that are continually renegotiated through history, personal experience, and subjectivity. Culture and cultural identities are a "production which is never complete, always in process ...
instead of an already accomplished fact" (Hall 1990, 222).[1] The
de-essentialized concept of culture relies on such epithets as "hybrid,"
"creolized," "hyphenated," which all aim at debunking the fiction of a
pre-given and reified culture from which the actors' ethnic or national
identities derive.

For most proponents of the anti-essentialist approach, the process of ethnic identity building performed by children of immigrants is bound to allow for negotiation, creative transformation,
and heuristic reappropriation. This argument needs to be taken into
account; for it rightly challenges the traditional view that members
of the second generation necessarily experience an identity crisis as
a result of being positioned in between two cultural camps that are
competing to gain their allegiance. Baumann remarks that the
expression "between two cultures," as applied to the children of
immigrants, is in keeping with the essentialist view of culture: "The
image it evokes is not of young people performing culture as a process of making sense of each other and of adult others, but of a
culture-less flock lost between two immutable objects named *cultures* (Bauman 1996, 212)." Baumann argues that what makes the
in-betweeness thesis most problematic is that it wrongly presup-
poses the existence of homogeneous and bounded cultures. Indeed,
the notion that children of immigrants are floating somewhere in
between two cultural blocks becomes obsolete once the idea of a
pure bounded culture has been rejected. Pina Werbner (1997),
acknowledging the full implications of such an argument, suggests
that the notion of "cultural hybridity," as applied specifically to
migrant youths, should be deserted as well, since by definition culture is hybrid. Similarly, Caglar rejects the notion of "cultural
hybridization" understood as a process by which elements from dis-
parate cultural systems are fully synthesized without their contra-

dictions and specificities being eroded. Therefore, in keeping with postmodernism, the term "ambivalence" is often substituted for hybridity in poststructuralist theories of ethnic identity (Werbner 1997). It is deemed that such a notion better reflects the fluid, unfixed, and equivocal character of postmodern identities, which are then seen as open fields in which actors are manoeuvring in response to their environments (Melluci 1997).

Once the notion of culture has been deconstructed with a view to exposing its fluid and ambiguous nature, research on the ethnic identities of migrant youths undergoes a radical shift: from the study of how migrant children are socialized into one cultural community or another, it is redirected toward strategies by which these children move away from the prefabricated ethnonational boundaries of host society and ethnic community alike. Although sociologically relevant in many respects, this "actor-centred" perspective should not be embraced uncritically.

To begin with, the antiessentialist approach to ethnic identity highlights how migrant youths can reappropriate the dominant social significations attached to ethnic categories. More generally, it emphasizes the social interstices through which the individual can pass so as to turn to his or her advantage the norms of the dominant discourse. This perspective derives from the notion that individuals are autonomous agents – rather than predetermined social beings – who are able to appraise and even transform social norms. It implies that actors are not bound to follow to the letter a prewritten "social script" but can improvise around it. In other words, the subjects are continually engaged in a (virtual) dialogue with the prescriptions attached to the social roles they are called to "play" – a process through which they can produce new creative interpretations of the dominant social norms (Werbner 1997; Melluci 1997; Calgar 1997).

That being said, the poststructuralist view that ethnic identity is a purely open space that actors can shape and transform at will in a social vacuum needs to be challenged. Proponents of this argument often claim to be indebted to Fredrik Barth's definition of ethnicity. In Barth's conception, "ethnic groups are categories of ascription and identification by the actors themselves" (Barth 1969, 10). But Barth never implied that ethnic categories were totally disconnected from the sociocultural environment in which actors are enmeshed. Rather, he argued that ethnic groups selectively draw certain defining characteristics from a pool of shared symbolic resources rooted in a common history. Once these characteristics are "socially activated," they become symbolic material available to members of the group for purposes of identity construction.

This perspective, to which my research is indebted, is largely in keeping with the "situational," or "contextual," approach to ethnicity as developed by such authors as Joane Nagel (1994) and Jonathan Okamura (1981). These authors, drawing on Barth's seminal work, recognize the unstable and changing nature of ethnic identity, which can take different forms depending on which culturally shared items are mobilized by individuals in their quest for meaningful self-definition. Ethnic identity then becomes a flexible structure that can be modified depending on the context in which actors perform social interactions. Thus, says Nagel (1994, 14–15), "as the individual (or group) moves through daily life, ethnicity can change according to variations in the situations and audiences encountered ... The chosen ethnic identity is determined by the individual's perception of its meanings to different audiences, its salience in different social contexts, and its utility in different settings." Culture must then be seen as a tool kit providing actors with various sources of meaning from which they can draw to create and recreate identities on a day-to-day basis. The notion of situational identity is particularly well suited for the study of ethnic identity formation among migrant youth. Children of immigrants indeed learn very quickly how and when to switch cultural codes appropriately depending on the different arenas in which they move (Wilpert 1989; Vertovec 1998).

However, although the construction of a social self requires a degree of personal latitude, the "negotiability" of identity is necessarily constrained by the pregiven symbolic universes produced by the social groups in which individuals have been socialized throughout their life. In other words, there is a finite set of meanings, roles, and discourses that people can activate for the purpose of identity formation. Various predetermined forms of sociality, based, for example, on ethnicity, gender, class, age, etc., all play a part in restricting the range of identity choices.

To sum up, poststructuralist theories of ethnicity, in stressing exclusively the almighty power of agency, fail to take into account the structural and external factors that restrict an actor's power to mould freely his or her ethnic self. The notion of a freely self-constructed identity must be refined to acknowledge the role played by the competing social roles that help to shape the identity choices people make in various contexts. In fact, the subjectivist/objectivist opposition may become irrelevant if ethnic identity is to be seen as the result of an interactive and creative dialogue between agents and the various sociocultural universes to which they have (collective) access. In the following section, I will sketch out a theoretical approach to ethnic consciousness that takes into account the power dynamics between personal agency, the ethnic community, and the majority group.

Self-Definition versus Outside Categorization

As stressed above, the situational approach to ethnicity avoids essentializing culture and identities, but it should not drift into an excessive subjectivism that overlooks the structural constraints on the power of actors to choose their identity. In particular, the position of one's group in the socioeconomic power structure, as well as the way members of the group are perceived by the host society, affect one's ability to adopt, or opt out of, ethnic labels.

In this respect, it must be kept in mind that the members of any ethnic group possess an ethnic self-concept that has both external and internal boundaries. Ethnic self-definitions (internal boundaries) should be analyzed in relation to the process of outside labelling and representations (external boundaries) whereby the majority group categorizes and perceives members of the categorized group (Juteau 1997, 1999a). Internal boundaries emerge through the shared memory and history that provide the ethnic group with the symbolic material it needs for the construction of its collective self ("us"). This process generates self-definitions that draw upon an inexhaustible reservoir of symbolic materials, of which certain items are selectively mobilized at different periods in order to provide the ethnic group with a historically situated self. Inversely, external boundaries consist of that part of an ethnic group's self-image that is defined through a (virtual) dialogue with the majority group. More specifically, external boundaries are formed *in relation* to the system of categories through which the majority group constructs and organize the ethnic group's cultural otherness. Furthermore, the external and internal sides of any group's boundaries are interrelated, cross-fertilizing each other in a dialectical relationship woven throughout history (ibid).

It should also be emphasized, following Colette Guillaumin (1972) and Christopher Jenkins (1997) that any form of majority/ minority relations entails from the outset symbolic violence as a result of social categorization. From this perspective, minority group members are construed as mere specimens of their group, for all their actions, speeches, and attitudes are perceived as manifestations of their group's essentialized cultural differences. In other words, the categorizing gaze of the majority group locks minority group members into an irreducible otherness, which is embodied in a cultural or physiological feature that is regarded as an expression of their quintessential being By doing so, categorization suppresses the multiple facets of minority group members' psyches and social selves, thus failing to acknowledge their humanity in all its complexity.

Members of ethnocultural and racialized minorities are particularly vulnerable to being assigned membership in broad categories that, first, are not always significant for the people so categorized and, second, obliterate the rich human and cultural diversity prevailing among the numerous subgroups encompassed by the category. Think for example of the following categories: "Black," "Asian," "Latino," "Hispanic" (in the US), "South Asians," or "Arab." These all help majority groups, in Canada and in the US, to translate minority groups' otherness into an intelligible and simplified language, one that conjures up stereotypical and socially recognizable features. But categorization is not merely affecting minority groups because of the generalization process it entails. Many of the stereotypes attached to ethnic and racial categories tend to be derogatory, or to carry a social stigma in popular imagery.

But what about the capacity of minority groups to resist the majority group's categorizing framework? On the one hand, minority groups tend to fight social categorization and stigmatization by raising the profile and bolstering the image of the stigmatized category (for example, women's liberation, gay pride, the US civil rights movement, etc.). Of course, the capacity for resistance varies depending on the political, economic, and symbolic resources at the minority group's disposal. Furthermore, groups that have been stigmatized often have the power to turn the negative stigma into a badge of pride. But they can hardly define themselves without reference to the ready-made categories bestowed upon them by the majority group.

They rather engage in counter-discourses of resistance by making use of the very same essentializing categories through which the majority group defines them (Guillaumin 1972; Gilroy, Hall 1991; Juteau 1999b). For instance, in the 1970s the state of race relations in the United States and Great Britain gave rise to a black movement that actually "learned" from racist discourses how to pitch against each other essentialized notions of "blackness" and "whiteness" as two antagonistic entities.

These theoretical assumptions are crucial to an understanding of the formation of Arab identity in a North American context, where ethnic profiling and categorization help to crystallize the notion of "Arab" into a "one size fits all" category used by majority groups to "imagine" Arab otherness. Arab Canadians can hardly remain neutral toward this pan-ethnic category as many of them embrace it proudly while others try to dissociate themselves from it, largely because of the stigma attached to it in the West. What's more, Western images of Arabs and Muslims largely overlap, fusing into a single integrated representational system. As a result, Muslim Arabs are led to negotiate their "Arabness" in relation to their Muslim identity since Islam and Arab cultures are inextricably intertwined in the majority group's popular imagery. Ironically, Christian Arabs find that their relation to "Arabness" is mediated by an Islam-laden categorizing frame of reference made up by the majority group.

Thus, the self-definitions delineating Arab consciousness – or any other form of ethnic consciousness – emerge through a complex "dialogue" with the majority group's system of representation. This points to the more general notion that self-definitions (i.e., internal boundaries) among minority groups cannot be properly understood without taking into account outside definitions (i.e., external boundaries). The last chapter of this book will investigate perceived stereotypes and discrimination, with a view to understanding how these perceptions influence the ethnoreligious consciousness of second-generation Arabs.

Ethnic Identity and Integration

At this point, it is important to theorize about the notion of ethnic identity in a more systematic manner, for there seems to be much confusion surrounding this concept in the literature. The most commonly found shortcoming is generally that the objective (behavioural) and the subjective dimensions of ethnic identity are not analytically differentiated. Following Isajiw (1974, 1997), Breton et al. (1990), and Isajiw, Sev'er, and Driedger (1993), I conceive of ethnic identity as a varying situational structure comprising both a subjective and an objective dimension. Whereas the former refers essentially to a sense of attachment to an "involuntary group" and its commonly shared cultural universe, the latter refers to the processes whereby individuals are socialized into one or more of these groups. The processes by which individuals establish subjective ties to one or more ethnic groups and their corresponding shared cultural universes (the subjective aspect of identity) should necessarily be analyzed *in relation* to the processes of sociocultural incorporation by which these same individuals become socially and culturally competent actors within one or more community (the objective aspect of identity). The rationale behind this approach is that a self-concept analyzed in isolation from the objective social processes in which it is rooted is of little sociological relevance. As Isajiw puts it, "locating oneself in relation to a community and society is not only a psychological phenomenon, but also a social phenomenon in the sense that the internal psychological states express themselves objectively in external behaviour patterns that come to be shared by others (1990, 35)." Such a definition allows researchers to take into consideration the complex dynamic that comes into play between these two processes. Even more interesting, from the perspective of research into the second generation, is that it allows identification of the possible discrepancies existing between the objective and the subjective aspects of ethnic identity (this point will be further discussed below).

Also, the phenomena encompassed by the subjective and objective aspects of ethnic identity relate to two different sorts of processes, social and cultural. The cultural domain of ethnic identity refers to the processes of learning, accepting, and internalizing some or all patterns of behaviour of one or more ethnic group (Isajiw 1974, 1997). The social processes pertain to the entrance of individuals into primary groups such as family and circles of friends, as well as into secondary groups such as systemic institutional organizations (economic, political, educational, etc.), and voluntary associations (cultural, professional, religious, etc.). These two sets of conceptual distinctions, subjective/objective and social/cultural, inform the notion of ethnic identity employed in this book.

Thus, the concept of ethnic identity includes, on the one hand, the (subjective) commitment to an ethnic group and its culture and, on the other, the (objective) processes of socialization by which one becomes familiar with one's ethnic culture and is incorporated into ethnic primary groups and formally organized ethnic networks.

One important question remains: what happens to ethnic culture and community over a prolonged period of contact with majority group culture and social networks? Today, most contemporary researchers in the field of ethnicity have rejected the old linear model of assimilation, which exerted a dominant influence in the field of ethnic studies up to the 1970s. Such a model, generally associated with Robert Park's Chicago School of Sociology, took the form of a "straight-line theory" positing an ineluctable process of assimilation for the first and subsequent generations of migrant settlers. Thus, the seven-step linear model of Milton Gordon (1964) posited that ethnic identity loss would naturally lead to assimilation into the social fabric of the host society.

Over the past three decades, several authors have challenged the hypothesis of a mechanical relationship between socioeconomic integration and ethnic identity retention (Glazer and Moniyan 1975; Reitz 1980; Breton et al. 1990). In Canada, for instance, a study conducted in Toronto by Breton and his colleagues has empirically invalidated the assumption that "if members of a group are fully incorporated in Canadian society, they have (necessarily) abandoned all elements of their ethnic identity and background. Similarly if a group shows a low degree of ethnic retention, it does not necessarily follow that they are highly incorporated in the social fabric of the society (1990, 263)." More recently, in the United States, in a comprehensive study of second-generation youth conducted in San Diego and Miami, Portes and Rumbaut (2001) found very divergent incorporation paths for children of immigrants. Each incorporation trajectory is a function of the amount of social and economic capital that the first generation passes on to their children. Three ideal types of incorporation are identified: consonant, dissonant, and selective acculturation. Consonant acculturation, which is very similar to what classical assimilation theory usually predicts, occurs when both the first and the second generations relinquish the old culture, adopt American ways, and undergo upward mobility at an even pace. Dissonant acculturation occurs when the children quickly acculturate into American society and culture while their generally working class parents remain staunchly anchored in their ethnic culture. In such a case, the children are left on their own to accumulate social capital, which puts them at risk of "downward assimilation." As a result, members of the second generation, lacking guidance and capital inherited from their parents, can potentially end up swelling the ranks of "the masses of the dispossessed ... of America's inner cities" (ibid., 45). According to Portes and Rumbaut, the third possible path, selective acculturation, takes place when both immigrants and their children are embedded in an ethnic community that, through co-ethnic support and networks, mediates and cushions their incorporation into American society. According to the authors, this is the ideal case scenario since it is characterized by a lack of intergenerational conflict and the harmonious coexistence of socioeconomic incorporation and ethnic identity retention.

This new brand of scholarship poses a serious challenge to the assumption of the old assimilation model that the incorporation of immigrants across generations follows a unidimensional and linear trajectory. It rather appears that ethnic identification, the maintenance of an ethnic culture, and socioeconomic incorporation should be considered as relatively autonomous processes that do not necessarily evolve in the same direction, nor at the same pace.

Children of Immigrants and Symbolic Ethnicity

These analytical distinctions are particularly relevant to the study of ethnic identity among children of immigrants. Numerous pieces of research show that, among the second generation, a strong ethnic self-concept is often coupled with a low degree of retention of the ethnic culture and a high degree of structural incorporation into the host society. Put differently, even though members of the second generation have generally gained significant access to majority-group institutions, become predominantly socialized into the host society's primary groups, and grown more familiar with the dominant culture than with their own ethnic cultural background, they persist in identifying strongly with their ethnic group and culture (see Alba 1990; Breton et al. 1990; Waters 1990; Gans 1994; Nagel 1994). This well-documented phenomenon led several authors to invoke the notion of "symbolic ethnicity," a lingering ethnic self-concept largely cut off from the cultural and social environment that would normally sustain and reinforce it. Herbert J. Gans argues that "symbolic ethnicity, and the consumption ... of ethnic symbols is intended mainly for the purpose of feeling or being identified with a particular ethnicity, but without either participating in an existing ethnic organization (formal or informal) or practicing an ongoing culture" (1994, 578). Thus, ethnic identity becomes increasingly symbolic as its objective basis is superseded by its subjective dimension. It should be noted that, whereas the objective dimension implies strong social obligations to a larger community, the subjective dimension can be sustained with a minimum amount of sociocultural investment in socialization groups (Waters 1990).

The symbolic ethnicity hypothesis also implies that, once estranged from an actual "ethnic community," people are to a large extent left to themselves in recreating and maintaining their (almost mythical) ethnic identity. The reproduction of a symbolic ethnicity thus obliges one to imagine, by means of numerous cultural amalgamations and collages, what it means to be "ethnic." This phenomenon is well captured by the notion of "invented tradition" as understood by social historian Eric Hobsbawm (1983). Invented traditions, Hobsbawm argues, are regularly produced by nations as well as by social groups, which often need to adapt their old collective identities when a rapid transformation of society weakens or destroys the social patterns for which old traditions had been designed. Likewise, because children of immigrants attempt to maintain an ethnic identity uprooted from its corresponding sociocultural environment, while lacking the necessary competence to carry on their ethnic culture, they are sometimes obliged to reinvent traditions and mores to give meaning to their reborn ethnicity. To do so, they need to draw from a pool of symbolic material various cultural items that are recycled into a viable form in an immigration context. In the process, ethnicity becomes largely symbolic since these "ethnic markers" are often picked from a "cultural grab bag" that contains a mix of (sometimes stereotypical) traits, practices, and attitudes reflecting the youth's image of what he or she believes to be ethnic (Waters, 1990).

Thus, the symbolic approach to ethnicity embraces the poststructuralist acknowledgment that agency plays a critical role in the creation of ethnic identity. However, contrary to what is assumed by a radical anti-essentialist perspective, it distinguishes ethnic self-definitions that are derived from an actual socialization process from the more "symbolic" ones whose communal basis has been seriously

eroded. In line with this approach, I suggest that, although members
of the second generation indeed have much latitude in the construction of their ethnic identity, the repertoire from which they can draw
to invent ethnic behavioural and attitudinal patterns diminishes as
they get culturally and structurally incorporated into the host society.
As Gans remarked (1994), while micro cultural inventions are
devised all the time, most members of the second and third generations are incapable of macro cultural inventions because of the dramatic depletion of the pool of symbolic material on which they can
rely for the purpose of reinventing a new ethnicity.

The case of French youths of North African descent (also called
"Beurs" in French street slang) exemplifies this phenomenon.
According to several authors, a significant proportion of these
youths appear to be well on their way to developing a symbolic
ethnoreligious identity as a result of structural and cultural incorporation into the majority culture. The French Beurs are portrayed
as a highly acculturated group whose relation to Arab and Islamic
cultures is rather remote and desubstantialized. Roy (1994) and
Leveau (1997), for example, both found that, among the second
generation, not only are the loss of Arabic and the shift to French
very rapid but Arab and Islamic cultural models also compete and
clash with the new youth subculture that has emerged within the
marginalized suburban ghettos (also known as "Cités"). Thus,
says Roy, the typical Beur of the Cité speaks more "Verlan" (urban
street slang used by French youth) than Arabic, listens to rap, and
goes to McDonald's. Bastenier (1998) argues along the same lines
when he points out that young Belgians of North African descent
increasingly opt for the street as their primary space of socialization, thus drifting away from the codes and norms of the family.
Leveau (1997) reported the results of a 1989 survey[2] that showed
that young Beurs identify with and embrace French culture at very
high levels. Seventy percent of the survey respondents wished to
settle permanently in France, while seventy-one percent said that
they felt closer to the way of life and culture of French people than
to that of their parents. Furthermore, between twenty-five percent
and thirty percent of the sample fully adhered to secular values
and norms.

It would be reductive, however, even inaccurate to conclude, as
French author Olivier Roy does, that "even though the Beurs conduct themselves and want to be perceived as Arabs, or Maghrébins,

yet they portray virtually no signs of the Arab culture or the Muslim religion (1994, 65)." Other authors more cautiously suggest that although the Beurs' cultural incorporation into French society seems to be well underway, their attachment to Islam and their ethnic culture is not completely fading away. In a recent case study, Venel (2004) sheds light on the multifarious ways in which French youths of North African ancestry combine religion and ethnicity in the reinvention of their French civic identity. Her findings help to deconstruct the well-entrenched notion among French scholars studying immigration issues that ethnoreligious allegiances and civic identification are two mutually exclusive phenomena. Begag (1990), along with Nijsten (1996), Bastenier (1998), and Cesari (2002), among others, acknowledge the prevalence of a situational use of religion and tradition among the North African youth living in Europe; religion and culture come to the foreground, not as a fixed set of behavioural models and norms but rather as symbolic materials used selectively for the (re)enactment of a distinct ethnoreligious identity. In the process, these children of immigrants often come to maintain two or more separate spheres of interaction, each corresponding to a different aspect of their multiethnic self. For instance, school and family call for two different types of attitudes and behaviours.

Authors such as Isajiw and Mary Waters have offered interesting explanations for the emergence of a symbolic situational ethnicity among the second and subsequent generations of "ethnic" individuals born and raised in Western societies. They argue that, because the ethnic identity of these groups has ceased to be driven by a process of socialization perpetuating the ethnic culture, it has largely become a matter of personal choice that fulfills sociopsychological needs. Mary Waters (1990), for example, suggests that the rapid development of symbolic ethnicity in the United States stems from the fact that American culture is characterized by two opposite trends: exacerbated individualism on the one hand, and conformity resulting from the standardization of mass society on the other. A symbolic ethnicity, she argues, perfectly mitigates the contradictions resulting from this conflicting situation; for it provides individuals with a sense of community, which they lack as a result of American individualism, while at the same time giving them the feeling of being different (as "ethnic-Americans"), which they also lack because of their conformism within a mass culture.

According to Waters, the main advantage of a symbolic identity is that it provides a sense of belonging to an imagined, and therefore costless, community. Indeed, because no commitments or obligations are required from an imagined community, symbolic ethnicity becomes a convenient identity marker and meaning provider that does not threaten American values such as individuality and flexibility. Similarly, Isajiw (1977) suggested that the instrumental rationality permeating Western societies' contemporary technological culture has created a symbolic vacuum in the life of agents who, through ethnic rediscovery, attempt to replenish the meaning in their identity structure.

However, once again, the notion of an optional ethnicity that agents can discard at will may not be applicable to all ethnic groups, nor to every situation. Visible minorities have less latitude than white immigrants and their offspring in deciding whether they will downplay or emphasize their race or ethnicity. The structural ethnoracial discrimination that still permeates Western societies can potentially magnify the importance of race and ethnicity among non-white groups, regardless of whether their members want to define themselves in ethnic or racial terms. It must then be re-emphasized that ethnic boundaries can sometimes be set from outside the group (Isajiw 1974; Juteau 1997). Also, ethnic-based prejudice, discrimination, and categorization can lead to the growth, among the second generation, of a "reactive ethnicity," that is, a defensive ethnic consciousness primarily activated in response to racism and exclusion (Portes and Zhou 1993; Waters 1996, 2004). I will discuss this point at greater length in the last chapter which is dedicated to the role of prejudice and discrimination in ethnoreligious identity formation.

WHEN RELIGION AND ETHNICITY MEET

My approach to religious identity is very much informed by the conceptual and theoretical framework put forward in my discussion of ethnic identity. What I mean is that from a sociological perspective, religious identity can also be broken down into its objective, subjective, social, and cultural dimensions. Correlatively, religion can be thought of not only as a spiritual relation between the believer and his or her God but also as a collective identity that, to varying degrees, can shape in group and out group boundaries. In such cases, it can be said that religion meets ethnicity or national selfhood as both overlap and cross-fertilize each other. Pre-Quiet Revolution Quebec provides a good example of this. Culture was so deeply rooted in religion at the time that it was impossible to think of the French-Canadian and Catholic identities as separate entities. Now since the 1960s, language (i.e., French) has clearly replaced religion as the primary identity marker underlying the modern notion of "Quebecois."

In a migratory context such as Montreal, certain immigrants and their children hold on to an ethnocultural identity that is still replete with religious symbols and meanings, even though the majority group's own collective identity and public institutions have been largely secularized. But what happens to religious practice and beliefs in such cases? In other words, what's left of God when ethnicity meets religion in a secular world? In this section, drawing on the sociology of religion, I look at how the shifting place of religion in contemporary Western societies can account, in part, for what could be referred to as the "ethnicization" of religious identity among Arab-Canadian youth.

Religious Identity:
A Sociological Approach

One possible way to measure the concept of religious identity is to examine the subjects' familiarity with beliefs associated with their religion on the one hand, and their level of observance of religious practices on the other (see for instance Glock 1973). From this angle, the researcher's task consists in measuring the extent to which the subjects' religious practices and beliefs actually conform to the frame of rules prescribed by their religion. Such a research strategy leads the analyst to measure one's religious behaviours and beliefs against a set of socially approved criteria determining what ought to be proper religious behaviours and beliefs. The latter criteria are derived from, either the sacred book, or the socially dominant interpretation of this book. In other words, this approach understands religious identity as the internalization and observance of a given religious system, or again, in terms of the believer's level of religiosity. Questions such as "How often do you attend church, the mosque, or the synagogue?" or "Do you eat kosher?" or "Do you respect the Islamic ban on alcohol?" become highly relevant to the researcher's empirical inquiry. This approach partially informs my investigation into religious identity. Thus, the analysis to come provides a picture, although rough and incomplete, of the subjects' level of religiosity.

This book, however, relies also on another approach to religious identity, which puts the main focus on the social use of religion by believers. More specifically, I will look at the extent to which religion helps to strengthen (ethnic) group solidarity among members of the ethnoreligious community. The main question then becomes whether religion acts as an ethnic binder, or again, whether religion is an important factor in the structuring of the various ethnocultural relations and networks in which actors are enmeshed.

In order to measure the sociocultural use of religion in the construction of ethnic group boundaries, I rely on a scale adapted from the previously discussed Isajiw scale (1990) designed to measure ethnic identity. I will break down the concept of religious identity into its subjective and objective aspects. Whereas the subjective dimension refers to self-identification with one's religious culture and community, the objective aspect refers to the extent to which feelings of belonging are coupled with corresponding levels of religious practice, and with participation in groups and activities structured along religious lines. Second, as with ethnic identity, I shall distinguish between the social and cultural manifestations of the subjective and objective aspects of religious identity. In short, the subjective/social and the objective/social aspects relate, respectively, to people's identification, and levels of interaction, with their religious community. The subjective/cultural aspect of religious identity refers to the sense of belonging to one's religious culture, whereas the objective/cultural aspect refers to the level of observance of religious rituals and participation in religious activities or organizations. The concept of religious identity is thus measured using a scale that taps into four distinct yet interrelated dimensions, each referring to a different sociocultural use of religion.[3] This four- by-four matrix has the advantage of being sensitive to the various social and psychological functions that religion can fulfill depending on the social context of interaction. Moreover, because the scale encompasses the possible discrepancies between the subjective dimension of religious identity (internalized beliefs and feelings) and the objective (externalized behaviours), it is particularly well suited for measuring the religiosity of young people who may be little inclined to practise a religion but have faith nonetheless in a divine power.

Second-Generation Youth and the "Ethnicization" of Religion

Within the notion that religion intermingles with ethnicity, religiosity must be understood to serve the purpose of reinforcing distinct ethnocultural group boundaries. But in the process, what happens to religious practice and belief? Is an ethnoreligiosity more "secular" than a traditional form of religiosity, that is, one defined narrowly as the belief in God or in some form of transcendental force? This question is all the more relevant since the young adults studied here were either born, or spent most of their lives, in Canada, a sociocultural environment that is considered less religious compared to most contemporary Arab societies. In this context, the hypothesis of the ethnicization of religion is related to the secularization hypothesis. I will thus start by briefly examining how the secularization hypothesis both connects with, and departs from, the present argument.

During the 1960s and until the late 1980s, the secularization hypothesis – originally put forth by the founding fathers of sociology – was considered by most sociologists of religion as "fact" requiring no further debate. At the time, for most proponents of the secularization hypothesis such as Stark (1963), Berger (1967), Luckman (1967), and Bibby (1987), industrialization coupled with economic modernization would ineluctably lead to the demise of religion, whether measured by the declining institutional power of churches or by the tendency of actors to rely more on instrumental rationality than on religious structures of meanings to interpret their actions and the social world. In recent years, however, many of the very same sociologists who only a few decades ago confidently foretold the imminent demise of religion are now qualifying their initial predictions.

First, in certain Western countries, we are witnessing the "deprivatization" of religion at the institutional level. This expression, coined by José Casanova (2001), means that in some countries, such as Spain, Poland, and the United States, the Church, after having been evicted from state apparatuses, has now re-entered the public sphere in the past three decades or so, this time not as a pivotal force within the political community but rather as a civil society actor raising "normative issues, participating in ongoing processes of normative contestation" and acting as a "countervailing power to State power (ibid., 1,048, 1,044)". In the United

States, however, not only have religious organizations become increasingly influential in civil society, especially since September 11, 2001, but (right-wing) Evangelical Protestantism informs large segments of the political and ideological agenda of top-level politicians such as President George W. Bush.[4]

On another level, in most Western societies, including Canada (and even more so in Quebec), individuals participate in religion less and less through formally organized rituals and more and more on a private and personal basis. Indeed, believers are increasingly deserting the Church in growing numbers, though they continue to rely on it to officiate during specific rites of passages (e.g., births, marriages, funerals, etc.). In other words, the believers' religious beliefs and practices are increasingly relegated to the private sphere and are thus becoming disengaged from religious institutional control. But what many sociologists of religion have shown is that this privatization of faith does not necessarily imply that people are becoming entirely areligious or atheistic (see Stark 1999; Swatos, Jr., and Christiano 1999, Bibby 2002).

Thus, Canadian sociologist Reginald Bibby (2002, 138–9), using a large set of nationwide survey data, found that in 2000, ninety-one percent of Canadians were still, to varying degrees, turning to some sort of higher power in an attempt to give purpose or transcendental meaning to their own lives and to human life in general. It should be noted, however, that Bibby's figure is perhaps slightly exaggerated since, according to 2001 census data, 16.2 percent of Canadians report that they have "no religion," although some of them may believe in a higher power while being religiously non-affiliated. There has been a slow but steady increase in the proportion of Canadians claiming "no religion," since this category represented only 12.3 percent of all responses in 1991 (Statistics Canada 1991). In any case, even based on Statistics Canada's more conservative figure, it appears that the vast majority of Canadians still believe in God, at least for now.

What perhaps has changed most dramatically is that people all across the Western world tend to be deterred by rigid religious dogma. They are rather strongly inclined to pick and choose among the ideological material and the various beliefs that different religious discourses proffer. This phenomenon has been referred to as "religion *à la carte*" and the result as *bricolage* (Dobbelaere 1999, 239; Swatos, Jr., and Christiano 1999, 222; Voyé 1999, 275). However, the fact that people today are more likely to indulge in code mixing and engage in religion selectively does not mean that they are less religious. What it does imply is that religion tends to be increasingly relegated to the private sphere, where individuals are free to recompose their own religious frame of beliefs so as to meet their personalized spiritual needs (Bramadat 2005, 4).

That being said, the notion of a privatized religion does not mean that people's quest for the sacred and the transcendental takes place in a communal vacuum. Research findings show that eighty percent of mainline Protestants in Canada continue to identify with the religion of their parents (Bibby 2002, 41), while two-thirds of Americans claim membership in a religious congregation (Swatos Jr and Christiano 1999, 216). In other words, people still harbour a sense of belonging to a wider community of believers, with whom they share a common memory and common institutions, references, and rituals, whether performed regularly or only occasionally to give meaning to key life events. Today religion, whether organized or privatized, is no longer pivotal when it comes to people's behaviours and attitudes in social interactions related to "worldly" affairs (Dobbelaere 1999). Could such a religious community, in which most individuals claim membership, constitute what Mary Waters (1990) referred to as a symbolic, and therefore costless, community? Such an imagined community becomes all the more appealing since, without imposing normative obligations and roles on believers, it acts nonetheless as a convenient identity marker and provider of meaning in a world where meaning has been eroded by mass culture and narcissistic individualism.

Some students of ethnicity argue that the symbolic communal ties provided by such "low investment" religious membership are particularly appealing to children of immigrants, for whom religion often acts as a vehicle for the assertion of a distinct ethnic identity. In North America, the best analyses of the ethnicization of religion may be those pertaining to the maintenance of Jewish identity across generations. In fact, the very notion of "ethnicized religion" stemmed from Jewish studies. The argument, in its most radical version, is that, while the religious basis of Jewishness is fading away, its social, cultural, and ideological bases are successfully maintained. Herbert Gans, in his study of second- and third-generation American Jews (1994), referred to this phenomenon as symbolic religious identity, a concept drawn directly from his earlier research on symbolic ethnicity. According to Gans, symbolic religious identity denotes fragmented knowledge of religious norms, a low level of ritual observance, yet a strong feeling of identification with religion and the religious community. Along similar lines, Stephen Sharot (1997) argues that, for American Jews, Judaism constitutes mainly a vehicle for the reproduction of ethnic group solidarity and cohesion but is no longer the expression of religious fervour and devotion.

The picture is not overly different for Canadian Jews, although the social and communal basis of their Jewish ethnicity is much better maintained in comparison with their American counterparts.[5] Indeed, Canadian Jews are extremely successful in preserving across generations the communal and social basis underlying their strong ethnic self-concept (Weinfeld 2001; Cohen 2003). For example, when compared with the first, second, and third generations of other ethnic groups, Canadian Jews systematically obtain the highest scores on every measure of the strength of ethnic bonds at the communal level, that is, in terms of ingroup friendship and marriage, institutional completeness, and residential segregation (Breton et al. 1990; Weinfeld 2001). What is less clear, however, is the extent to which the ethnicity of Canadian Jews has been severed from its religious foundations proper. It is interesting to note that for a (significant) minority of Canadian Jews, Jewish identity represents a pure ethnic label devoid of any religious meanings. Thus, according to the 2001 census data, 11.6 percent of Canadians who identified themselves ethnically as Jews reported "no religious affiliation" (Statistics Canada 2001). As sociologically fascinating as these cases may be, however, they are not representative of the whole Canadian Jewish community.

As a matter of fact, religious practice and observance among Canadian Jews remain relatively high compared with other religious groups. According to two surveys conducted in the 1990s, about half of the Jewish households in Toronto, and as many as two-thirds in Montreal, belong to synagogues. However, sixty percent of Toronto Jews and eighty percent of Montreal Jews attend synagogue only for the main religious holidays and special occasions such as marriages or bar mitzvahs (reported in Schoenfeld 2001, 179). It must also be kept in mind that synagogues are attended less for the religious services they offer than for their broader services as (ethnic) community centres (Weinfeld 2001, 290). To sum up, although it is difficult to determine accurately the extent to which ethnic Jewishness flourishes without religious Judaism, it is clear that the two are, in general, intricately intertwined.

In Europe, the same phenomenon has been observed among children of Muslim families. In a study conducted by Yalcin-Heckmann (1998) on religious socialization among Turkish migrant families in Germany, a large majority (ninety-two percent) of parents stressed the need for their children to take Koranic courses given by mosques, other Islamic institutions, or qualified private instructors. Similarly, in Vertovec's work on young Muslim South Asians raised in England (1998, 98), as well as in Lans and Rooijackers' study of young Turks living in the Netherlands (1994, 113), it was found that the majority of the youths interviewed or surveyed had attended some form of Islamic class at one point or another in their childhood. In most cases, however, Koranic instruction had been dropped by the time the children reached their teenage years. In Yalcin-Heckmann's study, parents were asked what their motivations were for inculcating Islamic principles in their children (1998, 11). They responded that, among other things, it would allow their kids to acquire proper "social skills," develop a sense of attachment to and identification with their ethnic group, and learn proper moral values. Many parents also reported being dissatisfied with the religious instruction their children received. It thus appears that, to the Muslim parents in the study, Koranic teaching was more than a mere instrument of religious socialization; it was also a means of socialization into the ethnic community. These findings are in keeping with Haddad's contention that mosques in North America, like several other ethnic churches, serve as centres for community bonding and social integration. Haddad adds that the majority of Muslim parents who send their children to religious schools are not involved in organized religion (Haddad 1994). These case studies all confirm the view not only that Muslim migrants tend to be unwilling to separate religion from ethnicity but that most of them also actively attempt to transmit their ethnoreligious identity to their offspring.

If Muslim parents see little distinction between their religious and ethnic identities, Muslim youths tend to problematize prescribed notions of how ethnicity and religion should relate to each other. Muslim children often creatively reassign new meanings and roles to Islam as an ethnic identity marker, thus reappropriating and transforming the "ready-made" ethnoreligious identities originating from the community. The vast majority of case studies suggest the presence of a strong and generalized feeling of attachment to Islam among young Muslims born and raised in Western settings. They also offer strong indications that structural and cultural incorporation into the host society has dramatically affected the second generation's knowledge of, and commitment to, religious prescriptions and practices. Thus, while the French Beurs studied by Jocelyne Cesari (1998) have a positive perception of Islam and define themselves as Muslims, their religious identity is in fact a symbolic assertion that is largely disconnected from everyday life. According to Cesari, they are not practising Muslims, and Islam has few implications for their social life. Furthermore, Cesari remarks, the religious symbols and references used by young Beurs in the construction of their ethnoreligious identity are not uncritically derived from family and community. They are rather chosen among various "salvation goods" in a consumerist fashion, as French-born Muslims pick and choose which religious tenets, practices, and norms to retain and which to dismiss (Cesari 2002).

Leveau (1997) made a similar observation when noting that the French Beurs' theological knowledge is generally negligible and distorted; for what they perceive as Islamic is often an assortment of basic Koranic prescriptions, popular religiosity, folklore, and tradition. Similarly, Nimat Hafez Barazangi showed, with a sample of Canadian and American Arab Muslim families, that parents tended to interpret Islamic prescriptions "out of context" while, inversely, their offspring tended to contextualize and adapt these principles to make them consistent with their Western sociocultural environment (Barazangi 1998). Finally, in a study of young Muslims living in Keighley, England, Steve Vertovec (1998) concluded that there is a discrepancy between the subjective and objective dimensions of religious identity. Indeed, he found that most of his respondents firmly believed in God and were deeply attached to their Muslim identity, regardless of levels of ritual observance. Most respondents in Vertovec's study in fact showed poor religious knowledge and admitted to neglecting religious prescriptions but were nonetheless staunch in their Muslim identity. Likewise, Begag (1990) remarked that while French youths of North African ancestry have relinquished many of the religious norms and concepts of their parents, they are certainly not rejecting religion as an ethnic identity marker, though few among them have a deep knowledge of Islam or engage in devout religious practice.

These case studies show how Islam comes to the foreground among the second generation, not as a fixed set of religious rituals and behavioural rules but rather as a medium for the assertion of a distinct ethnoreligious identity that can be downplayed or emphasized depending on the context. This does not mean that the religious identity of these Muslim descendants of immigrants is devoid of genuine piety. What it does mean, however, is that, for them, religious membership is more than merely believing in God and observing rituals; it becomes harnessed to the production of ethnic boundaries. Furthermore, they tend to adopt a flexible and contextual religious identity (similar in this respect to their ethnic identity) that denotes their incorporation into the host society. Indeed, their understanding of religious norms and prescriptions, as is often the case with their majority group peers, is personally adapted in order to reflect their Western-style liberal values and lifestyle.[6]

The notion of symbolic religious identity, largely documented for second- and third-generation Jews in North America, and for second-generation Muslims in Europe, may turn out to be equally relevant to the sample analyzed here. In chapter 4, I examine how children of Arab migrants in Montreal perform heuristic reappropriations of religious labels and norms that are freely recycled into symbolic material feeding ethnic identity building.

METHODOLOGICAL CONCERNS

This section describes the nature of the population targeted in my research, the sampling method I used, and the main characteristics of both quantitative and qualitative samples. Further details on how the key concepts used in this study were measured into quantitative variables are supplied in appendices A and B. Appendix A shows how various indicators were combined to measure the dependent, independent, and control variables. Appendix B provides information about the coding and recoding of each indicator, and the choice of answers attached to each question in the questionnaire. Appendix C includes a copy of the questionnaire, while appendix D consists of the interview question sheet that acted as a guideline for the semistructured interviews.

Data

The target population for this study consists of Muslim and Christian students of Arab origin from five selected cegeps in Greater Montreal. The students, whose parents had both migrated from an Arab country,[7] were between seventeen and twenty-four years of age. The selected institutions were Cegep de Saint-Laurent, Collège de Bois-de-Boulogne, Collège Ahuntsic, Collège Montmorency, and Vanier College. Of these schools only one, Vanier College, is English speaking while the others are French-speaking establishments. Subjects included in this study were either born in Canada or migrated from an Arab country before the age of twelve. Arab-origin students who migrated after the age of twelve were excluded from the sample since their recent arrival made them more likely to maintain their ethnoreligious identity.

Sample Size and Methods

Both quantitative and qualitative methods were used for this research. Cross-tabulation analyses were performed using a sample of 250 respondents of Arab origin attending a Montreal cegep. Respondents filled out a questionnaire comprising eighty-five multiple-choice questions. If quantitative methods are of much help to measure the intensity of one's attachment to any given identity category, they fall short of tapping into the various motives and meanings underlying the subjects' identity choices and strategies. For that reason, the quantitative information provided by the questionnaires was complemented by a series of sixteen in-depth nondirective interviews conducted with subjects selected from among the 250 respondents.

Because this sample is made up exclusively of cegep students, of whom most are en route to university, it is not representative of the whole range of class background within the Arab-origin youth population in Montreal. More specifically, because this research excludes those Arab-Canadian youths who did not pursue a postsecondary degree, it primarily applies to second-generation Arabs originating from urban middle and upper classes. Thus, one cannot generalize to the whole population of Arab-Canadian youth based on this research. That said, given that Arab-Canadians constitute a highly educated group,[8] it is reasonable to assume that the proportion of Arab youths who do not pursue a cegep degree after high school is relatively low, or at least lower than the national average.

The cegeps in this sample were generally multiethnic and were selected on the basis of their average, or above-average, concentration of Arab students. Having no access to reliable statistics about the exact number of Arab students attending each cegep, it was difficult to determine accurately the ideal sample size for each of the five selected institutions. As a result, it was impossible to get a sense of the quantitative representativeness of each of the five subsamples.

The sample was drawn on a volunteer basis, and permission to discuss the research project and solicit volunteers was granted by teachers. To ensure that the largest range of students was reached in each cegep, brief presentations were given at the beginning of french and philosophy courses (compulsory at the cegep level in Quebec) between January 2000 and April 2001. Cross-table analysis was performed on the resultant sample of 250 students of Arab origin.

With every class visit, a meeting was arranged with those students who qualified for, and were interested in, filling out the multiple-choice questionnaire. Each respondent was asked, at the end of the questionnaire, whether he or she would eventually be interested in participating in an interview. Upon filling out the questionnaire, seventy-five respondents volunteered their names and phone numbers, allowing me eventually to seek an interview. Six months later, of these seventy-five individuals, twenty actually agreed to be interviewed. Of these twenty volunteers, however, fourteen were female and six were male. I thus decided to discard four female respondents to ensure that the female-to-male ratio would not be abnormally high. In other words, I opted for a sample made up of ten females and six males in order to keep the gender imbalance within acceptable limits. Of these sixteen participants, ten were Christian and six were Muslim, a ratio slightly overrepresenting Christians.

It should be reiterated that the findings yielded by this research are not easily generalizable to the entire Montreal population of Arab-origin youth. First, because it excludes those Arab youths with no more than a high school degree, the study applies more specifically to an educated middle-class segment of Montreal's population of second-generation Arabs. But one would also have to be cautious about generalizing to the whole Montreal population of educated middle-class Arab youth, since the five cegeps sampled here had average, and often above-average, proportions of Arab-origin students. This necessarily skews the sample by slightly over-representing subjects with a stronger inclination toward ethnic and religious maintenance. The sample can however be considered fairly representative (quantitatively as well as qualitatively) of the Arab student population found in cegeps where Arabs are present in significant numbers.

Quantitative Sample

The quantitative sample is made up of 118 females and 132 males, aged between seventeen and twenty-four years old. Of these 250 respondents, 64.8 percent reported Christianity as their father's religion, while 35.2 percent reported Islam. These figures slightly overrepresent Christians since, among Canadians who claimed membership in one of the top six Arab-related ethnic origins in the census,[9] 51 percent were Christian and 40 percent were Muslim (Statistics Canada 2001). The majority of respondents (64.8 percent) were born in an Arab country, while 35.2 percent were born in Canada. Canadian-born individuals are thus slightly under-represented in the sample since, as of 2001, 43 percent of Arab Quebecois aged fifteen to twenty-four are Canadian born (ibid.). The respondents' fathers come from various Arab countries. Lebanese respondents make up the majority of the sample (46.8 percent), followed by Syrians (16 percent), Egyptians (11.2 percent), Moroccans (10.4 percent), and Algerians (8 percent). The four other national groups represented, namely Palestinians, Iraqis, Saudi Arabians, and Tunisians, together accounted for a marginal portion of the sample (7.6 percent). Such a distribution mirrors relatively well the overall distribution of Arab Quebecois by national origin in the same age group, except for a slight overrepresentation of respondents of Syrian origin (+4 percent), and a slight under-representation of respondents of Moroccan (−6 percent) and Egyptian (−5 percent) origin (Statistics Canada 2001).

The class origin of respondents was measured on the basis of the father's level of education and occupation. While 31.6 percent of the respondents' fathers were professionals, 24.1 percent were blue collar, 23.5 percent were independent businessmen, 10.2 percent worked in retails, and 3.2 percent were executives. The educational level of respondents' parents was, on average, quite comparable to that found among Arab-origin adults in the entire province of Quebec. Thus, 59 percent of respondents' fathers held a university degree, as opposed to 51 percent among Quebec's population of Arab-origin males aged twenty-five and over. The proportion of university-educated mothers in the sample matched exactly the proportion of Quebec women of Arab origin aged twenty-five and over holding a university degree (30 percent in both cases).[10]

Individual Profiles of Interviewees

In order to ensure confidentiality, each interviewee was assigned an alphabetical letter that would identify him or her throughout the analysis. Listed below are sociologically relevant characteristics of each informant, namely, gender, age, parents' country of origin, parents' religious affiliation, and age at arrival in Canada. All the interviews were conducted in French and then translated into English, with the exception of the interview with informant J, which was conducted originally in English.

A: male; twenty-one years old; Lebanon; Christian; migrated to Canada at the age of eleven.
B: male; nineteen years old; Lebanon; Christian; Canadian-born.
C: male; nineteen years old; Lebanon and Palestine; Christian; Canadian-born.
D: male; twenty years old; Lebanon; Christian; migrated to Canada at the age of twelve.
E: male; twenty-two years old; Lebanon; Christian; migrated to Canada at the age of five.
F: male; twenty years old; Algeria; Muslim; migrated to Canada at the age of eight.
G: female; nineteen years old; Egypt; Muslim; Canadian-born.
H: female, seventeen years old; Algeria; Muslim; Canadian-born.
I: female; twenty years old; Morocco; Muslim; Canadian-born.
J: female; nineteen years old; Algeria; Muslim; Canadian-born.
K: female; eighteen years old; Algeria; Muslim; migrated to Canada at the age of seven.
L: female; eighteen years old; Lebanon; Christian; migrated to Canada at the age of nine.
M: female; eighteen years old; Syria; Christian; migrated to Canada at the age of ten.

N: female; eighteen years old; Syrian; Christian; migrated to Canada at the age of six.
O: female; eighteen years old; Lebanon; Christian; Canadian-born.
P: female; nineteen years old; Lebanon; Christian; migrated to Canada at the age of seven.

3

Ingroup and Outgroup Boundaries:
Structural Factors

THE ROLE OF PREJUDICE AND DISCRIMINATION

As previously discussed, although children of immigrants have the power to shape contextually the contours of their ethnic and religious selves through cultural innovation and *bricolage,* this power is not boundless. The religious and ethnic identity "scripts" they write for themselves are continually submitted to the majority group for social validation. According to Charles Taylor (1994), the type of public recognition sought by minority groups consists in either the acknowledgment of their "equal dignity" and equal rights, in keeping with universal republican principles, or conversely, the recognition of their cultural uniqueness as legitimate grounds for differential treatments in the public sphere. And as mentioned earlier, if non-racialized[1] ethnic minority members have at their disposal much leeway in deciding when to make their ethnic difference salient or, inversely, when to downplay their cultural distinctiveness to enjoy difference-blind treatments and status, racialized minorities tend to be unwittingly confined in pre-ascribed categories that not only depart from their own self-representations but also place them socially and symbolically apart from the majority group (Waters 1996; Jenkins 1997). In other words, as far as most racialized minorities are concerned, prejudice and discrimination deny them equal consideration – and sometimes treatment – on the basis of a stigmatizing category defined for them from the outside.

Clearly, this process has a strong impact on the identity choices made by members of racialized groups when constructing their minority identity through an (unequal) dialogue with the majority group. In Europe, the reappropriation of religion as an ethnic marker by young European Muslims is regarded by several authors as a reaction to prejudice and discrimination. In fact, when prejudice is coupled with socioeconomic exclusion, the situation becomes ripe for either the development of Islam-based communal behaviours, the Islamization of one's ethnic self-concept, or both. Again the case of French Beurs is particularly illustrative of this phenomenon, since a large fraction of them are known to share with the African-American underclass the same bleak socioeconomic profile. For instance, a study conducted in 2002–03 in a suburb of Lyon on French males of North African descent aged twenty to twenty-nine revealed that forty-six percent of them were unemployed (Santelli n.d.). In France's impoverished suburban zones, young people of North African ancestry, being denied decent educational opportunities and employment, are also significantly overrepresented among young offenders who commit random acts of violence and engage in petty criminality (Begag 1990; Roy 1994; Gross et al. 1997; Viprey 1997; Duprez 2002). When coupled with prejudice and discrimination, such an ethnically segmented socioeconomic structure constitutes fertile ground for the development of ethnoreligious consciousness and protest. This was well exemplified by the urban riots of November 2005 in France's pauperized suburbs, which are inhabited by large numbers of Arab and African migrants and their descendants.

However, for authors such as Lapeyronnie (1987), Dubet and Lapeyronnie (1992), and Bastenier (1998), this ethnoreligious "us" arising from discrimination and exclusion, although fed by a common experience of racism, is not derived from a culturally distinct community. The high degree of acculturation experienced by young Beurs exacerbates their frustration at being left at the periphery of mainstream socioeconomic structures. More precisely, when realizing the wide gap between the cultural goals they have internalized and the scarce means at their disposal to attain them, French Beurs are retreating into a reactive ethnic and religious consciousness. Thus, according to many French authors, paradoxically, the idea of cultural distinctiveness increasingly gains support among French Beurs as their actual cultural differences fade away in the course of their cultural integration into French society.

So should ethnic mobilization and protest among French youth of North African origin be read solely as a demand for inclusion and equality, and not as a factor reinforcing ethnic allegiances and communalism? This reading may resonate in the French context, where the prevailing radical Republican/universalistic ideology is rather hostile to the presence of parochial identities in the public sphere. However, the same ideology that promotes a difference-blind notion of citizenship blinded some French sociologists to the fact that many French Beurs are not prepared to embrace a national identity that does not make room for their North African heritage.

Anti-Arab and Anti-Muslim Prejudice in Canada

In Canada, the Arab-origin youth experiencing discrimination may react differently, since multicultural policies in this country actively foster ethnic identity retention across generations. Therefore, if confronted with symbolic or material exclusion, many Arab-Canadian minorities may be tempted to hold on more strongly to their ethnocultural identity.

On the other hand, contrary to North Africans in France and other Muslim ethnic groups scattered elsewhere in Europe, North American Arabs are not negotiating a migrant identity with a majority group that once symbolized to them colonial domination. Nor do they suffer from structural discrimination and socioeconomic exclusion to the same extent as their European counterparts. Therefore, in their case it is not clear to what extent religion and ethnicity emerge as a similar reactive force, or as a protective buffer, in the formation of group consciousness.

One thing that is clear, however, is that in North America as much as in Europe, Muslim and Arab minorities are particularly affected by ethnic prejudice at the representational level. Anti-Muslim and anti-Arab prejudices tend to be highly contingent upon international politics, especially in relation to the Middle East (Antonius 2002). Certain world events aggravated stereotypes against Arab and Islamic cultures in North America. First, as previously mentioned, the 1967 Arab-Israeli war and the pro-Israeli US policies that ensued contributed significantly to the emergence of a reactive ethnoreligious identity among the Arab diaspora (Suleiman 1988, 1999). But Arab-origin youths born and raised in the West in the post-1970s era were particularly affected by more recent events, such as the Rushdie affair (1989), the first Gulf War (1990), and, more recently, the terrorist attacks on the World Trade Centre in 2001, the US-led invasion of Iraq in 2003, and the wave of Islamist terrorist attacks that have shaken the world since then, particularly those in Madrid in 2004 and London in 2005.

What these events have in common is that they helped to spark negative and distorted portrayals of Arabs and Muslims in the media, which in turn reinforced racist stereotypes and prejudices directed against these groups. There is a strand of discourse in the mainstream media that explains (away) Islamic terrorism or armed struggles in the Middle East by singling out cultural factors as the main cause of violence. Although most journalists are careful not to resort to this sort of "culturalist" explanation, some of them sporadically argue that Islam and Arab "civilizations" are bound to beget violence and terrorism because of their intrinsic incompatibility with, and even hostility to, Western values of liberty and equality. Here is an example of such dubious amalgamations in an article published on 2 April 2002 under various names in most Canadian newspapers owned by CanWest Global Communications, including Montreal's *Gazette*. In this article, the editorial team put forth the following explanation of Islamic terrorism in general, and Palestinian terrorism in particular: "Why can't some Muslims agree that killing innocent non-Muslims is unacceptable? *Part of the problem lies with Muslim civilization itself.* As Samuel P. Huntington writes in *The Clash of Civilizations and the Remaking of World Order*: 'Wherever one looks along the perimeter of Islam, Muslims have problems living peaceably with their neighbours' ... But *even by the barbaric standards of the Arab Middle East*, Yasser Arafat and the Palestinian terrorist organizations that operate freely under his writ have hit new lows."[2] In another piece published in several newspaper and magazines, including *Maclean's* and the *Ottawa Citizen* (11 November 2000), editorialist Barabara Amiel offered her own historical account of the Israel-Palestine conflict. At one point she wrote: "But the Arab countries take a somewhat different view of life on this earth from that of the West. Arab culture appears to put the glory of the tribe or Allah before the individual's suffering or happiness."[3] In the aftermath of the London terrorist attacks of 7 July 2005, editorialist Gil Courtemanche wrote in *Le Devoir*: "We [well-intended Westerners] believed that Koranic precepts fostering religious and male violence would be turned into obsolete folklore from coexisting with the human rights values offered by Western democracies. We were seriously wrong, including me ... Being exposed to modernity did not soften Islam, it radicalized it. As for our willingness to understand [radical Islam], it prevented us from seeing that the religion of Ben Laden and that of 'Madrasa' [Koranic schools] do not constitute a perversion of the Prophet's message, it is part of it."[4]

These articles – all published in prominent Canadian newspapers and magazines – convey notions of Arab and Muslim cultures constructed as ahistorical and essentialized monoliths that are inherently prone to breed intolerance, violence, and bigotry. The problem with this perspective is that the social context and power relations in which, historically, particular embodiments of Arab and Muslim cultures emerge are completely ignored. The conflation of Islamic and Arab cultures on the one hand and extremism and fanaticism on the other becomes almost "natural" once political domination and socioeconomic inequalities have been dismissed as potential explanatory factors for armed conflict and violence. As discussed earlier, the recent burgeoning of Islamic extremism in the 1970s and the tremendous political capital that these movements have gained throughout the Muslim world during the past decades cannot be properly understood without taking into account the political and economic backdrop against which the dissemination of religious fundamentalism took place (Eid 2002; Esposito and Burgat 2003). But most importantly, the generalizations about Arab and Muslim cultures expressed in the above quotations disregard the numerous intragroup disagreements within Arab communities over which interpretation of religion and culture to embrace, and which political norms and lines of action to follow (Yuval-Davis 1997, 58). These omissions help to fuel Westerners' simplistic tendency to associate *all* Arabs and Muslims with religious fanaticism and terrorism.

Not surprisingly, therefore, there is a strong feeling among Arab-origin and Muslim North Americans of the first and second generations that their ethnoreligious cultures are disparaged by Westerners at the representational level. For instance, Baha Abu-Laban and Sharon M. Abu-Laban's Edmonton study (1999, 150) showed that 63 percent of their sample of Muslim and Christian Arab-Canadian youths felt that television either often (19 percent) or sometimes (44 percent) portrays Arabs or Arab culture in a biased and unfair manner. Ibrahim Hayani (1999, 299), reporting the findings of a 1993 survey of Arabs in Ontario, pointed out that 80 percent of respondents consider that Canadians regard Arabs rather poorly. More recently, in a survey conducted by the Canadian chapter of the Council on American-Islamic Relations (CAIR-CAN) during the summer of 2002, it was found that 60 percent of the Canadian Muslim respondents reported having experienced "bias or discrimination since the 9/11 terrorist attacks" (cited in Helly 2004, 42). In another poll conducted in the spring of 2002, 41 percent of 253 Arab-origin respondents thought that Canadians "do not like Muslims," while 84.6 percent believed that Canadians regard Muslims as violent (cited in Helly 2004, 42).

The perception of Arab and Muslim Canadians that they are misportrayed and denigrated by Canadians is largely confirmed by various survey results measuring Canadian attitudes toward them. Interestingly, dominant representations of Arabs and Muslims have remained relatively stable in recent decades. Thus, as far back as 1977, a national survey of Canadian attitudes already showed that Arabs fared very poorly at the level of popular imagery. In a list of twenty-seven ethnic groups to be evaluated on an attitudinal scale, Arab Canadians were ranked twenty-fourth by Anglo-Canadians, and twenty-third by French Canadians (cited in S.M. Abu-Laban and B. Abu-Laban 1999, 115). Years later, a 1983 survey of two hundred French-speaking cegep students found that respondents had a much more positive opinion about white English or anglophone ethnic groups (such as Jewish and German Canadians) than about blacks and Arabs. In fact, out of a list of various ethnic groups to be ranked in order of preference, blacks and Arabs occupied the last positions. Furthermore, the cegep students thought that Arabs were sly, dishonest, cruel, and whining (cited in McAndrew 2002, 135).

Negative representations of Arabs and Muslims remain prevalent. According to a survey commissioned in August 2002 by the Association for Canadian Studies, 43 percent of respondents thought that Canada accepted too many immigrants from Arab countries, 40 percent from Asian countries, 24 percent from Africa, 21 percent from Latin America, and 16 percent from Europe. In November 2002, a nationwide survey sponsored by *Maclean's* magazine, Global TV, and the *Ottawa Citizen* revealed a similar trend: 44 percent of Canadians and 48 percent of Quebecois[5] were in favour of curtailing immigration from Muslim countries (cited in Helly 2004, 35). According to a July 2002 CROP survey, 17 percent of Quebecois and 13 percent of Canadians considered that "Islam promotes confrontational relations" (ibid., 34). In August 2002, according to an IPSO-Reid survey, 45 percent of Quebecois, 37 percent of Albertans, 22 percent of Ontarians, and 22% of British Columbians agreed with the statement: "The September 11 attacks made me more mistrustful of Arabs or Muslims coming from the Middle-East" (ibid., 35). Then by mid-March 2003, the week that the Americans and British invaded Iraq, a poll commissioned by the Association for Canadian Studies (ACS) from the Environics Research Group revealed that 30 percent of the 2,002 Canadians surveyed felt that Arabs project a negative image, while 33 percent held the same opinion about Aboriginals, 13 percent about blacks, and 11 percent about Jews (Jedwab 2003).[6]

Even more recently, a survey conducted by Leger Marketing for the ACS in the midst of the armed conflict between Israel and Lebanon in July 2006 revealed that 24 percent of Canadians had a negative view of Muslims, while only 9 percent had a negative opinion about Jews, and 10 percent about Christians. What's more, Islam seems to fare even more poorly in public opinion since 37 percent of Canadians have a negative impression of this religion, according to a survey conducted by Environics Research Group in the Fall of 2006 for the ACS and the Pierre-Elliot Foundation. But the good news is that 75 percent of respondents to this latter survey agree to say that "Muslim immigrants make a positive contribution to Canadian society," which suggests that Canadians make a distinction between Islam as a religion and the individuals who embrace it (Environics Research Group, 2006).

These cultural biases toward their ethnoreligious culture and communities are likely to deter Arab-origin and Muslim Canadians and Americans from identifying with their respective majority groups. Even second-generation Arabs, regardless of their level of social, cultural, and economic incorporation, can be led to retreat into their ethnoreligious identity in reaction to what they perceive as Western-made misrepresentations of their cultural heritage. This detrimental ideological climate obliges first- and second-generation Arab-Canadians to problematize their feelings of identification, first, with a majority community whose popular imagery is suffused with prejudicial stereotypes against their ethnocultural background, and

second, with an ethnocultural community proffering a socially compromising identity to its members.

Anti-Arab and Anti-Muslim Discrimination
in Canada

The above data reveal that Arab and Muslim individuals, in both
Quebec and Canada, perceive themselves to be portrayed negatively by Canadians and Quebecois. And, as shown earlier, most
national polls and surveys seem to prove them right. One may wonder, however, to what extent these prejudicial representations translate into discriminatory practices in the public sphere. There is
evidence to suggest that immigrants of Arab origin experience
ethnoracial discrimination like any other racialized groups in Canada (see for example Lians and Matthews 1998; Renaud et al.
2003). In a recent longitudinal study, Renaud and his colleagues
(2003) showed that during their first ten years of settlement in Canada (1989–1999), immigrants from the Middle East, North Africa,
Lebanon, Haiti, Vietnam, South America, and the Caribbean
remained at a significant disadvantage in terms of occupational status and income compared with immigrants from North America
and Europe, even after a large array of other variables were controlled for, including gender, age, years spent in Canada, educational credentials, professional qualifications, languages spoken,
social class, and job experience. This means that visible minorities,
including Arab migrants, need to invest up to ten more years than
their non-racialized counterparts to secure a profession reflecting
their actual value on the job market. Since groups with equal qualifications and experience were compared in this study, it can be
hypothesized that this income and occupational gap may be produced and sustained, at least in part, by discrimination on ethnic
and racial grounds.[7]
    Paradoxically, Hayani reported that the Arab-Canadian respon-
dents participating in the 1993 Ontario study cited earlier felt that
there was relatively little discrimination directed against them. As
Hayani rightly remarked, these relatively low rates of self-reported
discriminatory experience are surprising given "how poorly Canadians regard Arabs, their culture, and their way of life (Hayani
1999, 300)." These findings contrast especially with the general
perception among Arab Canadians that their group is regarded neg-

atively by Canadians. We are thus reminded that perceived prejudice and discrimination are two distinct phenomena that cannot be considered as being necessarily codependent. But the fact that visible minorities do not perceive themselves to be discriminated against does not mean they are not actually exposed to discriminating attitudes and practices. In fact, the existence of discrimination targeting visible minorities on the labour and housing market is strongly suggested by empirical research.

How can we account, then, for Hayani's finding that Arab Canadians report low levels of discrimination? Nowadays, those who are denied access to socioeconomic resources (e.g., jobs, housing) on ethnic or racial grounds are rarely aware of it, and when they are, they do not possess sufficient evidence to substantiate their case since ethnic and racial discrimination has largely retreated underground as a result of being socially and legally condemned. In a compelling case study conducted by Quebec's Human Rights Commission, two hundred black and white "actors" with identical job qualifications and social characteristics were paired and then asked to answer the same newspaper advertisement announcing an apartment for rent. In thirty-three percent of cases, the Haitian actor, upon betraying his accent on the phone or when showing up in person, was not invited to visit the apartment, whereas his "white twin," calling minutes later, was granted a meeting with the landlord and invited to step inside the apartment for a tour. Of particular interest to the researchers was the fact that only two of the black actors were under the impression that the landlord was racially biased against them (Quebec, Human Rights Commission 1988). These findings suggest that the victims of ethnoracial discrimination can easily be misled into believing that they were dealt with on an equal footing with majority group members when in fact they were not. Because blatant manifestations of overt racism are no longer socially tolerated, racial exclusion is now perpetrated more covertly and is thus much harder to detect.

However, since the terrorist attack September 11, anti-Arab and anti-Muslim discrimination fuelled by prejudicial attitudes, discourses, and representations is emerging from the shadows and acquiring a newborn legitimacy (Antonius 2002). As a result, Arab Canadians, and especially the Muslims among them, tend to report unprecedented levels of discrimination since 2001. For instance, according to data collected from 1995 to 2004 by Quebec's Human

Table 1: Number of Ethnic Discrimination Complaints Filed by Arab-Origin
Individuals with Quebec's Human Rights Commission

	1995	1996	1997	1998	1999	2000	2001	2002	2003	2004
No of ethnic discrimination complaints filed by Arab-origin individuals	21	22	18	25	16	23	49	50	44	48

Rights Commission,[8] the number of alleged anti-Arab discrimination complaints filed with the commission has increased dramatically from 2001 onwards.

While Arab Quebecois filed on average 20.8 ethnic discrimination complaints per year for the 1995–2000 period, they filed on average more than twice as many (47.8) for the 2001–04 period. The sudden increase from 2001 onwards can unquestionably be considered a byproduct of September 11. What's more, the upsurge in self-reported anti-Arab discrimination seems, so far, to be outliving the immediate aftermath of September 11 since the average number of complaints has never reverted to pre-2001 levels. It should also be noted that the Canadian Islamic Congress (CIC) reports a 1,600 percent increase in hate crimes against Muslim-looking individuals or places between September 2001 and September 2002. The Toronto Police Service Hate Crime Unit noted a 66 percent increase in hostile acts against Muslim or Arab-looking individuals in 2001, 90 percent of that increase was most probably related to the September terrorist attacks since they occurred between September and October 2001 (cited in Helly 2004, 26).

One wonders whether perceived discrimination and prejudice are as prevalent among the first as among the second generation of Arab Canadians. Are children of immigrants more likely to be spared discriminatory and prejudicial attitudes given that they are more extensively incorporated into majority group culture(s) and social networks? Finally, do prejudice and discrimination, to the extent that they are perceived as such, contribute to ethnic and religious identity formation among second-generation Arabs in Canada? If so, how? I will attempt to untangle these questions in chapter 7.

GENDER TRADITIONS AS ETHNORELIGIOUS
IDENTITY MARKERS

As noted earlier, one can hardly ignore how tightly entangled religion and ethnicity became in the post-1970s Arab world. As several authors argue, in many Third World nations, anti-(neo)colonial nationalisms are not only articulated along religious and traditional lines but are also powerfully gendered. More precisely, in the postcolonial logic, women are often required to be the repositories of the nation's cultural authenticity, which is considered to have been corrupted through colonial domination (see McClintock 1997; Yuval-Davis 1997; Loomba 1998; Nagel 1998). In the case of Arab and other Muslim countries, the emphasis placed on the issue of women in this context of cultural resistance was particularly strong (Ahmed 1992; Abu Odeh 1993; Shukrallah 1994; Eid 2002). The intertwining of nation, religion, and gender intensified during the post-1970s era, following the rise of Islamist movements and discourses. As a result, traditional gender relations came to represent the epitome of a genuine Arab and Islamic identity in the view of many religious nationalists. This close connection between gender and nationalist issues in newly independent Arab countries was captured by Lama Abu Odeh (1993) through the telling image of the woman's body as "a battlefield where the cultural struggles of postcolonial societies were waged" (1993, 27). As Shukrallah states, "women, as a category, were central to the process of the recreation of the [Arab] community due to their role as symbolic cultural bearers of national traditions" (1994, 16). Homa Hoodfar offers a premium example of this cross between religion and ethnicity in the Arab world, through the case of the hijab: "The veil ... since the nineteenth century has symbolized for the West the inferiority of Muslim cultures" (1993, 5). She then adds that, in resistance narratives, "the mostly man-made images of Oriental Muslim women continue to be [seen as] a mechanism by which Western dominant cultures re-create and perpetuate beliefs about their superiority" (ibid). Therefore, in postcolonial Arab social imagery, the new veil (hijab) came to symbolize, not the inferiority of the native culture but, on the contrary, the recovered dignity of native customs.

Several studies in Europe and North America underscore how women's role as the repository of the group's cultural authenticity often results, within Arab and Muslim migrant families, in gendered child-rearing practices that force the second generation, both males and females, to engage traditional gender roles in the negotiation of their ethnic and religious identities (see for example Begag 1990; Afshar 1993; Lacoste-Dujardin 1994; Rooijackers 1994; Brouwer 1998; Kucukcan 1998; Ajrouch 1999, 2004). Arab or Muslim parents living in Western societies often feel the need to be more vigilant and controlling when it comes to childrearing. The underlying objective is to shield children from behaviours and norms that are deemed too liberal when measured against the cultural and moral standards held by the parents.

However, family socialization patterns within migrant Arab families indicate that parents are not equally strict with children of both sexes; girls appear to be more constrained than boys. The issue that is central to Arab parents, and to Muslim parents in general, is their daughters' sexuality; one commonly held view is that the honour and reputation of the family are dependent upon the "purity" of its female members. By extension, controlling and policing women's sexuality appears to be construed as a means of preserving the group's identity within the diaspora. As a result, the spatial mobility and freedom of young female teenagers is often fettered within Arab families living in Western settings. For instance, stricter social control over these girls' conduct is deemed necessary to make sure they do not date or engage in premarital sex. As Begag points out, controlling female mobility and sexuality "appears to be in the males' minds, a means of preserving [the group's] identity. It remains above all, a means of avoiding contact with Western society and ensuring a certain impermeability, symbolic of the purity of the inherited culture" (1990, 7). Furthermore, there is evidence to suggest that the use of traditional gender role models in the building of ethnic and religious group identities in a migratory context prevails not only among Arab-origin men but also among Arab-origin women. Thus, Read's quantitative study (2003), based on a sample of 501 Christian and Muslim Arab-American adult women from all over the United States, showed that both ethnicity and religiosity are statistically associated with inegalitarian gender role attitudes among the respondents.

But what about the children of Arab and Muslim migrant parents? Do they buy into the rhetoric of gendered traditions construed as cultural safeguards? Are there sex-based variations in the reception of such discourse? Lacoste-Dujardin (1994), in a study of religious identity among French girls of North African descent, argued that "Beurettes" tend to reject any parental prescriptions they deem incompatible with the liberal norms and views prevailing in French society. This too-simplistic view overlooks the complexity of the contradictory gender patterns and roles in which the girls are enmeshed. In fact, the literature suggests that if Muslim girls do tend to question more than boys the older generation's traditional norms and values, they can hardly dispose at will of the gender role models fostered by their parents and their community. Young Muslim girls living in the West are torn between two competing social influences; on the one hand, they are still considered by their community to be the bearers of tradition and culture, while on the other, they are expected by the host society to engage with new and more liberal Western-based cultural models.

According to Cécile Nijsten (1996), a majority of Dutch-Moroccan youngsters of both sexes do not endorse traditional views on gender relationships. Several case studies showed, however, that young Muslim girls schooled and socialized in Western societies have greater difficulty than boys in dealing with parental expectations, which they often experience as encroachments upon their freedom. In a quantitative study of attitudes among British-Turkish teenagers toward their parents' cultural and traditional values, Kucukcan (1998) found that girls (73 percent), more than boy (33 percent), feel that they are subjected to excessive parental control. Similarly, when asked whether they had disagreements with their parents, 69 percent of males, compared with 90 percent of females, answered positively. Also, whereas only 14 percent of males declared that their parents did not approve of their having a girlfriend, 88 percent of females said their parents were opposed to their having a boyfriend. Thus, these Muslim parents seem to be more concerned with their daughters' chastity than with their sons', because, as one father said, "girls are responsible for the honour of the family, and honour must be protected" (quoted in Kucukcan 1998, 111). Kucukcan reports that the young girls he interviewed were particularly critical of such gender-based double standards. Likewise, both Rooijackers (1992) in her research on young Turks living in the Netherlands, and Leveau (1997) in his study of French Beurs, concluded that girls tend to oppose traditional values and norms more than boys do. Lenie Brouwer (1998) reported that many among her sample of Dutch-Moroccan and Dutch-Turkish female teenagers underlined that boys were sending them mixed signals; for while boys do not mind sleeping with girls before marriage, they are adamant in their intention to marry a virgin.

It should not be assumed, however, that second-generation Muslim girls have altogether rejected the gender models derived from their family culture. Rooijackers, for instance, reports that when her sample of second-generation Dutch-Turkish females were asked what it meant to them to feel Turkish, forty percent mentioned constraining rules and restrictions as defining cultural features of their community, which none of the male respondents did (1994, 104). According to Raissiguier (1995), young French-Algerian girls, while often rebelling against the controlling attitudes of their male kin (perceived as "double standarded"), are not willing to embrace unquestioningly Western views on female sexuality. In particular, says Raissiguier, French-Algerian girls disapprove of French girls' sexual attitudes, which they perceive as excessively promiscuous (1995, 86).

On the one hand, family and community play a significant part in regulating young girls' behaviours and attitudes. Morck, who interviewed young Muslim girls living in Copenhagen, concluded that gossip is a major contributing factor in this control system. One of Morck's subjects, for example, speaking about members of her community, said in the interview: "They are faster than CNN" (1998, 137). However, according to both Brouwer (1998, 150) and Afshar (1993), the level of social control exerted on the behaviour of young Muslim girls varies across class: "As we move up the social ladder, there is a less strict approach to daughters' activities" (Afshar 1993, 62).

On the other hand, school is a place where young Muslim girls and teenagers can escape the controlling gaze of family members. It is mainly through school that they come to adhere to models of gender relations that at least depart from those prevailing at home, if they do not clash with them. School gives young girls access to important power resources that, if necessary, can be mobilized to challenge parental authority. In this respect, according to several authors, the fact that French Beurettes are far more successful in school than Beurs has to be understood as a female strategy, albeit an unconscious one, to escape family control and pressure (Begag 1990; Kuusela 1993; Raissiguier 1995; Brouwer 1998). It can thus be said that young Muslim girls are actively engaged in the work of positioning themselves somewhere between, within, and against different competing discourses.

The few Canadian and American case studies on the relation between gender, ethnicity, and religion among Arab families largely confirm the research results pertaining to European settings. Kristine Ajrouch, who undertook in-depth qualitative studies of Muslim Arab families in Dearborne, Michigan, concluded that, for both the first and second generations, gender constitutes a foundational pillar of Arab identity in a diasporic context (Ajrouch 1999, 2004). She suggested, on the basis of interviews and focus group discussions, that female virtue, dignity, and reputation are tied to ethnic and religious identity maintenance among second-generation Arab Americans. Sharon Abu-Laban and Baha Abu-Laban's study (1999) on young people of Arab ancestry in Edmonton revealed that seventy percent of girls and forty-nine percent of boys felt that Arab-Canadian women face more problems than Arab-Canadian men in adapting to Canadian society. In-depth interviews revealed that these perceived problems of adaptation – considered by informants to be by-products of the inherited ethnoreligious culture – involve a wide range of restrictions exclusively applied to women. Furthermore, some female informants lamented the double standards that apply in the raising of boys and girls in Arab culture. Lois T. Keck (1989) found that most of the Egyptian-American girls she interviewed opposed the gender-specific standards governing child-rearing practices within their ethnic community. Several of the females interviewed by Keck saw in their parents' conservative values an attempt to enforce in America a moral code directly imported from the motherland, a code that some believed was probably even outdated in modern Egypt (1989, 109).

To recapitulate, most authors share the assumption that Arab parents' attempts to instil traditional models of gender relations in their children helps to maintain a distinctive group identity in a migration context. What remains unclear, however, is whether such gendered socialization represents a religious identity marker, an ethnic identity marker, or both. It is of critical importance to my research, therefore, to examine how gender, ethnicity, and religion intersect in the repertoire of identity of these second-generation Arabs, and how parental models are reappropriated and recomposed in the process.

4

The Place of Ethnicity
in Their Lives

Chapters 4 and 5 analyze quantitative and qualitative findings relating to ethnic and religious identities. It is important to bear in mind certain questions derived from the theoretical framework articulated earlier. Do these young adults of Arab origin harbour strong feelings of identification with their ethnic community and culture? Similarly, do they regard religion as a critical component of their personal identities and social selves? What is the significance of the Arab category for these young Arab Canadians?

Most importantly, are their subjective bonds with their ethnic and religious communities detached from sociocultural practices or are they sustained through repeated contacts with ethnic and religious networks and cultures? I shall also look at the relation, if any, between the ethnic and the religious components of these Arab-Canadians' identity structure. Is it sociologically relevant to use the notion of "ethnoreligiosity" to describe the ways in which religion and ethnicity intersect in the minds and lives of these second-generation Arabs?

Chapters 4 and 5 are organized along similar lines. Each of the following sections examines the respondents' scores on an identity retention index made up of four distinct subdimensions: objective-cultural, objective-social, subjective-cultural, and subjective-social. Quantitative and qualitative materials are then analyzed more specifically for selected indicators relating to each of the subdimensions as they pertain to ethnic and religious identity.

Table 2: Percentage Distribution for "Ethnic Identity's Global Index"

Ethnic Identity Strength	Distribution (%)
Very strong	3.0
Strong	45.4
Average	41.9
Weak	8.4
Very weak	1.3
TOTAL	100

Table 3: Compared Means of the Four Subdimensions of the Variable "Ethnic Identity"*

	Objective/ cultural	Objective/ social	Subjective/ cultural	Subjective/ social
Mean Score	0.42	0.50	0.19	0.55

*The lower the coefficient, the stronger one's ethnic identity.

THE GLOBAL INDEX OF ETHNIC IDENTITY: A QUANTITATIVE OUTLOOK[1]

As shown in Table 2, respondents show relatively high levels of ethnic identity retention. The majority (45.4 percent) have a "strong" ethnic identity, while an almost equal proportion (41.9 percent) fall into the "average" category. A very small proportion fall into the extreme categories, as only 3.1 percent scored "very strong," 1.3 percent "very weak," and 8.4 percent "weak." When breaking down the variable "ethnic identity" into its objective and subjective aspects, the latter appear to be more developed than the former. Thus, on a scale from zero to one – where zero equals the highest degree of identity retention and one the lowest – the mean coefficient for the subjective dimensions of ethnic identity is 0.37, as opposed to 0.46 for the objective aspects.

When comparing the means of all four aspects of ethnic identity (Table 3), it turns out that the most developed dimension by far is "subjective-cultural" (0.19), followed by "objective-cultural" (0.42), "objective-social" (0.50), and finally, "subjective-social" (0.55). It thus appears that the youths in this study have a stronger propensity to harbour pronounced feelings of identification with their ethnic culture than to maintain any other aspects of their ethnic identity, as indicated by the pronounced gap between "subjective-cultural" and each of the three other subdimensions of ethnic identity.

These findings confirm a trend ascertained by previous research, namely that a very strong ethnic self-concept tends to persist over time among the second generation (see Alba 1990; Breton et al. 1990, Waters 1990). Furthermore, these strong feelings of identification with the ethnic culture stand in contrast with the other significantly less developed aspects of their ethnic identity. These results lend partial support to the symbolic ethnicity hypothesis, insofar as they reveal an ethnic self-concept that is hypertrophied in comparison with the youths' less-pronounced incorporation into ethnic primary and secondary socialization groups. It cannot be said, however, that the communal basis underlying their ethnic identity is completely eroded. Indeed, the coefficients that are slightly below 0.5 relating to the "objective-cultural" and "objective-social" dimensions indicate that respondents are still, to a large extent, effectively socialized into their ethnic culture and community.

Another interesting finding in Table 3 is that these second-generation Arabs tend to retain their ethnic identity more at the cultural than at the social level. Put differently, respondents' identification with, and socialization into, their ethnic culture seem to be more pronounced than their identification with, and socialization into, their ethnic community. The notion of costless community, as understood by Mary Waters (1990), may help to account for this phenomenon. The process by which one becomes familiar with one's ethnic culture (its codes, language, values, etc.) does not necessarily involve intensive socialization into ethnic networks, or indeed any involvement at the social level. Waters argues, and I concur, that belonging to this form of "costless" and "symbolic" ethnic community is appealing to second-generation youth because it is not as demanding as building ties with an actual community of ethnic peers. Being enmeshed in social networks, be they ethnic or otherwise, means conforming to a socially binding framework of shared roles and obligations. In the case of second-generation Arabs, taking on "ethnic" roles and cultural obligations generally entails more restrictions upon one's liberties than taking on roles and obligations relating to Canadian society and culture.

Once again, however, it cannot be said that the communal basis on which the ethnic self-concept of these young adults of Arab descent rests has completely faded away. Since they are relatively familiar with Arab culture and language, while also being minimally enmeshed in a web of Arab primary and secondary groups, these Arab-origin youngsters depart from those "ethnic Whites" described by Waters (1990) and Alba (1990), who are largely cut off from their ethnic culture and community. In other words, their ethnic identity is not completely symbolic. During social interactions, however, they may be deploying a situational ethnic identity that allows them to activate or downplay at will symbolic materials drawn from their ethnic culture (Okamura 1981; Nagel 1994). I shall explore this question further.

SELF-LABELLING PATTERNS

The variable "self-labelling" is meant to determine the preferred source of collective identification for second-generation Arab youth. In a close-ended question, respondents were asked to choose from among a series of labels the one that best reflected their identity. They were asked "How do you usually think of yourself first and foremost?" and were provided with the following options:

a) Arab
b) Member of a National community (e.g. Egyptian, Moroccan, Lebanese, etc.) If so, specify which one.
c) Arab-Canadian (or Québécois[2])
d) National community-Canadian (or Québécois)
e) Canadian (or Québécois)
f) Other _____

The underlying objective of this question was to assess, first, the relative weight of ethnic identities in contrast with majority group identities, and second, the importance given to the Arab category as a source of identification compared with national origin. Table 4 displays percentage distributions for the variable "self-labelling" by "time spent in Canada," "religious affiliation," and "gender."

Contrary to what might be expected, the most popular answer to this question turned out to be "Arab," as opposed to national membership, both for the whole sample (40.8 percent), and within each "time-spent-in-Canada" bracket. However, the proportion of those who chose the Arab label was the lowest (34.4 percent) among

Table 4: Percentage Distributions for "Self-Labelling" with Selected Independent Variables

				Self-identification (percentages and frequencies)			
	Arab	_National Group_	_Arab Canadian (or Quebecois)_	_National Group – Canadian (or Quebecois)_	_Canadian (or Quebecois)_	_Other_	_Total_
Whole sample	40.8	28.0	21.2	2.8	1.2	6.0	100% (250)
By religious affiliation**							
Christians	35.2	30.2	24.1	3.7	1.9	4.9	100% (162)
Muslims	51.1	23.9	15.9	1.1	0.0	8.0	100% (88)
By time spent in Canada**							
Less than 10 years	44.0	34.5	13.1	4.8	0.0	3.6	100% (84)
Between 10 and 15 years	45.3	24.0	18.7	4.0	0.0	8.0	100% (75)
More than 15 years	34.4	25.6	31.1	0.0	3.3	5.6	100 (90)
By gender							
Males	43.9	27.3	18.9	2.3	1.5	6.1	100 (132)
Females	37.3	28.8	23.7	3.4	0.8	5.9	100 (118)

* = $p < 0.1$
** = $p < 0.05$

respondents who had spent the longest period of time in Canada (fifteen years or more), whereas 44 percent of respondents who had lived in this country for less than ten years identified as Arabs. National membership was the second most popular choice for those respondents who had spent ten years or less in Canada (34.5 percent), as well as for those who had lived here for between ten and fifteen years (24 percent). The second most popular choice for respondents who had spent the longest period of time here was "Arab-Canadian" (31.1 percent), followed, in third position, by national membership (25.6 percent).

A majority of respondents thus favoured the "Arab" label over national membership regardless of time spent in Canada – and this was true even among respondents who were born here or had lived more than fifteen years here. Also, very interestingly, although Muslims were more likely than Christians to identify as Arabs (51.1

percent as opposed to 35.2 percent), the fact remains that the Arab label turned out to be the most popular answer among both religious groups. This shows that Christian Arabs, despite being more ambivalent toward the notion of Arabness, tend nonetheless to anchor their ethnic consciousness firmly in Arab culture and community. I will discuss this finding in greater detail in the qualitative analysis.

The above figures are, for the most part, consistent with the results of a 1993 Ontario survey of Arab Canadians of both first and second generations (cited in Hayani 1999). In this survey – which included the same "self-labelling" question and choice of answers as those provided in my questionnaire – the "Arab" label also turned out to be the most popular answer for the whole sample. Among respondents who had been living in Canada for more than ten years, the most popular answer was "Arab-Canadian" (note that "Arab" actually came in second place among this group). Thus, in both my research and the Ontario survey, the "Arab" label, whether taken alone or as part of a hyphenated Canadian identity, was favoured over national membership, regardless of time spent in Canada.

These findings, however, need to be interpreted with caution, especially in light of some divergent results yielded by the qualitative data. Most interviewees, when asked to expand on their answer, made it clear that their home country was the primary group or community with which they identified. At the same time, almost all of them considered themselves as belonging as well to the Arab community, and as sharing a broader Arab culture. In other words, the majority of them identified with the label Arab, while being aware of the numerous differences existing between the various Arab groups.

Thus, subject N, a Christian woman of Syrian descent, declared: "Arab is a very general term. When one speaks about the Arab people, one speaks of a people who live under the same conditions ... Maybe at the political level, it is the same, the language also... There are several things that unite us. But essentially, at the cultural level, the mentalities and all that, it's very different. Even if we take, for example, Syrians and Lebanese, who are neighbours, it's a completely different mentality ..." Informant P, a Christian woman of Lebanese origin, said: "For sure, I'd be more inclined to say I am a Lebanese but, at the same time, I am Arab ... Of course there are

differences but ... It's like if you take Europeans, such as a Spanish
and a French, there are a lot of differences, but they remain Europeans. But for them, it's more at the geographic level – it's the same
continent – whereas for us [the Arabs], it's more than merely geographical: It's really ... the culture, there are several commonalities:
the traditions, the mores ... There are differences, that's for sure,
but still."

Several Christian informants reported that they identify as Arabs
only insofar as it is understood that the label does not apply exclusively to Muslims. They resented both the host society and Muslim
Arabs for tending to equate Arab culture with Islam. Informant B, a
Canadian-born Christian man of Lebanese descent, declared that he
is first and foremost Lebanese. But when asked whether he also
identified as an Arab, he added: "Being Lebanese is one part of the
Arab community, but only as long as it is made clear that there are
Christians among Arabs. Once this point is stressed, yes, I consider
myself as an Arab. I have no problem with that." Informant P, when
asked whether she makes a distinction between her Lebanese and
her Arab identities, gave the following answer: "Perhaps a Muslim
Algerian would say that I am not Arab because Lebanon has undergone too much Westernization and because there are Christians
there. You know what I mean? ... But I say I am Arab because I speak
Arabic, I listen to Arab music. We are Arabs in my country after all.
To me, being Arab, it's not only being Muslim. It's really more, like,
the Arab culture."

Thus, when contrasted with these narratives, the quantitative
finding suggesting that the Arab label is preferred over national
membership should be put in perspective. More specifically, Arab
identity is endorsed by most informants for what it actually is,
namely, an overarching identity that, far from superseding national
membership, is coupled with it (as mentioned, however, many
informants, particularly Christians, identify with this pan-ethnic
label only insofar as it does not negate their national and religious
subgroups). How can we account, then, for the fact that in the questionnaire, a majority of respondents chose the Arab label over
nationality as a main source of self-identification?

First, as stressed earlier, ethnic identity, like any other form of identity, is not only multidimensional but also situational (Okamura
1981). Thus, depending on the social context and on the person to
whom they are speaking, these second-generation Arabs are likely

to emphasize or downplay different aspects of their identity. This could explain in part why a majority of respondents chose the Arab label over national membership in the specific context of this study; knowing that the research focused on Arab identity, respondents may have felt expected to stress, first and foremost, their identification with the Arab community. Nonetheless, it is safe to say that, although national membership constitutes a chief identity provider, respondents make significant room within their identity structure for their Arabness, understood as a broader pool of cross-national cultural references.

Another explanation for the respondents' choice of the Arab label is that, as previously mentioned, ethnic identity is generally delineated by both internal and external boundaries (which structure each other dialectically). To reiterate, internal boundaries refer to a group's self-produced definition, shared memory, and culture. It was also said – and this is central to the present argument – that the collective Us forming internal boundaries is always defined in relation to Them, which contributes to the shaping of external boundaries (Barth 1969; Juteau 1997, 1999). Furthermore, it must be remembered that minority groups' internal boundaries always result from an unequal dialogue with the categorizing frame through which majority groups construct the cultural otherness of minorities. As far as minority groups are concerned, this unequal dialogue can translate into either alienated self-definitions or symbolic emancipation. In any case, self-images stemming from the periphery are always constructed in relation to a symbolic framework defined by the "centre" (Guillaumin 1972; Jenkins 1997).

Before analyzing the pan-Arab identity detected among the present sample in relation to this internal/external boundary hypothesis, it will be useful briefly to examine the literature on pan-ethnicity, which can be divided into two camps offering slightly divergent readings of the phenomenon. Some authors, embracing a post-Marxist perspective, stressed the detrimental power dynamic resulting from pan-ethnic labelling in some instances. For example, Alejandro Portes and Dag MacLeod (1996) consider that the adoption of the American-made "Hispanic" label by Hispanic-American youth should be understood as a form of symbolic violence, whereby external definitions are imposed on minority or disadvantaged groups who lack the resources (symbolic, material) needed "to resist outside labelling and construct a more positive image of

themselves" (Portes and Macleod 1996, 544). Inversely, Deirdre
Meintel (1993) and Gerd Baumann (1996), among others, under-
line the positive aspects of pan-ethnic labels. Baumann noted that
his South Asian informants (Pakistanis, East Indians, Sikh, etc.)
who live in a highly multiethnic London suburb reappropriate the
"South Asian" label by turning this overarching designation –
under which the British usually lump together various culturally
heterogeneous national groups – into a symbol of pride.

Some authors tend to adopt an in-between posture on this issue.
Most notably, Yen Le Espiritu, in *Asian-American Panethnicity*
(1992), demonstrates how in the us, the "Asian" label, initially
forced upon Asian-American minorities through outside labelling,
eventually came to act as a meaningful identity provider for the individuals so labelled. Anti-Asian racism, argues Espiritu, obliged the
targeted groups to mobilize as Asians to put up resistance in a form
that was compatible with the majority group's frame of reference.

Most scholars who reflect on pan-ethnicity among the Arab diaspora generally espouse a view akin to Espiritu's. As seen in chapter
1, authors such as Abraham (1983, 100), Suleiman and Abu-Laban
(1989, 4–5), and Kayal (1983) argue that the derogatory connotations conveyed by the Arab label as framed by the Western mind
help to foster Arab consciousness and solidarity among the Arab
diaspora in North America. This approach, in keeping with that of
Espiritu (1992), shows how a derogatory outside label can be
reappropriated by the group to which it is applied and turned into a
symbol of resistance against symbolic domination. However, following Portes and Macleod (1996), it must be stressed that the
emergence of, say, "Arab-Canadian pride" implies an ongoing and
unequal struggle against the overwhelming influence of the derogatory connotations conveyed by the dominant representations of
Arabs in Canada.

In fact, both perspectives are relevant to the case of second-generation Arab Canadians. In Canada, as in any other Western country,
Arab nations are presently construed as undifferentiated entities, all
lumped together in popular imagery as well as in a host of official
publications and statistics. With this in view, the popularity of the
pan-ethnic Arab label among this sample has to be understood in
part as an overdetermined identity mirroring a definition imposed
from the outside. But one important question remains: if the out-
side-labelling hypothesis is true, have Arab-Canadian youth also

imported from the outside, along with the label, the web of dominant significations attached to it? If this were the case, then one would be largely justified in referring to this external influence as a form of "symbolic violence," since Canadian perceptions of the "Arabs" are in general highly negative and culturally disparaging[3] (note that in this respect Canadians are not exceptional within the broader Western context).

However, the informants who expounded on the meaning they give to their Arab identity substantiate Meintel's (1993) and Baumann's (1996) portrayal of pan-ethnic identity as a positive badge of pride. It could be, then, that the assertion of a shared Arab identity and memory by these second-generation Arabs represents a form of reactive ethnicity triggered by Canadian-made stereotypes and prejudices. In other words, set against the reductive and derogatory representations of "Arab" is a counterimage that is meant to challenge Western-made neocolonial perceptions. But as mentioned above, the reappropriation of a category so laden with negative connotations necessarily entails the subversion of the dominant significations attached to it. This is precisely the kind of symbolic subversion that informant H, a Canadian-born Muslim Algerian woman, performed during the interview. When asked whether she identified with the Arab label, she said: "Well, it depends on what you have in mind. Because often the Arab label [means] that they [the Arabs] are all Mafioso's, thieves, you know, delinquents. There is a lot of that in the label 'Arab.' But me, it is not with this label that I identify."

The inversion of the polarity attached to external definitions of Arab is facilitated by the fact that, in contrast with Hispanic or Asian identities, Arab identity has a history of its own rooted in the country of origin of these young Canadians of Arab descent who make use of it in a Western context. Indeed, this pan-ethnic identity derives from a nationalist movement that goes back to the end of the nineteenth century. Furthermore, Arab peoples were once united under a common political, religious, and cultural block from the seventh to the fifteenth century under the Umayyad and Abbassid dynasties. As a result, second-generation Arab Canadians today can forge their pan-ethnic identity by drawing on a large array of Arab-made positive symbolic markers and historical references. This is illustrated by the responses of informant E, a Canadian-born Christian Lebanese male:

INTERVIEWER: "Is your cultural heritage important to you?"
INFORMANT E: "Yes."
INTERVIEWER: "Despite the criticisms you voiced previously?"
INFORMANT E: "I was talking about a certain mentality. But there
   are [many] good things in our culture. Because I find that being
   an Arab ... there is a history, you know what I mean? The Arabs,
   it's a people with a history, they left their mark on Earth. I am
   proud to be Arab!"

Thus, the Arab label can also be associated with an internal form
of ethnic boundary. Informants can indeed draw on their group's
own symbolic resources to resist external derogatory definitions
imposed on them by the host society. And these symbolic resources
allow second-generation Arabs to subvert, for purposes of self-identification, the signified externally attached to the signifier "Arab."
However, as noted above, the emergence of an "Arab-Canadian
pride" implies an ongoing unequal struggle against anti-Arab stereotypes and prejudice in Canada. I pay special attention to this
question in the last chapter.

Interestingly, complementary data that are not displayed in Table 4
indicate that self-labelling patterns do not differ significantly across
national groups, even after having controlled for religious affiliation.[4] The Arab label was chosen by a majority of Algerian-origin
(55 percent), Moroccan-origin (53.8 percent), and Syrian-origin
(67.5 percent) respondents, while the most popular answer for Egyp-
tian- origin respondents (53.6 percent) was "Arab-Canadian (or
Québécois)," followed by "Arab" (21.4 percent).[5] The only exception to this dominant trend would be Lebanese-origin Christians, for
whom national membership was the preferred answer (42.7 percent),
followed by "Arab" (24.0 percent), "Arab-Canadian (or Québécois),"(21.9 percent), "Lebanese-Canadian (or Québécois)," (4.2
percent), and finally, "Canadian (or Québécois)," (1.0 percent).

The Lebanese exception can be accounted for by the fact that in
Lebanon, the emergence of group consciousness among Christian
Maronites has been historically inseparable from nation-state
building. Moreover, ever since Lebanon's religious civil war in the
1970s and 1980s, Christian Lebanese nationalism has become even
more cut off from pan-Arab sentiments and rhetoric because Muslim Lebanese were prompt to play the pan-Arab solidarity card to
foster their own nationalist agenda throughout the civil war.

That being said, the data pertaining specifically to Christian Lebanese reveal that the "Arab" and "Arab-Canadian (or Québécois)" categories, when merged, yield a percentage (45.9 percent) almost equivalent to the combined percentage of answers falling into the "Lebanese" and "Lebanese-Canadian (or Québécois)" categories (46.9 percent). It thus appears that, even among Christian Lebanese, Arab identity (taken alone or in a hyphenated form) is almost as likely as national membership to be mobilized for ethnic identity building purposes in a Canadian context.

Finally, as seen in Table 4, the variable "gender" does not have a statistically significant impact on self-labelling patterns. The Arab category was favoured over national membership among both gender groups, although this preference was stronger for males than for females (44.3 percent as opposed to 37.3 percent). More interestingly, "religious affiliation" (Christian or Muslim) was slightly correlated with "self-labelling." Although the Arab label was the most popular category for both religious groups, Muslim respondents were significantly more likely to identify as Arabs, compared with their Christian ethnic peers (51.1 percent versus 35.2 percent). This could be accounted for by the fact that the great majority of Christians in this sample are Lebanese, who, once again, tend to identify more with their national group than with the Arab community as a whole. But perhaps the chief contributing factor to this discrepancy is that Christian Arabs in general tend not to feel as close to the Arab community as their Muslim counterparts since, in most Arab countries, the notion of Arabness is laden with Islamic references in the popular imagery of majority groups.

In conclusion, I wish to draw attention to the dramatically small proportion of respondents (25.2 percent) who selected the Canadian or Quebecois categories (taken alone or in a hyphenated form) as their preferred self-defining label, compared with the much higher proportion of respondents (68.8 percent) who chose to define themselves solely in "ethnic" terms. This finding raises interesting questions concerning the way second-generation youngsters relate to Canadian and Quebecois identities. In any case, it is consistent with the findings yielded by previous research on other racialized groups of second-generation youth in Quebec. In an interview-based study, Micheline Labelle (2004) observed that second-generation Haitian and Jamaican Quebecers show extremely weak levels of emotional and symbolic attachment to Quebecois and Canadian identities, which they tend to consider as labels denoting nothing more than a territorial-based citizenship. Furthermore, the participants Labelle interviewed shared an ethnicized and non-civic view of Quebec identity, "which is reflected by the recurrent and pejorative image, markedly present in their discourse, of Québécois pure laine – old-stock Quebecers or Quebec-born residents of French descent" (2004, 57). She concludes that despite the relentless efforts of the Quebec government and nationalist elites to de-ethnicize the "Québécois" label, visible minorities continue to regard the latter as referring exclusively to Quebecers of French descent .

Could Labelle's findings apply also to second-generation Arab Quebecers who, like blacks, tend to be perceived as racialized Others in the majority group's popular imagery? In other words, could the low propensity of Arab Quebecers to resort to majority group labels in constructing their cultural identity be a reflection of their perception that, in Quebec, the national "Us" is saturated with ethnic symbols and memory excluding those citizens whose ancestry is non-French? The sections to come provide insight into how Arab-origin youth relate to, and identify with, majority groups and cultures in Canada and Quebec. This issue will be touched upon indirectly as I analyze how participants account for their feeling of belonging to a culturally distinct ethnic community in Canada and Quebec. Shedding light on the making of a group's collective Us (ingroup boundaries) begs the question which groups come to be construed as Them in the process (outgroup boundaries), and why.

ATTITUDES TOWARD ETHNIC ENDOGAMY

In a migratory context, commitment to ethnic identity maintenance is perhaps best signalled by one's intention of marrying an ethnic peer. Indeed, the importance attached to ethnic endogamy uncovers the extent to which children of immigrants feel the need to structure their most intimate relationships along ethnic lines.

As seen in Table 5 below, a majority of respondents (41.7 percent) deem it "important" to marry inside their ethnic group, whereas 32.8 percent consider ingroup marriage as an ideal but not necessary, option. Finally, 22.3 percent stated it was "not important" for them to marry inside their ethnic group, while a meagre

Table 5: Percentage Distribution for "Attitude towards Ethnically Endogamous Marriage"

Level of Importance	Distribution (%)
Important	41.7
Ideally but not compulsorily	32.8
Not important	22.3
I don't want it	3.2
TOTAL	100

3.2 percent reported they did not want to marry an ethnic peer. So generally speaking, ingroup marriage seems to be a highly popular option among these second-generation Arabs.

Interestingly, Baha Abu-Laban (1980, 161) found that 42 percent of his 1974 sample of both first- and second-generation Arab Canadians reported that ethnicity was "not important" in their choice of spouse. By contrast, only 22.3 percent of my sample gave the same answer. Also, while 54 percent of Abu-Laban's respondents identified ethnic endogamy either as a preference or a necessity, as many as 74.5 percent of my sample either prefer or insist on marrying an ethnic peer. At first sight, these discrepancies appear counterintuitive since there was a much higher proportion of immigrants in Abu-Laban's sample than there is among the group of second-generation Arabs comprising the present sample. But this anomaly suddenly makes sense once cohort variations are taken into account. Abu-Laban's respondents, in 1974, must have belonged to a cohort of Westernized or Western-schooled Arab migrants who, as a result, were little inclined to engage in insular patterns of ethnic behaviours and attitudes. Inversely, most Arab-origin youngsters making up my sample originate from families that migrated to Canada from the 1970s onwards. Therefore, their parents are far more likely to be staunchly committed to ethnoreligious identity maintenance than previous migratory cohorts. It could thus be that, at present, the stronger inclinations of second-generation Arab youths toward endogamous marriage are the result of stronger parental commitment to ethnic and religious identity transmission. Also accounting for these cohort variations is the fact that, today, Arab Canadians who are committed to ingroup marriage can choose from a much larger pool of potential mates than they could twenty-five years ago.

The interviews yielded a wide array of reasons for wanting to marry an ethnic peer. Those committed to endogamous marriage often argued that sharing a common cultural background facilitates mutual understanding between spouses. The importance placed by these informants on "cultural connectedness" is justified by various motives. Informant K, a Muslim woman of Algerian descent who had been in Canada for eleven years, stated that she could not marry a Canadian or Quebecois because he would not be able to understand her, given their cultural differences. When asked to specify what she meant by cultural differences, she mentioned family values: "They [Canadians and Quebecois] don't have the same values. They do not place as much importance on the family as we do. There are many different things." Likewise, informant B, a Canadian-born Christian male of Lebanese origin, mentioned that he could not marry a Canadian or Quebecois woman because they were not sufficiently family-oriented. However, his understanding of family-oriented values departs from that of the female participant quoted above: "I find that the difference [between Arab and Canadian women] lies in the family, family values ... I don't know, I find that here [in Canada] they [women] want too much freedom. There is 'not free at all,' and 'too free.' I am not saying that they [women] should all be left inside the house, but there are limits in all, I find."

Similarly, informant C, a Canadian-born Christian male of Lebanese-Palestinian origin, prefers to marry an Arab woman because, according to him, Canadian women are more likely to "ask for divorce." Thus, for these two men (informants B and C), marrying an ethnic peer is important in order not to end up with a wife who is too liberty-hungry in one case, or prompt in asking for a divorce in the other. Their preference for ethnic endogamy is fuelled by their uneasiness with women's freedom and autonomy, which, for them, is epitomized by Canadian women.

Three female participants (informants N, I, and M) outlined that it was important for them to marry an ethnic peer so that their parents would get along with their son-in-law. Two respondents (N and L) mentioned that they would prefer an Arab spouse to ensure that their children knew Arabic later in life.

Several interviewees who wanted to marry an ethnic peer stated their preference for a spouse who shared the same national background or was Arab at the very least. Informant M, a Christian woman of Syrian origin who had been in Canada for eight years, explained it in this way: "First, he has to be Christian ... Wait, I'll tell you: First, Christian, and second, I prefer him to be Arab because I want him to get along with my family ... So, Christian and Arab. But what I prefer personally would perhaps be a Syrian because my mentality is Syrian. And the people whose mentality is going to coincide with mine are Syrians." Informant N, another Christian woman of Syrian origin who had been in Canada for twelve years, declared that she used to want to marry only a Syrian, but that she is now willing to compromise by marrying someone from a different national background, as long as he is Arab: "He has to be Arab, but who knows whether he'll be Syrian, Lebanese, even Armenian, or Iraqi, or Jordanian. It doesn't matter."

Interestingly, this Syrian-origin informant only mentioned Middle Eastern nations as possible countries of origin for her ideal spouse, leaving out North African countries. Conversely, informant H, a Canadian-born woman of Algerian descent, stated that if she could not find an Algerian husband (her preferred option), she might also be content with an Arab Canadian from another North African nation (Tunisia or Morocco): "He has to be Muslim. Maybe not Lebanese, but from the Maghreb. Because Middle East and North Africa: I think these are two different things. We are all considered as Arabs, but I think we are all different from one another. It's really ... The religion, the values ... I think it's different."

Thus, in general, these informants would like to find a husband who shares their national background, but if such a thing is impossible, their second choice would be to marry either another Arab or, more specifically, an Arab sharing the same regional culture (i.e., from North Africa or the Middle East). Informants H's and N's narratives are a reminder that pan-ethnic Arab identity among the second generation can in some cases be subordinated to national and regional subgroup identities. However, there seems to be sufficient identification with, and cultural integration into, the broader Arab community for Arab-Canadian youths to consider marrying members of other Arab groups. Finally, the narratives suggest that religion is considered to be even more crucial than ethnicity in choosing the right mate, but this point will be further discussed in the next chapter.

Of the female subjects prioritizing ingroup marriage, two made a comment that is worthy of particular interest. Informants H and M both specified that they could not marry compatriots who had just recently migrated to Canada and would prefer to choose their future spouses from among their Canadianized ethnic peers of the second generation. They both disliked the prospect of marrying a "typical" Algerian or Syrian who, they argued, might be too dominating and controlling. To explain why she could not marry a Syrian from Syria, informant M remarked: "They [Syrian men] have conserved a mentality that I don't have anymore. For example, there are guys [in Syria] who say: *My wife doesn't need to work, and she should stay home.* No, this is nonsense! I want someone who is open- minded and who will share the household chores half and half with me." Informant H stated at first that men should have the last word with regard to family matters, but she added: "It would be complicated if I were to marry an Algerian from Algeria because he would be too controlling."

Thus, informants H and M both felt that they could not share their lives with an ethnic peer who had just recently migrated to Canada, since such a husband would be likely to hold views on gender relationships that depart significantly from theirs. In this respect, informants H's and M's comments are indicative of a desire to find in their future husbands traces of the very same hybridity that characterized their own cultural identity. A similar trend was observed in a recent interview-based study of second-generation Arabs living in Western Canada (Wanna-Jones 2003). This study showed that, although participants wished to marry people who shared their ethnicity (i.e., Arabs), they were not interested in marrying people who had lived all their lives in the Arab world; for such people would be unable to understand their "experiences within and between two cultures" (p.117).

Children of immigrants are solicited by different communities, primarily the ethnic community and the host society, which both provide them with essentialized definitions of culture and community. But whereas at the discourse level second-generation youths often choose their identity camp in a very definite manner, in effect their ethnocultural identities and practices result from very fluid processes that cannot be traced back once and for all to a single cultural framework (Baumann 1996, 1997). In this respect, the reservations of informants H and M about marrying an "ideal-typical" Algerian or Syrian – or people they perceived as such – illustrate the ambiguous character of their relation to their own ethnicity, which they want to maintain, but in a form consistent with the more liberal and Westernized models they have internalized.

In fact, the relative levels of ethnic over Canadian culture these second-generation Arab women wish to find in their Canadian-born husbands of Arab origin are hardly measurable. For instance, informant H, having stated her preference for an Algerian-Canadian husband, as opposed to an Algerian from the motherland, added the following: "But I don't want a Canadian-born Algerian who lost too much [of his Algerian culture] either, like my brother for example. You see, I couldn't marry someone like my brother. Well, not my actual brother but ...You know what I mean?" By this informants' standards, the line between an Algerian who has dropped the proper undesired cultural features and one who has dropped "too much" seems to be very fine. Again, such comments indicate that Arab-Canadian youths tend to strive for latitude and flexibility in the (re-)construction of their nuanced and heterogeneous ethnic selves. Kristine Ajrouch made a similar observation in her study of second-generation Arab-Americans. The youngsters she interviewed insisted on dissociating themselves from those whom they called the "Boaters," that is, recent Arab immigrants who symbolize *"that part of ethnicity which captures the originating immigrant culture"* (2004, 379), while also wanting to differentiate themselves from "White Americans."

As shown in Table 5 above, however, a significant minority of respondents (22.3 percent) do not consider it important to marry someone of the same ethnic background. Most interviewees who articulated this view did not set up ethnicity as a central axis of their identity structure. Informant J (a Canadian-born Muslim female of Algerian origin) even stated that she would be more comfortable with a non-Arab, whether as friend or spouse: "Arabs are too much into their religion, their ethnic group. Whenever you see a student who is Arab, even here [in the school], most of the time they are with another ten Arab students ... I find that Canada is such a multiethnic country that you have to interact with other countries, other ethnic groups. If you restrict your vision, your attention on, I guess, the Arab heritage, then ... you are not exploring other fields."

Children of immigrants can push their ethnic world aside for different reasons. They can either distance themselves from their ethnic community and culture, or sociopsychologically rebel against

Table 6: Percentage Distribution for "Attitude toward Endogamous Marriage" with Gender

| | Attitude toward Endogamous Marriage | | | | |
	Important	Ideally but not compulsorily	Not important	I don't want it	TOTAL
Gender					
Females	45.7	31.0	21.6	1.7	100
Males	38.2	34.4	22.9	4.5	100
Whole sample	41.7	32.8	22.3	3.2	100

them (Isajiw 1999). The above narrative clearly belongs to the former category. Indeed, informant J does not reject her ethnic culture and community so much as ethnic cliquishness and ethnicity taken as a defining axis of identity.

As outlined in Table 6, although women are more likely than men to favour endogamous over exogamous marriage, the difference is not statistically significant. Nonetheless, it is revealing that 45.7 percent of women find it "important" to marry an ethnic peer, while only 38.2 percent of men hold the same view. This difference can be accounted for by the fact that, within Arab communities, women are often considered to be the repositories of cultural authenticity and tradition. Therefore, the weakening of ethnic culture that inevitably results from exogamous marriage is seen as less problematic in the case of boys, since identity maintenance is considered to be transmitted essentially through women. For this reason, it is often the case that more social pressure is exerted on females to prevent them from marrying outside their ethnic group.

Finally, as shown in Table 7, Muslims are more inclined than Christians to favour ethnic endogamy, although this difference is not statistically significant. Indeed, 49.4 percent of Muslims versus 37.5 percent of Christians reported that it was "important" to them to marry inside their ethnic group. Also, 25 percent of Christians, as opposed to 17.2 percent of Muslims, consider that it is "not important" to marry within their own ethnic group. Such findings are not surprising since, for Arab Muslims, as opposed to Arab Christians, marrying outside their ethnic group in a Canadian context significantly increases their chances of marrying outside their religious group as well. Moreover, at present, there are considerable perceived cultural differences between Muslims and Christians,

Table 7: Percentage Distribution for "Attitudes towards Endogamous Marriage" with "Religious Affiliation"

	Attitudes towards Endogamous Marriage				
	Important	Ideally but not compulsorily	Not important	I don't want it	TOTAL
Father's religion					
Christian	37.5	35.6	25.0	1.9	100
Muslim	49.4	27.6	17.2	5.7	100
Whole sample	41.7	32.8	22.3	3.2	100

both groups construing each other as their prime religious out-group. This could explain, at least in part, why Muslim respondents are more reluctant than Christian respondents to marry outside their ethnic group in Canada.

Thus far, the cultural and social manifestations of the subjective dimension of ethnic identity have been addressed. In the coming sections, I shall examine whether the ethnic identity building strategies deployed by second-generation Arab youths are coupled with personal "investments" in their ethnic culture (objective-cultural), and with social contacts with their ethnic community (objective-social).

CULTURAL EXPOSURE AND PRACTICE

Language Proficiency

This section deals with Arabic language acquisition among Arab-Canadian youth. In Montreal, francophones and anglophones compete fiercely to ensure that language shifts among allophones turn to their advantage. In this context where language constitutes the principal terrain on which political struggles between majority groups are played out, considerable pressures are exerted on minority groups to choose the "right" linguistic camp. It then becomes interesting to examine the place left to minority languages within this complex (linguistic) power dynamic. Respondents were asked to self-assess their knowledge of spoken Arabic on a scale of four (Table 8). Because language choices and uses vary markedly depending on who is addressed, respondents were also asked to report the language they are most likely to use in various conversational contexts (Table 9).

Table 8: Percentage Distribution for "Proficiency in Spoken Arabic" with "Time Spent in Canada"

Time spent in Canada*	Self-Assessed Proficiency in Spoken Arabic	%
Less than 10 years	Good	78.6
	Average	14.3
	Poor	7.1
	I don't speak it	0.0
	TOTAL	100
Between 10 and 15 years	Good	54.7
	Average	32.0
	Poor	6.7
	I don't speak it	6.7
	TOTAL	100
More than 15 years	Good	41.8
	Average	26.4
	Poor	19.8
	I don't speak it	12.1
	TOTAL	100

* = $p < 0.01$

As seen in Table 8 above, a "good" knowledge of Arabic is reported by most respondents, regardless of the number of years spent in Canada. This suggests that ethnic language transmission among Arab communities is successful to a considerable extent. However, quite expectedly, the proportion of respondents whose proficiency in Arabic is "good" decreases as time spent in Canada increases – and this relationship is significant at the 0.01 level. The data thus point to a gradual and steady tendency toward ethnic language loss in the long run, a finding confirmed by most ethnic identity studies on the second generation (see B. Abu-Laban 1980, 202–26; Isajiw 1990).

As shown in Table 9, the longer the time spent in Canada, the more likely respondents are to resort to a Charter language (English or French) when speaking to their siblings, parents, or Arab friends. Inversely, the longer they have been living in Canada, the more likely they are to speak Arabic in all three conversational contexts. Among respondents who have spent the shortest amount of time in Canada (ten years or less), Arabic is the most widely used language for addressing parents, siblings, and Arab friends. Among those who have spent between ten and fifteen years in Canada, as well as among those who have spent more than fifteen years here, the same

Table 9: Percentage Distributions for "Most-Used Language" by "Time Spent in Canada" and by "Interlocutor Status"

Time spent in Canada	Most-used language	With Arab friends	With siblings	With parents
Less than 10 years	Arab	54.8	51.2	85.7
	French	26.2	31.0	9.5
	English	15.5	11.9	1.2
	Other	3.6	6.0	3.6
	TOTAL	100	100	100
Between 10 and 15 years	Arab	41.3	30.7	68.0
	French	38.7	50.7	22.7
	English	17.3	13.3	5.3
	Other	2.7	5.2	4.0
	TOTAL	100	100	100
More than 15 years	Arab	36.3	20.9	48.4
	French	34.1	56.0	34.1
	English	23.1	17.6	11.0
	Other	6.6	5.5	6.6
	TOTAL	100	100	100

pattern is at work, with one noticeable difference: Arabic is the language of choice with parents and Arab friends, but French is more often spoken with siblings.[6] Thus, with the exception of recent immigrants who use primarily Arabic in all three conversational contexts, second-generation Arab youths tend to communicate slightly more in Arabic with their Arab friends (French is not far behind) but prefer French over Arabic when talking with their brothers and sisters. It could be that children of immigrants tend, when interacting with second-generation ethnic peers (siblings and friends), to use a language that is less likely to be understood by other people in their surroundings, namely, their parents at home, and their non-Arabic schoolmates at school. This hypothesis would of course call for further (qualitative) investigation.

Based on some informal exchanges I had with respondents, one important remark deserves to be made. All the language-related questions in the questionnaire are phrased as follows: "Which language do you use *first and foremost* when speaking to ... (only one answer)." It was thus made clear to respondents that they were not allowed to choose more than one answer. Despite this restriction, an important minority of respondents asked whether they could circle more than one answer, arguing that they just could not choose one language over another as their most frequently used language

of interaction. This indicates that it would have been more sociologically and methodologically relevant to authorize the circling of
more than one answer.

Most importantly, this observation reveals, apart from the well-
established fact that bilingualism is widespread among children of
immigrants, that these youngsters resort to more than one language
simultaneously in certain contexts. Indeed, they often reported practising linguistic code switching in the course of the same conversation
and, at times, in the same sentence. Perhaps this phenomenon is more
pronounced in Montreal than in any other Canadian city. It was
demonstrated that Montreal's double majority status (French and
English) contributes to both greater ethnic language retention (Anctil
1984), and greater trilingualism rates among second generation
youth (Jedwab 1999). Put differently, in Montreal, not only have
children of immigrants been efficiently "Frenchified" (thanks largely
to Bill 101) but the double majority status of the city leaves much
room for other languages to flourish concomitantly (Meintel 1998;
Jedwab 1999). Inversely, in the rest of Canada, English tends more to
engulf minority languages in the long term, due to its hegemonic
position in the North American context (Anctil 1984). These factors
could account in part for the relatively marked tendency of second-generation Arabs to resort to code switching.

Consumption of Cultural Goods

The second-generation Arabs' contacts with the material and symbolic "goods" derived from their parental culture is another good
indicator of the degree to which they have been exposed to, and
socialized into, their ethnic culture (the objective/cultural aspect of
ethnic identity).

As highlighted in Table 10, respondents indulge to a large extent
in various cultural practices associated with their ethnic background. The most common ethnic-related cultural practice among
these second-generation Arabs is eating ethnic food, that is, food
pertaining to the respondent's ethnic origin. Indeed, the overwhelming majority of them eat ethnic food "often" (at least once a week),
and this majority remains very high and stable across all three
"time-spent-in-Canada" brackets (between 87 percent and 91 percent). Such a finding is consistent with Isajiw's observation that
"the tradition of eating ethnic food is maintained from generation

Table 10: Percentage Distributions for "Consumption of Cultural Goods" with "Time Spent in Canada"

			How Often Do You		
		Eat ethnic food	Listen to ethnic music	Watch/listen to ethnic programs	Read ethnic newspaper
Less than 10 years	Often	89.3	64.6	42.9	9.5
	Occasionally	6.0	23.2	33.3	21.4
	Rarely	4.8	8.5	19.0	27.4
	Never	Not an option	3.7	4.8	41.7
	TOTAL	100	100	100	100
Between 10 and 15 years	Often	90.5	41.1	21.3	8.0
	Occasionally	8.1	34.2	36.0	10.7
	Rarely	1.4	19.2	22.7	18.7
	Never	Not an option	5.5	20.0	62.7
	TOTAL	100	100	100	100
More than 15 years	Often	86.8	41.1	20.9	4.4
	Occasionally	9.9	31.1	34.1	12.1
	Rarely	3.3	17.8	23.1	22.0
	Never	Not an option	10.0	22.0	61.5
	TOTAL	100	100	100	100

Time Spent in Canada (row label for the table)

to generation more than any other ethnic pattern of behaviour" (Isajiw 1990, 67).

The second most widely retained ethnic-related practice in all three "time-spent-in-Canada" categories is listening to ethnic music, followed by watching and listening to ethnic programs.[7] Regardless of time spent in Canada, most respondents declared listening "often" to ethnic music. However, time spent in Canada matters somewhat as far as the consumption of ethnic programs is concerned. Thus, most recent immigrants (42.9 percent) reported that they "often" watch ethnic programs on television or tune in to ethnic radio. However, the majority of respondents who have been living in this country for more than ten or fifteen years watch or listen to ethnic programs only "occasionally." The only ethnic pattern of behaviour that is clearly uncommon among all three "time-spent-in-Canada" brackets is reading newspapers and magazines that cater to one's ethnic group. This could be accounted for by the fact that the proportion of children of immigrants who read and write well in their ethnic language is commonly low, in particular when the alphabet of the ethnic language differs from the majority group's alphabet. It must also be kept in mind that, in this age of multimedia, reading is largely neglected by teenagers and young adults irrespective of ethnicity.

Interestingly, the interviews have disclosed that, whereas the practice of eating ethnic food goes back to early childhood, watching ethnic programs and listening to ethnic music are often part of a process of ethnic (re)discovery that takes place at the end of adolescence, that is, at a time when children of immigrants often try to become more familiar with their ethnic culture (Laperrière 1994). Indeed, the narratives suggest that listening to ethnic music – a popular activity according to quantitative data – is a key element in the ethnic revival experienced by second-generation youth. Thus, informant P said that she feels more Lebanese than before, in part because of her renewed interest in her country's musical heritage: "Last year, I have started being more interested in my country's political affairs, the music ... To me, the music is also the culture. That's why it [the music] is very important to me."

INGROUP FRIENDSHIP

The objective/social dimension of ethnicity relates to the degree of social interaction and involvement with the ethnic community. Ingroup friendship constitutes a premium expression of ethnic-based social interactions in the private sphere. Respondents were asked the following question: "I would like you to think about your three closest friends who are not relatives. Of these friends, how many belong to your ethnic group (or to any another Arab group)?" As seen in Table 11 below, most respondents (49.8 percent) reported that their three best friends were ethnic peers, while 24.5 percent reported that two out of their three closest friends were ethnic peers. Only 8.8 percent reported that none of their three best friends were ethnic peers.

In a Toronto study (Isajiw 1990), a sample of first-, second-, and third-generation respondents from six different ethnic groups were asked the same question. At 51 percent, Jews turned out to be the group with the highest proportion of second-generation youth whose three best friends were ethnic peers (Isajiw 1990, 57). This is

Table 11: Percentage Distributions for "Ingroup Friendship" with "Gender," "Religious affiliation," and "Time Spent in Canada"

		No. of friends of same ethnicity				
		3	2	1	None	Total
Whole sample		49.8	24.5	16.9	8.8	100
By gender	Males	54.5	23.6	12.9	9.1	100
	Females	44.4	25.6	21.5	8.5	100
By religious	Christians	54.7	21.1	16.1	8.1	100
affiliation	Muslims	40.9	30.7	18.2	10.2	100
By time spent in	10 years and less	63.1	19.0	13.1	4.8	100
Canada*	Between 10 and 15 years	49.3	26.7	18.7	5.3	100
	15 years and more	37.8	27.8	18.9	15.6	100

* = $p < 0.05$

only one percent higher than the proportion of second-generation Arabs within my sample whose three best friends share the same ethnic background. This suggests that these second-generation Arabs tend to be markedly engaged in endogamous patterns of friendship. The variable "time spent in Canada" has some impact on ingroup friendship (the relationship is significant at the 0.05 level); the proportion of respondents who have three ethnic peers as their best friends drops from 63.1 percent to 37.8 percent as we move from the highest to the lowest "time-spent-in-Canada" category. Within each of the three groups, most respondents declared that their three best friends were ethnic peers. This suggests that second-generation Arabs tend to be rather cliquish in their patterns of friendship, a trend that prevails (while declining) as more time is spent in Canada.

Throughout the interviews, informants accounted in various ways for the predominance of ethnic peers within their circle of best friends. However, nearly all subjects who engaged primarily in endogamous friendships explained that they were not purposely avoiding non-Arabs. Most of them mentioned that the majority of their good friends were of Arab origin (often countrymen or women) because they believed that ethnic peers were more likely to have the same "mentality" and would thus understand them better:

INFORMANT N, Syrian-origin: It's an ambiguous question because I don't choose my friends based on their ethnicity. I choose my friends based on who they are. But necessarily, because of my mentality, because of my tastes, what I like to do, and all that, I am gonna meet ... I am gonna choose people who have the same cultural background as mine, or even the same religion.

INFORMANT B, Lebanese-origin: I feel more comfortable with Lebanese, but it is not because they are Lebanese. It's just that our mentality, our way of thinking coincided. That's all. But I could have connected with non-Lebanese.

INFORMANT I, Moroccan-origin: No, not necessarily [she does not look for Arab friends], except I tend more to choose my friends among people of my culture. This way, it's easier: we better understand each other. The things we talk about. We know what the other is talking about.

INFORMANT H, Algerian-origin: "My close friends are Arabs. Because we have the same values. It's when it comes to values that we are gonna be on the same wave length, you know what I mean? Like, there are some Quebecois who are very open-minded and all ... but they don't understand [us]. They say they do, but they don't."

INFORMANT M, Syrian-origin: It's because our mentalities coincide. If the mentalities coincide.... Maybe it's the Arab mentality that brought us together. But it's not because you're Arab that you are gonna be a friend of mine. No, it means nothing. It just proves that they [the Arabs] have the same mentality.

Few participants elaborated on how exactly this strong ethnocultural connection operates with ethnic peers. Informant I, a Canadian-born Muslim female of Moroccan descent, argued that she has a majority of ethnic peers as best friends because "Arabs are more generous and welcoming towards newcomers. Their heart is wide open." Similarly, informant F, a Muslim male of Algerian origin who has been in Canada for twelve years, states that he is inclined to make Algerian friends because they are "warmer" than Canadians. But most other subjects who favoured ingroup friendship were more evasive, simply saying they did not feel comfortable with Quebecois, who they considered were too culturally different.

However, interviewees were asked a question (not covered in the questionnaire) that provides more information on these perceived differences between what was often referred to as the Arab "mentality" on the one hand, and Quebecois or Canadian cultures on the other. This perceived cultural gap could account to a large extent for the fact that a majority of interviewees said not only that they were more inclined to befriend ethnic peers but also that they had very few Quebecois within their circle of best friends. Interviewees were asked, "Do you think your ethnic group's culture is much different from Quebecois or Canadian cultures? If so, in which ways do you think it is?" Three recurring themes emerged from their answers: 1) respect versus disrespect of parental authority, 2) community-oriented versus individualistic values, and 3) strict versus liberal education (which, we shall see below, is a strongly gendered issue).

Relationship to parental authority was considered by five informants to be a crucial cultural difference between Arabs and majority groups. For instance, informant C, a Christian male of Lebanese and Palestinian origin, declared that he was afraid of Quebecois values, especially where child-parent relationships were concerned: "Once I saw a girl shouting at her mother, and the mother didn't answer back. Me, if I shout at my father, I get a slap right in the face. So, for sure it was shocking." Similarly, informant K, a Muslim female of Algerian origin remarked: "Respect of the family. Especially respect of the father. Here [in Canada] sometimes, when I go at my Quebecois girlfriends' place, and that they answer back to their parents ... I am surprised. Me, I'd get a slap. Also, here, if you hit your child, it's considered as something dramatic. But my father was slapping me when I was young. But he was not beating me."

Another perceived cultural difference that was frequently brought up by participants is that Canadian culture is too "liberal," particularly with respect to types of permission granted to children and gender relations. Thus, says informant K: "You see, when you're in elementary school, you want to be like them [the Quebecois]. It's easy in elementary school to adapt. But when comes a time where there are things that are not accepted by your parents, but that are accepted by your friends' parents, it's a whole different thing."

In the same vein, informants B, a Christian male of Lebanese ancestry, and H, a Muslim male of Algerian descent, both consider that female teenagers in Quebec are libertines or too sexually liberated. Informant B thinks that women here have too much "freedom." When asked to elaborate, he said: "For example, when I see a thirteen-year-old girl who speaks about her sexual relations, I find this a little bit exaggerated. And when girls here think that this sixteen-year-old girl is bizarre because she is still a virgin, I find this to be exaggerated."

Likewise, informant H believes that female teenagers in Quebec are too promiscuous: "My Quebecoises friends, they go: *Haaa! We went to a Club last night, I got drunk, and I woke up in his bed. Ha! Ha Ha! Ha!* And for them, it's really funny. I really don't think it's funny! You know what I mean?"

Finally, it was commonly reported that Arabs place greater importance on family and community-oriented values than Canadians and Quebecois, who are deemed to hold on to more individualistic values. The three following statements illustrate this view:

INFORMANT E: Well if I look at my family … I have the feeling that family is very important for Arabs. And I think that they're absolutely right. They're more bound by family.

INFORMANT D: Of course Arab culture is different. First, in Montreal, people are more individualistic, you know? Whereas us [the Arabs], we are trying more to live in community. Take me, for example: I am twenty-one, my brother's twenty-seven, and my sister's twenty-four, and we still live at our parents'. Whereas here, as soon as they hit eighteen, they must leave the house and live on their own. I am not saying that they are all like this … But in Montreal, from what I've seen, it's like that.

INFORMANT F: Family, the extended family, and friends are so important in Algeria or in the Arab world. There is a human warmth [in Arab culture] that can be found within circles of close relations. And this cannot be found here, or not to the same extent.

Table 11 reveals that males are more likely than females to have ethnic peers as best friends (although this correlation is not significant). Inversely, females are more likely to have best friends who are non-Arabs. These findings are in keeping with S.M. Abu-Laban and B. Laban's observations (1999, 121), drawn from an Edmonton sample of second-generation Arabs. As the authors concluded, and as my data set confirms, young Arab-Canadian females can sometimes, through outgroup friendships, gain a sense of personal freedom and individuality that they say is lacking within their circles of Arab friends.

For Arab-origin females, outgroup friendship often implies the temporary lifting of normative constraints usually imposed on them in the name of ethnoreligious tradition, and socially reinforced through the controlling gaze of ethnic peers. Below is a citation that illustrates this phenomenon. Having said that she does not "hang" much with Quebecois, this Muslim female of Algerian origin (informant K) adds that she does not like to be surrounded by too many Algerians either: "I am afraid of the Algerian mentality. I wouldn't like to hang with too many Algerians. I avoid them, especially boys. I avoid Algerians because they think in a certain way: they're gonna judge you all the time, all the time, all the time. Their mentality ... It's as if you were at home 24/7, but even worse."

In an informal exchange, another female informant explained that she tries not to become too involved with Arab men: "You heard how they [Arab boys] talk about girls? They look down on you if you start going out with a boy, or just flirting around with him." It thus appears that the behaviour of Arab-origin females is under close scrutiny within certain circles of Arab friends, specifically those where traditional views prevail. This could in part explain why the females in my sample tend slightly more than the males to have non-Arabs among their three best friends.

Inversely, ingroup friendship can be appealing to a certain category of interviewees (both male and female) who hold to more traditional values, and who, as a result, show a preference for traditionalist ethnic peer friends. Informants in this category have internalized a traditional normative framework, which they often set up as a defining component of their ethnic identity. Therefore, contrary to those who stay away from ingroup friendship because they suffer from the weight of tradition and conservatism, this category of informants prefers to be surrounded by friends who share their traditional views regarding gender relations, parental permission, and other such issues. Interestingly, two interviewees mentioned that they get along better not only with ethnic peers but also with non-Arab youth who come from equally traditional religious cultures, or cultures that are at least perceived as such (e.g., second-generation Greeks, Italians, Portuguese, etc.). For example, informant C, a male, declared: "I have a Jewish female friend, a Muslim female friend, I have Lebanese friends, I have a lot of Greek friends, Armenian friends, which are all groups with a culture similar to mine." Informant H, a Muslim female of Algerian descent, articulates the same view when she argues that other Mediterranean women, such as Italians, are more likely to understand, and relate to, the type of parental restrictions she experiences at home: "Religion doesn't necessarily play a role in my choice of friends, because I have an Italian friend. One of my best friends is Italian. And Italians ... I find that they have a lot in common with Arabs. Like, Italian girls, you know, their father is a bit strict, and, like, they can't do anything they want. And we get along very well because we understand each other. Personally, I need someone who's going to understand me if I say: *No, I can't go out tonight, my mom won't let me.* You know, I'm eighteen. If I say that to a Quebecois, he's gonna tell me: *Come on! Who cares about your parents?* You know what I mean? They are gonna tell me this as if it goes without saying, they won't understand."

For second-generation Arab women, ethnic distinctiveness tends to be associated with parental restrictions, whether negatively perceived (as with informant K) or positively (as with informant H). In other words, for Arab-origin females, the structuring of ethnic identity, both in its behavioural and subjective forms, can hardly be dissociated from the restricted latitude they have in negotiating permissions at home. It thus appears that traditional values, and their attendant rules and restrictions, help to a large extent, especially among Arab-origin female youths, to delineate the contours of ethnic boundaries.

As also shown in Table 11, Christian respondents are more inclined than Muslims to have three best friends who share their ethnic background (54.7 percent versus 40.9 percent), though such a correlation is not statistically significant. This finding is interesting because it suggests that Muslim youths depart from the image that Westerners generally cultivate about Muslim communities: a group with a withdrawn attitude accounted for either by sentiments of hostility or what are perceived as insurmountable cultural disparities. These data show that, while most second-generation Muslim Arabs favour ingroup friendship, they do so to a lesser extent than their Christian counterparts. Therefore, based on this case study, Islam cannot be considered as a factor reinforcing self-segregation patterns among Arab communities.

Finally, four interviewees, of whom three are Canadian-born, mentioned that they only started making friends with ethnic peers when they entered cegep. These informants, who had mainly been acquainted with non-Arabs prior to cegep, reported switching to ingroup friendship once they found themselves in an environment with a critical mass of ethnic peers. Informant H reports: "To be honest, in high school, I had more Quebecois friends [than Arab friends]. It's more when I got to Cegep Bois-de-Boulogne that ... here, in Bois-de-Boulogne, there are only Arabs [laughter] ... that I started to join a specific group. It's not as if my parents ... We do speak Arabic at home, but we speak more often French than Arabic at my place. But I learned Arabic with my friends [in Cegep]."

Previous research has shown that attending a school with a high concentration of ethnic peers increases the students' likelihood of developing ethnically segregated circles of friends (McAndrew et al. 1999). In this respect, the fact that the institutions selected for my study all have a high concentration of Arab-origin students is important in accounting for the high ingroup friendship rates detected among second-generation Arabs.

But there could be more to it than a mere matter of ratios. As noted earlier, the late teenage years often coincide with a period of ethnic (re)discovery during which second generation youths attempt to become more familiar with their culture of origin (Isajiw 1990, 37–8). Of course, the fact that the respondents all attend schools with a high concentration of Arab-Canadian students is certainly an important condition, and perhaps even a trigger, for the Arabization of their circle of friends. However, they probably would not have turned to ingroup friendship had they not developed, around the same time, an interest in their ethnic cultural heritage. Informant P puts it this way: "I don't know, during the past year, I got closer to ... I have started being more interested in my country's politics, and to the music. Even the people ... Before, I had no Arab friends, you know? Not even one Arab, really! I couldn't even get along well with an Arab. Now, like, I almost only hang with Arab people. My boyfriend is Arab. It's really a big change!"

PARENTAL COMMITMENT TO ETHNIC IDENTITY TRANSMISSION

This section examines how respondents perceive, and relate to, parental strategies, attitudes, and behaviours (conscious or unconscious) aimed at ethnocultural identity transmission. Except for a brief discussion of the results yielded by the global index of parental commitment to ethnic identity transmission,[8] this section is devoted essentially to qualitative data analysis. The collected narratives

Table 12: Percentage Distribution for "Parental Commitment to Ethnic Identity Transmission"

Strength of Parental Commitment	Distribution (%)
Very strong	35.8
Strong	35.8
Average	14.8
Weak	9.9
Very weak	3.7
TOTAL	100

turned out to be far richer than the quantitative material in terms of how the socialization process experienced by this group of second-generation youths contributed to the shaping of their ethnic identity.

As far as quantitative data are concerned, only one of the indicators measuring this variable (variable 17 in appendix B) taps into parents' *actual* attempts to socialize their children into their ethnic culture. As mentioned, they focus instead mainly on parental *commitment* to ethnic culture and identity transmission. Table 12 shows that a large majority of respondents consider that their parents prioritize the transmission of their ethnic culture and identity to their children: 71.6 percent of the respondents' parents fall into either the "strong commitment" (35.8 percent) or "average commitment" (35.8 percent) categories. Only 13.6 percent of the sample fall into the "weak commitment" and "very weak commitment" categories.

As previously stressed, the qualitative material provided precious information regarding which aspects of their ethnic culture respondents thought their parents most wanted them to retain. Interviewees were asked "Which aspects of your ethnic culture [do] your parents want you to retain in particular?" and "How do your parents let you know about it?"

Three females informants (informants H, I, and K) mentioned constraining rules as aspects of their ethnic culture their parents most wanted them to retain. Once again, it is not coincidental that all subjects associating ethnic identity transmission with parental restrictions were women. Parental transmission of the ethnic culture usually implies far fewer interdictions and restrictions for boys than for girls. In Arab cultures, at least in their traditional forms, it is not uncommon for girls to be burdened with extra controlling rules, which they eventually come to perceive as being synonymous with ethnic boundary maintenance. For instance, when asked which aspects of her culture her parents wanted her to maintain, informant H replied: "The values that they instilled into me. For my mother, it's fundamental ... You know, my mom was always telling me *Haa! In Algeria, you know, they don't do that, they don't go out with boys, they don't drink, they don't dress this way, yada yada yada.*" The parental "values" reportedly instilled in this informant all amount to a series of parental interdictions. Implied in this view is the notion that rules and restrictions are important foundations on which ethnic identity is laid. This perceived relation between cultural identity and normative restrictions could not be more clearly expressed than by informant K, a Muslim female of Algerian origin. When asked, "Do you speak Arabic?" she replied: "I tell them (my parents): *You are teaching me the mentality and that sort of thing. You give me rules. But when it comes to language, the interesting part of culture ... Well, I am not entitled to the interesting parts of culture.* That's the problem in my family: I only get the negative stuff of the mentality. And the nice part of culture, well, I don't get it." Informant K thus considers that her parents provide her with the "negative" sides of their ethnic culture, namely rules (equated here with the "mentality"), while depriving her of the interesting aspects of the same culture (namely, the language).

Migrant parents often cling to the very same standards with regard to child-rearing practices as those they embraced at the time of their migration (Isajiw 1999, 193). This is precisely the idea that informant H, a Canadian-born female of Algerian origin, conveys in the following excerpt:

Hmm, I don't know exactly what they [my parents] want me to conserve. The values that they instilled in me I guess ... These are not necessarily Algerian values ... Well they are, but they are kind of specific to the values my parents inflicted[9] on me. Because it's been thirty years now that my parents are in Canada, and they still have the mentality that their parents had when they raised them. That's why they raised us the way they were raised ... That's why I developed preconceived notions. I used to think: *In Algeria, people are really straight!* I went to Algeria two years ago. It was a big shock! When I got there, I realized that they [the girls] all did fifty times more stuff than I did: A lot of them drink, go out with boys. Ho yeah! The thing is that their parents evolved a little bit, whereas my parents raised me the way they were raised. So when I go to Algeria, I am told: *It's funny, but you are more Algerian than the Algerians we have here ...* I was born in

Quebec, you know, so logically, I should have turned Québécoise, but I turned more Algerian than the Algerians from Algeria!"

As underlined by this female informant, there is often a wide gap between the inherited cultural and normative standards of migrant parents, and those currently prevailing in their country of origin (Khosrokhavar 2000, 95). In other words, tradition-oriented migrant parents tend to hold on to "outdated" values, that is, values ossified in time, unaffected by the cultural changes that have occurred in their home country since they left it. Furthermore, when traditional migrant parents settle in a Western environment such as Canada, they often feel the need to impose even more rigid rules on their children, so as to keep in check the numerous liberal influences that threaten to undermine the largely phantasmal "ethnic" culture they wish to transmit to their offspring.

Paradoxically, toward the end of her remarks, informant H implicitly validates the very same essentialism that she previously decried in her parents' understanding of Algerian culture. Indeed, having stressed that her parents' notion of Algerian culture is largely imagined and thus in need of a reality check, informant H argues, even boasts, that when she goes to Algeria her traditional behaviours and attitudes make her "more Algerian than the Algerians from there." This example confirms that the ethnic self-representations of children of immigrants are heavily indebted to (dominant) essentialized and fixed conceptions of culture, even though, in effect, their identity strategies as well as their cultural norms and references are characterized by fluidity, pluralism, and hybrid amalgamations (Bauman 1996, 1997).

Other cultural features were mentioned by participants as aspects of their ethnic heritage that their parents wanted them to preserve. Both informants F and M reported that family-oriented values, in particular respect due to parents, were the most important cultural features their parents tried to instil in them. Informants E and O declared that their ethnic language was regarded by their parents as the most important cultural legacy that could be transmitted to their offspring.

The issue of family reputation also emerged as a recurring theme throughout the interviews. According to informant K, a Muslim female of Algerian origin, her parents wanted her to be committed to preserving the family reputation above all. As a result, she became highly self-conscious of what other people thought of her, having internalized the notion that family reputation is dependent upon the proper behaviour of family members:

What other people think is very important for my parents ... My mom always tells me: *you are your father's daughter*. If someone sees me on the street, he's gonna say: *That's the Jammal* [fictitious name] *girl*. But in my mind, there were no other people to judge me. I wouldn't see the other people, my parents' friends and all. When you live in a Quebecois environment, there's no one to say: *That's Mr So-and-so's daughter*. My mom still tells me to watch who I talk to, what I do, how I dress ... Because people can judge you. But here [in Quebec], people don't think this way ... Take my [Quebecois] friends for example; they don't care about what other people think of them. But now I care a lot about what people think. And now it's in me: you cannot humiliate me publicly.

This statement illustrates how in Arab culture, as opposed to Canadian culture, family reputation constitutes a highly valuable symbolic capital that has to be conserved by ensuring that the conduct of family members, especially female family members, is proper. Of course, the value placed on family reputation by parents, and the pressures the latter exert over children to protect it, vary from one family to another. In general, parents who attach importance to reputation are those whose views, beliefs, and attitudes are more traditional.

In Arab countries, parental concerns with family reputation are usually fed by the community's collective and multifaceted gaze, which brings deviant individuals and families into social disrepute. Things are different, however, in a migration context, where this "ethnic gaze" needs to be largely reinvented, unless the migrant family is strongly anchored in ethnic social networks. For instance, as highlighted by the remarks quoted above, informant K's traditional parents attempt to present a virtuous image of their family to a public that is largely indifferent to their "performance"; hence the subject's ambivalence toward her parents' concerns about what other people think. To put it in Goffman's terms, this subject feels she does not "play" to the same public as the one her parents want her to perform for. Yet she admits that "now it's in me"; that in the end her parents succeeded in instilling in her their concern with family reputation.

Informant L, a Christian female of Lebanese descent, also
declared that the notion of reputation was very important in her
family, but she opposed this parental value more strongly and
openly than informant K. She criticized the hypocrisy of her parents, who boasted about her "irreproachable" behaviour while
refusing to admit to their friends that their daughter was dating
boys. "Image is more important than reality [in my culture]. It's not
only about what a single person thinks or does, it's the actions and
ways of thinking of the whole family which is at stake. That's why
you carry a weight on your shoulders all along; it's not only your
own reputation that you either build up or ruin, it's the whole
family's reputation."

It is certainly no coincidence that the two subjects who reported
having suffered under parental pressure aimed at protecting family
reputation were women. Again family reputation is particularly
dependent upon the preservation of the female family members'
respectability and good virtue in the public eye. Therefore, the task
of protecting family reputation tends to be approached more
serenely by sons than daughters. For instance, in the following
excerpt, a Christian male informant explains how preserving the
"family name" is a very important concern not only for his parents
but also for himself: "Your family name is gonna determine who
you are, how people are going to perceive you ... My uncle always
used to tell me that my grandfather worked very hard to establish
our family name. And I don't want to be responsible for giving a
bad reputation to the family."

Interestingly, this male informant, contrary to female interviewees K and L, talked about the importance of preserving family reputation as something positive, if demanding. Indeed, he regarded his
family name as a source of pride ("built by my grandfather"), and
viewed it as an exciting challenge that he shared the responsibility
of protecting that name. It thus appears, based on the narratives
examined here, that preserving family reputation is more likely to
be experienced as a burden by females than by males.

Of the three interviewees who stressed family reputation as an
important parental concern, two were Christian. The quantitative
data also show that religious affiliation does not make a difference
with respect to the importance that Arab parents are thought to
place on family reputation. Indeed, as shown in Table 13, Christian
respondents are almost as likely as Muslim respondents to believe

Table 13: Parental Agreement with the Statement "Female Virginity has to be Preserved for Family Reputation" by "Religious Affiliation"

	Parents would agree completely (%)	Parents would somewhat agree (%)	Parents would somewhat disagree (%)	Parents would disagree completely (%)	TOTAL
Christians	48.7	23.4	12.3	15.6	100
Muslims	51.1	22.7	14.8	11.4	100

that their parents endorse the statement that "a girl's virginity should be protected until marriage by her male kin for family reputation to be preserved."

This suggests that placing a high value on family name and honour is not necessarily a Muslim-specific cultural feature, even though the majority of studies on this issue focused on Muslim groups (i.e., Begag 1990; Afshar 1993; Lacoste-Dujardin 1994; Rooijackers 1994; Brouwer 1998; Kucukcan 1998). Therefore, it may be the case that parental emphasis on family honour and reputation, rather than relating to a specific religious group, is connected with communal and family-oriented cultures, in which personal life choices and group status are forged relationally, caught up in a complex reciprocity. This close connection between gender, family reputation, and group boundary maintenance will be discussed further in chapter 6, dealing specifically with second-generation Arab attitudes toward traditional gender role models.

Participants were also asked whether the Canadian part of their identity could be held responsible to some extent for disagreements, even conflicts, between them and their parents. The most frequently reported culture-related examples of intergenerational tension relate again to parental restrictions. The restrictions most commonly reported by informants are curfew, followed by dating (especially for girls), and unconventional body modifications (piercing, tattoos, hair dying, etc.). The common denominator of these issues is they all amount to permissions denied by parents. Clearly, denied permissions are factors of dissension between parents and teenagers in most societies, though probably more in Western ones. But what is of particular interest here is that these second-generation Arabs tend to construe their desire to gain more freedom as a specifically Canadian component of their identity that clashes with their parents' culture. As a matter of fact, it seems that parents themselves quite often help to reinforce this cultural dichotomy in their children's eyes. Thus, informant F, a Muslim male who had been in Canada for eight years explains: "I go clubbing quite often. And sometimes my mom tells me: How about staying home more often to be in good shape for school? Once she went a step further: If you were in Algeria, you wouldn't be doing this. It's not because you're in Canada that you are allowed to act like Canadians!"

Likewise, when informant I, a Canadian-born Muslim female, is denied permission to do something, her parents often use this justification: "They tell me: *Ha! You shouldn't follow what Canadians do. They do what they have to do, and we do what we have to do. It's their problem.* My parents tell us that, at bottom, we are lucky to be living here because we can come back at 9:00 PM, whereas back there [in Morocco], kids have to come back at 5:00 PM."

In these latter two cases, the informants are being signalled by their parents that they should not expect to be treated according to Canada's cultural and normative standards, for they remain, respectively, an Algerian and a Moroccan merely living in Canada.

Inversely, other parents, especially when they have been living in Canada for a certain number of years, compromise more easily on how much freedom they should allow their children. For instance, when asked whether the Canadian part of her identity sometimes clashes with her parents' culture, informant O, a Canadian-born female Christian of Lebanese origin, responded, "No, no. Because it's been eighteen years since my parents first got here. We share the same religious ideology, the same political ideology, the same social ideology."

The conflict management strategies to which interviewees resort are varied, ranging from compromise to provocation and confrontation. There is one strategy that deserves special attention since it was frequently reported by participants: keeping things secret in order to avoid conflict. According to these second-generation Arabs, the most taboo issues relate to dating and sex. As might be expected, the great majority of those who reported keeping their romantic life secret from their parents were women. Thus, informant I, a Canadian-born Muslim female of Moroccan origin, stated that she would like to be allowed to date boys, as opposed to remaining a virgin until marriage as her parents wished. But when asked whether she had voiced this concern to her parents, she said, "No. I tried to talk about it with them, but they don't want to.

Because they don't talk about this kind of thing. It's one of the biggest taboos at my place ... I guess you could say my mom trusts me. Maybe she knows [that I date boys], but she doesn't want to talk about it. She knows that I live like that, and that I am obliged to ... [because] here [in Canada], to be happy, you've got to be like everybody else. You can't stay in your corner, completely isolated. ...

Other female informants who kept their romantic life secret from their parents were even more uncomfortable with doing so. As the following excerpt shows, informant L, a Christian female of Lebanese origin, resented the hypocrisy of her parents, who chose to turn a blind eye to her romantic life: "What I like about the culture here [in Quebec], is that when you do something, your parents know about it. Even if they disagree, at least they know about it, and you don't have to do things in their back. Whereas Arab parents brag to their relatives about you being the best person on earth. And they fool themselves by pretending that certain things you do, which they don't like, don't exist."

Interestingly, informant I reported that some of her Arab female friends who were obliged by their parents to wear the Islamic veil (hijab), or simply to dress in a conservative fashion, waited until they arrived at school and then took off their veil or changed their clothes:

INTERVIEWER: "We don't see a lot of veiled girls at the cegep?"
INFORMANT I: "No. It's because, sometimes, those who are forced to wear it take it off once they get to the cegep. And after school, just a little bit before reaching home, they put it back on. It's the same with skirts: they can't wear them in front of their parents, so when they get to school, they go change in the bathroom."

The absence of dialogue on issues such as dating and sex is thus a problem frequently experienced by Arab-Canadian youths in their relationships with their parents. Some of them present a "virtuous" facade to their parents, while engaging in forbidden practices outside the home. This pattern applies particularly to young women, for whom the range of morally prohibited conduct is significantly wider than for males. As a result, in certain Arab migrant families – those in which traditional/gendered educational models prevail – there can be a large gap between the self that girls present at home and what they show at school. The discrepancy is compounded by the fact that parental expectations generally stand in vivid contrast to the more liberal expectations prevailing within the school environment. For these reasons, in traditional Arab-Canadian families, daughters who attempt to fit in at school while meeting parental expectations at home often have to set up hermetic walls between those two spheres of their life.

There is another possible scenario whereby second-generation females accept as their own their parents' conservative expectations and gendered double standards and consequently prefer to befriend like-minded ethnic peers, as we saw earlier. In such cases, parent-teenager conflicts are significantly mitigated. But it must be emphasized that in effect, there are no clear-cut distinctions between these two opposite scenarios. Somewhere in between disagreeing in secret with, and embracing unquestioningly, gendered traditions, there is a whole continuum of possible variations. Moreover, the subject's approach to conflict management can vary drastically depending on the social context of interaction and the type of issue at stake.

5

The Place of Religion
in Their Lives

I will now investigate the religious identity of my sample of second-generation Arabs using the same conceptual framework as the one applied to ethnic identity in chapter 4. First I will look briefly at the results relating to the global index of religious identity. Then, drawing on both quantitative and qualitative materials, I discuss the findings pertaining to four selected items making up the religious identity scale. Each of these parameters measures a different dimension of religious identity.

THE GLOBAL INDEX OF RELIGIOUS IDENTITY: A QUANTITATIVE OUTLOOK[1]

When comparing percent age distributions for ethnic and religious identity global indexes, it appears that the religions identity of the second-generation Arabs in my study is in general less salient than their ethnic identity. Indeed, as seen in earlier in Table 2, most respondents (45.4 percent) scored "strong" on the ethnic identity scale, followed by "average" (41.9 percent), whereas most respondents (49.2 percent) scored "average", followed by "weak" (27.3 percent), on the religious identity scale (see Table 14). This observation can be further corroborated by comparing the average means associated with each global index. On a scale from zero to one, where zero equals the highest degree of identity retention and one the lowest, the average coefficient for the ethnic identity global index is 0.42, whereas the one yielded by religious identity global index is 0.55, a difference of 0.13.[2]

Table 14: Percentage Distribution for "Religious Identity Strength's Global Index"

Religious Identity Strength	Distribution (%)
Very strong	0.8
Strong	14.3
Average	49.2
Weak	27.3
Very weak	8.4
TOTAL	100

Table 15: Compared Means of the Four Subvariables Forming "Religious Identity Strength" (Global Indexes)*

	Objective/ cultural	Objective/ social	Subjective/ cultural	Subjective/ social
Mean Score	0.58	0.73	0.43	0.48

* The lower the coefficient, the stronger one's religious identity

As seen in Table 15, when comparing the four subvariables measuring the strength of religious identity, the strongest aspect is subjective/cultural[3] (0.43), followed by subjective/social (0.48), objective/cultural (0.58), and objective/social (0.73). Thus, religious identity is much more salient in its subjective than its objective form among these second-generation Arabs. In other words, respondents tend more to have a strong sense of attachment to their religious culture and feel they are under an obligation to their religious community than to actually practise their religion and be involved with, and socialized into, groups of religious peers. The objective dimension of their religious identity also is significantly more developed at the cultural than at the social level. It follows that in general young Arab-Canadian adults are more inclined to observe religious rituals than to be enmeshed in social groups self-defined along religious lines.

In light of these results, Herbert Gans's symbolic religiosity hypothesis (1994) is lent partial support. On the one hand, the fact that respondents have a primarily subjective religious identity points to the gradual relegation of religious experiences to the private sphere, a trend typical of Western societies. Though it appears to be a premium building block in the development of self-concept, religion plays a relatively minor role as a structuring element of social interactions. However, levels of ritual observance (objective/cultural)

Table 16: Compared Percentage Distributions for "Religious Identity Strength's Global Index": Respondents and Their Parents

Religious identity strength	Respondents	Parents (assessed by respondents)
Very strong	0.8	42.6
Strong	14.3	34.8
Average	49.2	15.7
Weak	27.3	5.2
Very weak	8.4	1.6
TOTAL	100	100

seem sufficiently important to call for a qualification of the concept of symbolic religiosity. Indeed, the religiosity of the Arab Canadians in my sample, far from being salient only at the subjective level, is also minimally rooted in social practice, primarily in ritual observance. Later in this chapter, the parameters measuring ritual observance will be analyzed separately to determine whether some rituals are observed more than others. For instance, prayer frequency, a mostly solitary activity, is less socially involving and engaging than temple attendance, which requires stronger communal anchorages in the community.

As seen in Table 16, the data also clearly reveal that respondents consider that their parents' religious identity[4] is significantly stronger than their own. Whereas the majority of respondents (49.2 percent) have an "average" religiosity, the majority of their parents (42.6 percent) are thought to have a "very strong" religiosity. Furthermore, on a scale from zero to one, where zero equals the highest degree of religiosity and one the lowest, the mean coefficient associated with respondents' religiosity is 0.55, whereas the mean coefficient associated with their parents is 0.27. However, comparisons between these figures should be made with caution. First, the parent's strength of religious identity was assessed by their children, which is not a totally reliable measure. Second, the questions measuring respondents' religious identity are not exactly the same as those measuring parents' religious identity.

In the following sections, drawing on both quantitative and qualitative data, I address the findings pertaining to four parameters making up the religious identity global index. The subjective/cultural, subjective/social, objective/cultural, and objective/social dimensions of religious identity are examined in turn.

THE IMPORTANCE OF RELIGION
IN THEIR LIVES

How important is religion in these second-generation Arabs' lives? The previous section already suggested that their religiosity is expressed primarily at the subjective level. This section explores this issue in greater detail, with the addition of qualitative material on the meaning these young Muslim and Christian Arab Canadians attribute to their religious experience.

As outlined in Table 17, a majority of respondents (52.6 percent) stated that religion plays a "very important" role in their life, while 30.5 percent considered religion to have an "important" role. Only 16.8 percent of respondents found religion to be either "not very important" (10.8 percent), or "not important" (6 percent). These results are in agreement with the data displayed in Table 15, showing that the most salient dimension of these second-generation Arabs' religious identity is its "subjective/cultural" aspect.

Gender does not have any significant impact on the importance given to religion. Moreover, Christian and Muslim responses have a similar distribution in this cross-tabulation, with two noteworthy exceptions: a slightly larger percentage of Christians regard religion as an important component of their lives (54.3 percent versus 49.4 percent) while Muslims are slightly more likely to regard it as unimportant (9.2 percent versus 4.3 percent). These variations will be discussed later.

Finally, time spent in Canada does not significantly influence the respondents' views on the importance of religion in their lives. The only exceptions are that most recent immigrants (in Canada for fewer than ten years) are significantly more inclined than the two other groups to view religion as a "very important" part of their lives, and, surprisingly, that those who have spent the longest time in Canada (more than fifteen years) tend to be slightly more religiously inclined than the intermediate group (in Canada for ten to fifteen years). But in general, the subjective salience of religion does not seem to weaken much as years of socialization in Canada go by.

So based on quantitative data, it appears that the great majority of second-generation Arabs consider religion to be a highly important aspect of their lives. On the basis of the interviews, however, this should not necessarily be understood as the sign of a pious life committed to God. Although religion is indeed an important and

Table 17: Percentage Distributions for "Importance of Religion in Life," with "Gender," "Age at Arrival," and "Religious Affiliation"

		Very Important	Important	Not very important	Not important	Total
Whole sample		52.6	30.5	10.8	6.0	100
Gender	Males	53.4	29.0	11.5	6.1	100
	Females	51.7	32.2	10.2	5.9	100
Religious affiliation	Christians	54.3	29.6	11.7	4.3	100
	Muslims	49.4	32.2	9.2	9.2	100
Time spent in Canada	Less than 10 years	59.0	28.9	7.2	4.8	100
	Between 10 and 15 years	46.7	32.0	14.7	6.7	100
	More than 15 years	51.6	30.8	11.0	6.6	100

pervasive underpinning of the informants' identity structure, it often seems to be limited to providing general spiritual guidance, rather than offering a strict normative code governing life. As this Christian female (informant N) reports "Yes, religion is very important. I think it's one of the most important things for me. What's religion? It's a way to reach spirituality, and spirituality is very important in everyday life. Because it defines us as human beings. It would be very difficult to go through life – especially in the world we live in now – without spirituality to guide us. And religion is a way to bring us to this spirituality. That's why, to me, it's very important to preserve it."

Others see religion as a major contributor to personal and collective identity building. This is the case of informant C, a Christian male who conceives of religion as a symbolic framework colouring every aspect of family life: "Religion defines me as a person. And the way I have been raised, you know ... We always went to church on Sunday, I don't go anymore. The priest is well respected, despite the errors he makes. Always on a pedestal, the Church. You can feel that religion is ingrained in the family, in everyday life."

Many informants also seem to embrace a privatized notion of religion; for their responses often denote a desire to cultivate their faith outside of any formally organized structures. Informant O, a Christian female, puts it this way: "I am a believer. I would lie if I'd say I practise. I am a believer who ... Let's say I practice at home. It's between me and Him in fact." This position is echoed by informant M, another Christian woman: "When you reach adulthood, religion is not a heritage anymore, something you have been given. It's not about saying *I believe, yadda yadda yadda*. There comes a time when you ask yourself *Do I believe in God of my own will, because I want to, or do I believe because my parents influenced me*. Now, I start adopting the former approach. Religion is not a heritage: I made a new profession of faith, in a sense."

There appears to be a minority group that does not attach much importance to religion. These respondents justify their indifference in various ways. Of all the students I interviewed, only one identified openly as an atheist. Others, such as informants L and J, a Christian and Muslim respectively, said they drifted away from religion, which they regarded as too sectarian and exclusive, preferring a more universal system of beliefs. Informant L made this claim: "I want to give up religion in order to opt for more universal values. I don't want to end up in church praying to such and such divinity. I start to think that practising a religion is not that important. I still believe there is a God. But I start to find that practising a religion is too narrow-minded ... I've asked myself many questions, and I haven't found answers to these questions. So I may as well drop everything."

The case of informant J is particularly interesting. Although this Canadian-born Muslim woman of Algerian descent does not consider herself to be "religious", she wore a necklace with a cross on the day of the interview. I was surprised to see a self-declared "non-religious" person wear a religious symbol but was even more startled to see a person of Muslim background wear a cross. I said to her, "You told me your parents are Muslims. But I see you wear a cross." She replied, "Yeah, because it's pretty. I am not religious, so ... My friends got me this for my birthday, and if I don't wear it, they're gonna kill me (laughter)."

This case shows clearly that in today's Western societies, religious symbols have been largely severed from the collective framework that formerly infused them with sacred meanings. Informant J, who reported having been raised by fairly pious Muslim parents, reassigned, in a typically postmodern fashion, a merely aesthetic function to the cross she wore ("it's pretty"). By doing so she engaged, like many of her majority group age peers, in the free recycling of religious signifiers, which are cut off from their originally transcendental symbolism. Because informant J was raised in a Western secular society, she was given sufficient latitude to extricate her Christian cross from the meaning traditionally attached to it. Even more interesting is the fact that this Muslim informant felt comfortable casually crossing religious group boundaries, which she actually did not even regard as such. In most Arab countries, because religion generally occupies such a central position within individual and group identity structures, this casual boundary crossing would have been regarded as a (symbolic) transgression and would thus have been, if not impossible, at least very unlikely.

To sum up this section, religion is mobilized by second-generation Arabs selectively and contextually so as to give substance to their self-definitions. In general, Arab-origin youth highly value their religion as a structuring and defining component of their identity.

ATTITUDES TOWARD RELIGIOUS ENDOGAMY

Whereas the preceding section looked into the importance attached to religion as an identity marker (the subjective/cultural dimension), this section taps into the importance accorded to religion in mate selection strategies (the subjective/social dimension). Respondents were asked, "How important is it for you to marry a religious peer?" As seen in Table 18, 63.2 percent of respondents reported that it was "important" for them to marry a religious peer, while 19.4 percent considered the prospect of an endogamous marriage as an ideal, though not compulsory, option. For 17 percent of the students I surveyed, religion was not relevant to their choice of a future spouse. Only one respondent chose the option "I don't want to marry someone of my religious group." Thus, the majority (63.2 percent) of the Arab youths preferred to marry within their own religious group.

The findings suggest that these second-generation Arabs are more concerned with marrying a religious than an ethnic peer. Indeed, whereas 41.7 percent of respondents reported that marrying an ethnic peer was "important" to them (see Table 5), a much greater proportion (63.2 percent) reported that it was "important" for them to marry a religious peer (Table 18). Furthermore, the qualitative data also point to the prevalence of religion over ethnicity in mate selection strategies among Arab-origin youths. Several interviewees declared that they would not compromise on the issue of marrying

Table 18: Percentage Distribution for "Attitude towards Marrying a Religious Peer," with "Gender," "Age at Arrival," and "Religious Affiliation"

		Important	Ideally but not compulsorily	Not important	I don't want it	TOTAL
Whole sample		63.2	19.4	17.0	0.4	100
Gender	Males	57.7	24.6	16.9	0.8	100
	Females	69.2	13.7	17.1	0.0	100
Religious affiliation	Christians	63.4	19.2	16.8	0.6	100
	Muslims	62.8	19.8	17.4	0.0	100
Time spent in Canada	Less than 10 years	68.7	13.3	18.1	0.0	100
	Between 10 and 15 years	56.0	26.7	16.0	1.3	100
	More than 15 years	64.0	19.1	16.9	0.0	100

a religious peer, while merely expressing a preference for marrying inside their ethnic group.

As the respondents justified their desire to marry a religious peer, however, only one stressed the importance of sharing a common system of religious beliefs. The most common rationale was rather that a religious peer would be more likely to share the same cultural framework and mentality.[5] Thus, in the minds of several informants, religion seemed to be inextricably tied to culture. More specifically, in their view, the value of religion lies in its cultural effects, namely its propensity to colour and inform one's world representations and values. As this Christian female (informant P) put it, "Of course, religion matters in the choice of my future husband, because religion influences personal convictions and behaviours. I wouldn't say I'd never marry a Buddhist or a Muslim. But it would really depends on how his religion affects his character." Informant H, a Muslin female, expressed it similarly: "I want it [marrying a Muslim] also for me. If I were to marry a non-Muslim, we wouldn't be on the same wave length."

Among other reasons put forward by participants to justify their desire to marry within their religious group, two were frequently reported: passing on their religious heritage to their future offspring, and ensuring that parents would get along well with their son- or daughter-in-law.

The importance placed on marrying a religious peer varies slightly according to gender. As with ethnic endogamy (see Table 6), women are slightly more likely than men to favour religious endogamy, although the difference is not statistically significant. As shown in Table 18, 69.2 percent of female respondents said that it was "important" for them to marry a religious peer, as opposed to 57.7 percent of males. These gendered variations remain the same among Muslim and Christian respondents. Such a phenomenon may be attributed to the combined effect of two factors. First, as Kristine Ajrouch remarked in her study of Arab families in Dearborne, Michigan (1999), Arab parents living in a Western context often consider that group identity maintenance is contingent upon religious identity maintenance. As the author notes: "The most striking theme that emerged from the focus group discussions [with the parents] was the pervasiveness of religion as a major underpinning of ethnic identity" (Ajrouch 1999, 134). Religion is indeed often considered by Arab parents as a moral safeguard against Western values, which are deemed too lax and liberal. Second, since daughters are often considered as the repositories of the group's ethnoreligious identity, Arab female youths end up being subjected to greater pressure than boys to marry inside their religious group. Daughters more than sons are thus the target of the anti-assimilation efforts deployed by parents to ensure maintenance of ethnoreligious identity. Ajrouch (1999, 138) went so far as to argue that daughters come to bear almost the entire weight of identity maintenance within Arab families. This issue will be addressed more specifically in chapter 6.

Finally, neither "religious affiliation" nor "time spent in Canada" has a statistically significant impact on attitudes toward religious endogamy. Indeed, as shown in Table 18, the responses of both Christians and Muslims have an almost identical distribution in this cross-tabulation, and regardless of time spent in Canada, religious endogamy remains an "important" priority for a majority of respondents.

The two last sections of this chapter examine whether the importance attached (subjectively) by second-generation Arabs to religion is rooted (objectively) in cultural practices and social relations, which are measured, respectively, through ritual observance and participation in religious social affairs.

Table 19: Percentage Distributions for "Prayer Frequency," with "Religious Affiliation," "Gender," and "Age at Arrival"

		Once a day or more	Once a week	Once a month	Never or rarely	Total
Whole sample		51.4	20.1	8.8	19.7	100
Religious affiliation*	Christians	55.9	24.2	9.3	10.6	100
	Muslims	43.2	12.4	8.0	36.4	100
Gender	Males	45.9	24.4	9.9	19.8	100
	Females	57.6	15.3	7.6	19.5	100
Time spent in Canada	Less than 10 years	53.0	20.5	7.2	19.3	100
	10 to 15 years	53.3	21.3	8.0	17.3	100
	More than 15 years	48.4	18.7	11.0	22.0	100

* = $p < 0.01$

RITUAL OBSERVANCE

Prayer Frequency

Praying is a surprisingly popular practice among respondents. As Table 19 shows, a majority of them (51.4 percent) reported praying at least once a day. The options "once a week" (20.1 percent) and "never or rarely" (19.7 percent) were almost tied. The proportion of respondents praying once a day is quite high compared with Reginald Bibby's 2000 nationwide survey data on Canadian religious practices and beliefs. In Bibby's study, for example, only sixteen percent of Canadians aged eighteen to thirty-four reported praying on a daily basis, while most of this group, 35 percent, reported that they "never" prayed (Bibby 2002, 161). However, it must be kept in mind that, although praying is undoubtedly an expression of religious devotion, it does not necessarily have to be performed as part of an institutionalized and collective ritual; anyone can engage in it, anywhere, at any time, and in any place. In that sense, praying is particularly well fitted to a privatized approach to religion, or again, to a more symbolic form of religious identity.

As seen in Table 19, religious affiliation has a statistically significant impact at the 0.01 level on prayer frequency. The proportion of respondents praying at least once a day is 55.9 percent among Christians, as opposed to 43.2 percent among Muslims. What's more, the proportion of respondents who "never or rarely" pray is

10.6 percent among Christians, as opposed to 36.4 percent among Muslims (the second most popular answer for Muslims).

Certain considerations must be taken into account before concluding, on the basis of this observation, that Christians are more pious and devout than their Muslim counterparts.[6] One of the five pillars of Islam is the obligation to pray five times a day. The Bible, in contrast, does not prescribe any specific daily number of prayers. As a result, many Muslims consider that one should pray five times a day or not at all, whereas Christians are generally given more freedom to determine how often they need to pray to meet their own personal religious and spiritual needs. Islamic prayers, as opposed to Christian prayers, also require a praying area.

These distinctions could explain in part why the proportion of respondents praying "once a day or more" is less among Muslims than among Christians. They could also account for the fact that Muslims tended more to answer that they "never or rarely" prayed; praying is, in theory, much more demanding and time consuming for Muslims than it is for Christians. Moreover, in formal and informal exchanges, Muslim subjects often reported that they consider praying to be a serious enterprise that can only be undertaken as one reaches adulthood or at least a certain level of maturity. Informant I, a Canadian-born Muslim woman, provides a good illustration of this philosophy: "Well, my father prays, he went to Mecca and all. But if I tell my father that I want to start praying, he'll tell me *Wait, you're still young!* Yeah, he tells me, *Keep enjoying life.* Because for him, to start praying is a serious business. It has to be followed to the letter. Otherwise, you just don't do it at all." Similarly, because he has not yet started praying, informant F does not consider that he can call himself a practising Muslim, even though he actively follows all other religious prescriptions. When asked whether his religious heritage was important to him, he said, "Very important. Unfortunately, I do not practise. I am a Sunni Muslim. It's really important. I have faith in God, but I just don't practise the way a real Muslim should. It's because I don't pray, which is a very important aspect of religion. I fast, I have faith in God, I give money to the poor. It's just that the prayer ...."

Finally, Table 19 shows that gender and time spent in Canada do not have a statistically significant effect on prayer frequency. As might be expected, the group of respondents who have spent the

Table 20: Percentage Distributions for "Religious Service Attendance," with Selected Variables

		Religious Service Attendance				
		At least once a week	Once a month	For religious holidays only	Never or rarely	Total
Whole sample		20.9	20.5	36.9	21.7	100
Religious affiliation*	Christians	25.5	26.0	39.8	8.7	100
	Muslims	12.5	10.2	31.8	45.5	100
Gender	Males	22.9	22.9	37.4	16.8	100
	Females	18.6	17.8	36.4	27.2	100
Time spent in Canada	10 years and less	25.0	16.7	35.7	22.6	100
	10 to 15 years	20.3	18.9	33.8	27.0	100
	15 years and more	17.6	25.3	40.7	16.5	100

* = $p < 0.01$

longest time in Canada (fifteen years or more) are less likely to pray once a day than the two other groups (48 percent versus 53 percent). It should be noted, however, that more females tend to "pray at least once a day" than males (57.6 percent versus 45.9 percent).

Religious Service Attendance

It could be safely said that, today, a majority of Canadian youth only attend religious services for religious holidays or for major rites of passage (marriage, baptism, death, etc.), while many never attend at all. In this respect, the Arab Canadians surveyed here are not very different. Most of them declared that they attend religious services "only for religious holidays" (36.9 percent), while 21.7 percent said that they "never or rarely" attend (see Table 20). This suggests that a majority of them, like most young people in Canada, do not express their religiosity through significant involvement in formally organized religious rituals. In this respect, once again, their religiosity is clearly in line with the privatized approach to religion prevailing among their coevals in the majority group.

The only striking feature in Table 20, however, is that levels of service attendance are significantly higher among Christian than Muslim respondents (and this correlation is statistically significant at the 0.01 level). Even though most Muslims (31.8 percent) and

Christians (39.8 percent) report attending a religious service only for religious holidays, the latter group is at least twice as likely as the former to attend a religious service either once a week or once a month. For instance, 25.5 percent of Christians attend a service weekly, as opposed to 12.2 percent of Muslims. To most young Canadian adults, the mere thought of attending a religious service once a week – as many of their parents and most of their grandparents did at their age – would be unimaginable. Nowadays, only a minority of young people in this country attend church on a weekly basis. Thus, according to Reginald Bibby's 2000 nationwide survey data, only twelve percent of Canadians aged eighteen to thirty-four reported attending weekly a religious service, and the percentage dropped to five percent if one looked only at the province of Quebec (Bibby 2002, 77). It is worth emphasizing that, whereas the proportion of weekly attenders among Muslim respondents matches the national average for Canadians aged fifteen to thirty-four (12.5 percent versus 12 percent), the proportion of weekly attenders among Christian respondents is closer to the national average for Canadians aged fifty-five and over – 25.5 percent versus 30 percent (ibid.). But perhaps the most spectacular gap between Muslim and Christian response distributions is that as many as 45.5 percent of Muslim respondents reported that they "never or rarely" attend religious services (their most popular response), as opposed to only 8.7 percent for Christians (their least popular response).

More than one factor could account for this surprisingly large discrepancy. First, as with prayer, mosque attendance is perceived by Muslims as a serious undertaking that can only take place once the believer starts observing scrupulously Islamic rituals. Second, the greater propensity of Christian respondents to attend religious services may be explained by the fact that they tend more than Muslim respondents to live in ethnically segregated neighbourhoods.[7] Indeed, after levels of self-reported residential segregation were broken down into "high" and "low" categories, it appeared that 65.6 percent of Arab-origin Christians as opposed to 48.3 percent of Arab-origin Muslims live in neighbourhoods with high concentrations of ethnic peers. Ethnically segregated enclaves are commonly associated with higher levels of institutional completeness (Breton 1964) and ethnocultural identity retention (Kalbach 1990). A cross-tabular test was run to verify whether these variations between Christians and Muslims still held when controlling for eth-

Table 21: Muslim Respondents' Observance of Fasting (Ramadan) and the Ban on Alcohol

	Yes (%)	No (%)	Total
Do you fast when prescribed	82.6	17.4	100
Do you try NOT to drink alcohol	27.1	72.9	100

Table 22: Muslim Respondents' Observance of Food Regulations

	Almost all the time (%)	Ideally but not compulsorily (%)	Only for religious holidays (%)	Never (%)	Total
Do you eat "Halal" meat	46.3	23.9	11.9	1.9	100

nic residential segregation: Christians remained significantly more likely than Muslims to attend religious services. Perhaps a better explanation of this discrepancy is that Arab Christians' ethnic and religious identities are so closely entangled that their church tends to be an "ethnic" church, serving both as a space where formally organized religious rituals are performed and as a community centre where ethnonational bonds are reinforced.

In any case, though it is difficult to draw reliable conclusions at this stage, it seems that the objective/cultural dimension of religiosity, at least as measured by ritual observance, is more developed among Christian than Muslim respondents. The discrepancy is discussed in greater length in the conclusion. Once again, however, because the indicators used to measure the degree to which respondents practise their religion take on different meanings depending on whether one is Muslim or Christian, these results should be interpreted with caution.

Ramadan, Ban on Alcohol, and Food Regulations

The questionnaire includes a series of ritual observance indicators that concern Muslim respondents specifically. These parameters pertain to fasting,[8] the Islamic ban on alcohol, and food regulations. They were excluded from the scale measuring the global index of religious identity since their Islam-specific character would render comparisons between Christian and Muslim levels of ritual

observance methodologically problematic. However, it is interesting to look briefly at the results yielded by these parameters to tap
into Muslim respondents' religious experience, at the material and
symbolic levels.

The findings largely echo those typically found in other studies
on second-generation Muslim youths living in Western settings
(e.g., Roy 1994). For example, as Table 21 shows, the practice of
fasting during religious holidays is much more persistent over time
than the ban on alcohol; 82.6 percent observe the former prescription while only 21.7 percent observe the latter. As shown in Table
22, eating "halal"[9] meat is observed by the majority of Muslim
respondents "almost all the time" (46.3 percent), or "ideally but
not compulsorily" (23.9 percent).

It is not surprising that while the overwhelming majority of Muslim respondents fast during Ramadan (82.6 percent), very few
observe the ban on alcohol (27.1 percent). As opposed to the ban
on alcohol, which amounts to no more than an ascetic religious
restriction, the Ramadan holiday gives rise to the formation of
social bonds between community members, especially after dusk,
when the extended family gathers to share copious meals as the fast
is officially broken. As a social binder for many Muslims, Ramadan
may be more closely related to ethnic identity maintenance than to
religious devotion.

To corroborate this hypothesis, two percentage tables were produced, crossing the variable "fasting" with both "religious identity
strength" and "ethnic identity strength." The majority of those who
reported fasting during Ramadan scored either "weak" (39.7 percent) or "average" (38.2 percent) on the religious identity scale.
However, the majority of these same fast observers scored either
"strong" (43.8 percent) or "average" (42.2 percent) on the ethnic
identity scale. Therefore, it appears that Ramadan is more than just
a formal religious interdiction; it also acts first and foremost as a
group solidifier and thus should be understood more as a factor
that cements and reinforces ethnic identity than as a reflection of
strict religious orthodoxy. The social function of Ramadan is exemplified by this statement made by informant G: "Yeah, towards the
end [of Ramadan], it's like, we eat, we eat, and then we are tired.
But the prayer in the morning also helps. You see people hugging.
You don't see it often. I just see it during that time."

PARTICIPATION IN RELIGIOUS SOCIAL AFFAIRS

Respondents were asked whether they participate in religious events or social affairs "often," "occasionally," or "never." The majority reported participating occasionally (56 percent) in religious events or social affairs. This is a relatively high figure when contrasted with the low interest among Quebecois youth in formally organized religious activities (see Bibby 2002, 87–8). The second most popular answer was "never" (28.6 percent), followed by "often" (15.3 percent). This indicates that religion plays a certain role, if on limited occasions, in the participation of second-generation Arabs in formally organized social activities. It should be noted that, in the case of Christian respondents, the data do not reveal whether these religious social activities and events take place within mainstream, or ethnic-specific, Christian institutions and organizations.

Unfortunately, qualitative information was not collected on the nature and the significance of the respondents' participation in religious social affairs (events or activities). However, it was deemed relevant to look for possible correlations between attendance at religious social affairs and the strength of ethnic and religious identity respectively. Upon cross-examination of the data (see Tables 23 and 24), it appears, quite expectedly, that the majority of those who "often" attend their religious group's social affairs possess "strong" religious and ethnic identities. But what is particularly interesting is that, among occasional participants (the bulk of the sample), a majority scored "average" (67.2 percent) and "weak" (23.1 percent) on the religious identity scale, but "strong" (50.4 percent) and "average" (40.2 percent) on the ethnic identity scale.[10] In short, a majority of those who occasionally participate in religious social affairs tend to have a "strong" ethnic identity, but an "average" religious identity.

These findings suggest that the social affairs organized by religious institutions tend to draw (occasionally) a majority of second-generation Arabs who, though they may not be particularly devout or religious, nonetheless strongly hold on to their ethnic background. This is a reminder of the structuring role that religion can play in the maintenance of ethnic group solidarity, for it provides the community with a space, both literally and figuratively, where the subjective aspect of ethnicity can be retained through the necessary social and communal networks. These results also point to a

Table 23: Percentage Distribution for "Religious Social Affairs" by "Religious Identity Strength"

		Religious Identity Strength					
		Very strong	Strong	Average	Weak	Very weak	Total
Religious	Often	5.4	56.8	29.7	8.1	0.0	100
Social Affairs	Occasionally	0.0	9.7	67.2	23.1	0.0	100
Attendance*	Never	0.0	0.0	23.9	46.2	29.9	100

* $= p < 0.01$

Table 24: Percentage Distribution for "Religious Social Affairs" by "Ethnic Identity Strength"

		Ethnic Identity's Strength					
		Very strong	Strong	Average	Weak	Very weak	Total
Religious	Often	6.3	53.1	31.3	9.4	0.0	100
Social Affairs	Occasionally	3.9	50.4	40.2	3.9	1.6	100
Attendance*	Never	0.0	33.3	48.5	16.7	1.5	100

* $= p < 0.05$

symbolic religiosity that acts first and foremost as an ethnic boundary marker among the second generation. More specifically, it seems that those young adults of Arab origin who occasionally attend religious social affairs use religion as a social unifier reinforcing ethnic group solidarity. As shown, this use of religion as a way of cementing group solidarity in a migratory context does not necessarily require strong religious devotion. In other words, it appears that religion is being recycled by some of these youths into a social vector ensuring ethnic identity maintenance.

CONCLUDING REMARKS

In chapters 4 and 5, it was shown that both ethnicity and religiosity can assume different forms and take on different meanings. From an analytical point of view, it was fruitful to treat separately the various dimensions of ethnicity and religiosity (i.e., objective versus subjective, and social versus cultural aspects). These distinctions allowed us to examine the phenomena from a dual perspective fuelled by both structuralist and poststructuralist assumptions. More specifically, they permitted us to determine whether ethnoreligious consciousness – a relatively open space where identities are built, deconstructed, and recomposed – is accompanied by integrative moves to gain access to the social networks and cultural goods associated with the reference group(s).

It was found that, subjectively, the second-generation Arabs in this study are holding on strongly to their ethnic and religious backgrounds, which they regard as an essential and defining part of their identity repertoire. Also, ethnic identity, far more so than religious identity, appeared to be a multidimensional and contextually varying phenomenon – which makes sense since one generally adheres to a single religion[11] but can identify with more than one ethnocultural group. Indeed, the ethnic consciousness of these Arab-origin students is informed by several sources such as pan-Arab identity, national identities, and subnational identities (e.g., Berber, Kurd, etc.). Pan-Arab identity seems to be particularly salient among second-generation Arabs. This can be partly accounted for by the majority group's tendency to lock them into a monolithic and reductive notion of Arabness that is often suffused with prejudicial connotations. This issue is addressed at greater length in chapter 7.

It must be emphasized that, in theory, ethnic consciousness and self-identification with the majority group(s) are not mutually exclusive processes. However, although it is beyond the scope of this book to analyze how both forms of group allegiance combine, interrelate, and even sometimes merge, both quantitative and qualitative materials suggest that Canadian and Quebecois communities are not significant identity poles for second-generation Arabs. Further research is needed to lend support to this hypothesis.

The data also showed that ethnic and religious consciousness are not necessarily coupled with corresponding levels of integration into ethnic and religious cultures and networks. This is particularly the case for religious identity, whereas ethnic identity proved to be better sustained by socialization and cultural incorporation. For instance, the children of Arab immigrants have a good command of their ethnic language and a strong tendency to develop ethnically segregated circles of friends.

As for religion, it plays a relatively marginal role in the sociocultural practices of these Arab Canadians. Most notably, their strong identification with their religious community is essentially maintained outside of formally organized rituals. In other words, the shape and content of their religious community and culture is largely imagined on a personal basis, a trend similar to what can be observed among other Canadians of the same age group. Furthermore, even when religion does inform their life projects (e.g., mate selection) or activities (participation in religious social affairs), it does so mainly by fusing with ethnicity in the formation of distinct group boundaries.

The next two chapters explore structural contributing factors to ethnic and religious identity building. The emphasizing or downplaying of ethnic or religious identities is contingent not only upon human agency but also upon the broader social and historical contexts. More specifically, the range of identity and cultural options offered to individuals is not only a matter of personal choices but is also determined by structural factors such as intergroup power dynamics, social class, education, gendered traditions, prejudicial stereotyping, and discrimination. Chapters 6 and 7 focus on the three latter factors, which weigh heavily in ethnoreligious identity formation among the Arab diaspora.

6

Attitudes Toward Gender Traditions

In this chapter, I examine whether gender issues help to shape ethnoreligious identity, as the literature frequently suggests. The underlying assumption – which found strong support in chapter 4 – is that families of the Arab diaspora often find in traditional gender relations a cultural buffer delineating symbolic boundaries between Us and Them. Furthermore, since both the host society and Arab communities tend to construe gender politics as the key source of their intercultural differences, the second generation has no choice but to negotiate ethnoreligious identity in relation to gender traditions. It is not to argue that all second-generation Arabs are enmeshed in traditional gender role models but rather that they are led to engage with them, critically or not, as they attempt to define themselves in a Canadian context.

The notion of tradition, however, should not be understood in an essentialized manner. In other words, there is no such thing as a fixed set of traditions tied ontologically to a given community, that is, existing out of time. Indeed traditions are not anchored in some kind of immutable past waiting to be either perpetually re-enacted (as in traditional societies) or discarded in the name of modernity (as in modern liberal nation-states). Rather, they are social constructions that are always historically situated.

Moreover, traditions should not be understood exclusively as remnants of premodern times that can be (re-)activated only in opposition to egalitarian liberal ideas and models. As highlighted by Eric Hobsbawm and Terence Rangers (1983), traditions were mobilized in the West to legitimate nation-building in modern times as well. Although Western nationalism claims to have broken away from tradition en route to modernity, the construction or assertion of the political community is not, and has never been, solely understood as a civic contract between subjects bound by the rule of law; it is also presented by nationalist leaders as a quasi-ontological necessity allowing the nation to actualize its true collective self (Smith 1994, chapter 3). The use of the past and tradition by nationalists is crucial to the process whereby the imagined political community is (re-)constructed; history and culture are selectively arranged and rearranged so as to differentiate Us from Them and create internal group cohesion (Hobsbawm 1983; Brass 1991; Yuval-Davis 1997). Nationalists resort to the rhetoric of tradition to legitimize their political agenda, that is, to demonstrate that their political projects are in natural conformity with the alleged cultural authenticity of the nation.

Tradition and culture are used along the same lines by immigrants in the reconstruction of their ethnic community in a diasporic context. As mentioned earlier, traditional gender relations, particularly as they relate to female sexuality, constitute premium symbolic material feeding ethnic consciousness among the most recent cohorts of Arab and Muslim immigrants. This is due to the fact that, in the post-1970s Arab world, dominant models of gender relations were refocused along religious lines in the name of postcolonial resistance (Esposito 2001; Eid 2002). In the process, the political agenda fostered by religious nationalists (often fundamentalists) gained considerable social legitimacy. As a result, a return to traditional gender politics came increasingly to be viewed by the Arab masses as the *sine qua non* for the actualization of the nation's authentic self.

Once again, this is not to argue that all members of the Arab diaspora embrace a conservative reading of gender relations. Nonetheless, it must be acknowledged that, compared to previous migratory cohorts, post-1970s Arab migrants to Canada are more likely to draw on traditions – including gender traditions – when setting up ethnoreligious boundaries that define their minority Us.

The positioning of the children of Arab migrants vis-à-vis gendered traditions is likely to be complex. A plethora of scenarios is possible, ranging from pure rejection to reinvention, including, inbetween, a sort of à la carte collage in which traditional and Western models are amalgamated. This chapter thus explores how Arab-Canadian youths either critically engage or reappropriate gender traditions in the process of ethnoreligious identity formation. Since these young

Arab Canadians' relation to what they construe as tradition is largely mediated by their families, some of the data shed light on their perceptions of their parents' views and educational practices relating to gender issues. Throughout the analysis special attention will be paid to sex-based variations in the responses.

I will first briefly analyze the results yielded by the attitudinal tradition scales measuring respondents' levels of agreement with selected gender-related statements, and respondents' assessment of their parents' level of agreement with these same statements. I will then examine the quantitative and qualitative materials pertaining to the four selected indicators that make up these scales. These four indicators/statements are phrased as follows: a) "A woman should obey her husband," b) "Girls/boys should compulsorily remain a virgin before marriage," c) "A woman's virginity should compulsorily be protected until marriage by her male kin in order for family reputation and honour to be preserved," and d) "Male/female teenagers should be allowed to have a girlfriend before marriage if they want to."

GENDER TRADITION SCALE: A QUANTITATIVE
OUTLOOK[1]

In order to make it easier to understand the tradition scale, the measuring coefficients, ranging from zero (the highest level of traditionalism) to one (the lowest level of traditionalism), were broken down into five attitudinal categories: very traditional, somewhat traditional, borderline, somewhat liberal, and very liberal.

As seen in Table 25, the overall tendency among respondents is to embrace relatively liberal views on gender role models. Most of them (34.1 percent) fall into the category "somewhat liberal," while the second largest category is "borderline" (26.1 percent), followed closely by "very liberal" (24.9 percent). Only a small proportion of respondents are either "somewhat traditional" (13.3 percent) or "very traditional" (1.6 percent).

By contrast, respondents' perceptions of how parents would answer the same questions provide a different picture. Parents are perceived to be more attached to traditional values and attitudes than their children, at least as far as gender issues are concerned. Thus Table 25 shows that, according to the respondents, most parents (37.3 percent) would fall into the "somewhat traditional" category. The second most popular category would be "borderline"

Table 25: Percentage Distributions of Youth's and Parents' Mean Scores on the Gender Tradition Scale

Gender-related traditionalism	Respondents	Parents (as reported by respondents)
Very traditional	1.6	5.9
Somewhat traditional	13.3	37.3
Borderline	26.1	33.2
Somewhat liberal	34.1	17.8
Very liberal	24.9	5.8
TOTAL	100	100

(33.2 percent), followed by "somewhat liberal" (17.8 percent). This generational gap is also confirmed by the fact that respondents' estimations of their parents views on gender role traditions yield a mean coefficient of 0.64 on the tradition scale (where one equals the highest level of traditionalism), whereas the respondents' own mean coefficient is 0.47.

MARITAL POWER RELATIONS

This sections taps into second-generation Arab attitudes regarding the division of decisional power within the family unit. In particular, respondents were asked to report the extent to which they agree or disagree with the notion that a wife should submit to her husband. As we see in Table 26, most respondents (45.6 percent) "strongly disagree" with the statement "A wife should obey her husband." It should be noted, however, that the second most popular answer is "somewhat agree" (23.2 percent), followed by "completely agree" and "somewhat disagree," each with 15.6 percent. Thus, although the predominant trend is strongly to oppose the idea of a wife "obeying" her husband, there is also an important minority, made up of those who "somewhat agree" and somewhat disagree" (38.8 percent in total), who seem to have a more ambivalent position on this issue.

The following narratives illustrate the rationales underlying the respondents' positions on the issue of gendered power relations. First, corroborating the quantitative data, the majority of informants stressed that they believe in gender equality in every aspect of life. Most of them argued that couple relationships should be based on mutual respect, and that husband and wife should have equal rights within the family unit. In that respect, the positions of infor-

Table 26: Percentages of Agreement with the Statement "A Woman Should Obey Her Husband"

Level of agreement	Respondents	Parents (estimated by respondents)
completely agree	15.6	20.7
somewhat agree	23.2	24.1
somewhat disagree	15.6	22.8
completely disagree	45.6	32.4
TOTAL	100	100

mants M, a Christian female of Syrian descent, and D, a Christian male of Lebanese descent, are quite representative:

INFORMANT M: OK, I think that gender relationships are all really ... about respect, and only respect: It's like: I don't want to force anything on you that you don't want, and hmm ... I cannot force you either. You are an individual. True, we live together, and we make decisions together, but we must find a solution together.

INFORMANT D: No. Both men and women have to obey each other. It's mutual respect for both of them. I mean, why should a wife obey her husband while he can do whatever he wants? No, no, no, to me, both of them have to talk to each other to know ... And if someone is not comfortable with something, the other shouldn't do it. It's called respect. It's not about obeying the husband.

Only informant C, a Christian male of Palestinian and Lebanese descent, stated unequivocally that a woman should submit to her husband under any circumstance. But as indicated in Table 26, this extreme position was endorsed only by a minority of respondents (15.6 percent). Moreover, informant C's black-and-white view contrasts strongly with the more nuanced opinions provided by most other informants, nuances that, in the questionnaire, found expression in the answers "somewhat agree" (23.2 percent) and "somewhat disagree" (15.6 percent). The narratives associated with these intermediate positions should be given particular attention since they make up 38.8 percent of the sample altogether.

At least six informants, three men and three women, agreed with the statement "A woman should obey her husband," but with certain reservations. The general idea expressed by these subjects was that, although both gender groups owe each other mutual respect, men should still have the last word in most family matters (except for children's education, according to some informants). It was also stressed by these informants, especially by the females, that while he should have the last word, a good husband is still expected to consult his wife and to take her opinions into account before making any important decisions. For instance, informants F (a Muslim male of Algerian origin) and B (a Canadian-born Christian male of Lebanese origin) both consider that, as husbands, they should have the final say over their wives. Yet they would allow, even encourage, their wives to voice their concerns, and to have a chance to prove their husbands wrong whenever they disagree. Informant F put it this way:

Women should obey their husband. But let's not push this too far! Take my parents, for instance. If my father decides something, in general, it's gonna happen. But there are always discussions between the two of them. For instance, the day I wanted to come to Canada, my mom was OK with it, but my dad was not ... So there's been a discussion between them, and my mom was able to convince my father. But if my father had said *No, he is not going* ... The decision is final! But there are always discussions. Some people say that women do not have the right to voice their opposition. I really don't get this! Even the Koran doesn't say that. It says that men are the leaders of the house, that they have the last word, [but] it doesn't say that this word is right.

Thus, according to male informants B and F, a good husband, while having full control over family matters, should not make unilateral decisions without first consulting his wife. In other words, these subjects agree with the notion that men hold the ultimate power within the family unit, but they nonetheless believe that this power differential is only legitimate to the extent that the husband takes his wife's views into consideration.

Interestingly, three female informants held views largely consistent with those expressed by male informants B and F. Thus, informants H and I (two Muslim females), while recognizing the ultimate authority of the male, strongly disapproved of a domineering husband who would confiscate their freedom of speech and disregard their points of view. Female informants who took this in-between position tended to offer more complex answers than their male counterparts, answers that expressed certain contradictions at times. The following exchange with informant H illustrates perfectly this ambivalence resulting from Arab-Canadian females' attempts to reconcile two conflictual concerns: on the one hand, their desire to be free and self-assertive wives and, on the other, their belief that their husband should nonetheless conserve the ultimate decisional power in the household:

INTERVIEWER: For the statement *A woman should obey her husband*, you chose *I somewhat disagree* ... Do you want to comment on your answer?

INFORMANT H: Well, I am not really gonna obey my husband. It's not ... I don't want to be a submissive woman. I have a good head on my shoulders, and I have things to say. I won't tolerate anything like No, you won't wear this, you won't see this. It doesn't work like that with me. Definitely not!

INTERVIEWER: OK, then why didn't you choose the option *I completely disagree* in the questionnaire?

INFORMANT H: Well, of course, there are limits! For sure, your husband ... It's not that he's gonna tell me *don't do this and that*, but you know, I still have to take into account what he's gonna tell me. I mean, I am not gonna marry a loser, you know? The guy I am gonna be with, it's gonna be because he understands me, we understand each other. That's why if he tells me to do something, well maybe it's because he's right. It depends."

INTERVIEWER: So could you say that, to you, a man and a woman are completely equal in a relationship?

INFORMANT H: Hmm ... I don't know. I don't know if it's stupid but, you know, my parents taught me: *Your brother ... Your brother, well, it's not the same. Your brother is a guy, and you are a girl.* Whether I want it or not, it's there. Even if deep down inside, I don't like it, it's still there.

This exchange is illuminating for several reasons. Informant H attempts to resolve the possible contradictions resulting from her dual belief in male dominance and womanpower. She does so by stressing that it is unlikely that she would marry "a loser" in the first place. The man she will choose, she argues, will understand her so well that his decisions will be naturally in tune with her own desires and interests. It then becomes harmless to surrender her freedom to a husband regarded as an "enlightened master," so to speak. Informant H's reasoning should not be considered as an unequivocal sign of disempowerment; her power lies in the fact that her future husband will only come into being thanks to her own enlightened judgment in choosing the right egalitarian mate. This perspective is articulated in a similar fashion by informant K, a Muslim female of Algerian origin: "I agree that he [my husband] should make the decisions for the family, you see. So if he decides something, if he wants to do this or that, I agree that the husband should make the decisions ... But I won't marry a guy who wants to discipline me, and who will require obedience from me because he's the master. However, if I marry a guy who is on the same wavelength as me, technically, I think that the decisions he'll make will be good for me."

Now what about the parents? What do respondents think their parents' positions would be on the issue of female obedience in the couple? As a reminder, according to respondents, most parents (32.4 percent) would completely disagree with the notion that wives should obey their husbands in the household (see Table 26). This finding suggests that both respondents and their parents have relatively liberal views on this topic, though the proportion of individuals strongly opposed to female submission is reportedly higher among respondents than among parents (45.6 percent versus 32.4 percent). But besides this significant discrepancy, both percentage distributions are comparable.

During the interviews, the contrast between the informants and their parents on this matter became clearer. In certain cases, the perspectives of parents and children diverged radically, the parents being allegedly more conservative than their egalitarian children. But none of the informants reported that such disagreements translated into parent-child conflicts at home. Informants who were committed to gender equality but whose parents' relationship was structured along patriarchal lines tended to be resigned to the unequal division of power at home. They recognized that their parents belong to another culture and time, in which female obedience in the household is construed as something natural. As a result, they were not personally affected by the unequal gender role models prevailing among their parents. Informant J is representative:

INTERVIEWER: First of all, do you believe that men and women are equal in the couple.

INFORMANT J: Me? Yeah! Yeah!

INTERVIEWER: What about your parents?

INFORMANT J: Hmm ... No, there is always that sense of male superiority, whatever, that I don't agree with. Completely not! Yeah but that's probably from their heritage, or from where they came from. Maybe that's the way they were raised.

There was another scenario in which the informants and their parents both advocated gender inequality in the couple. In that case, parental influence was readily acknowledged by participants as a factor shaping their view. For instance, informant C, a Christian male who overtly embraces the notion of male dominance in the couple, traced his conservative attitude to his parents' and grandparents' patriarchal models of gender relationships. Thus, when asked why he "completely agrees" with the statement "a woman should obey her husband," this informant answered as follows:

INFORMANT C: My father was the type of man ... and I guess the same is true with my grandfather, I can picture him with my grandmother. Once my father and my mother got married, my mom gave up everything. She became a housewife. My grandmother did the same thing. My aunt did the same thing. My other grandmother did the same thing. All my aunts, whether they are blood-related or not, all became housewives ... I don't know, I have always lived with my parents, and it was always: If my father decides something, my mom would follow. Same thing for my grandfather, on my father's side. Of course the mom is consulted ... like *What do you think?* But no advice. Just your opinion.

INTERVIEWER: And you want to reproduce the same model with your wife?

INFORMANT C: That's it. When my uncle decided to leave for the Arab Emirates, he told his wife "We leave." His wife left with him. She didn't have a choice.

Four variables that, according to the literature, could have an impact on one's likelihood of agreeing with the notion of female obedience were tested. First, many case studies showed that second-generation Muslim females living in Western settings are more likely than their male counterparts to, if not resist, at least oppose, traditional gender role models (Rooijackers 1992, 70; Lacoste-Dujardin 1994; Leveau 1997, 153; Kucukcan 1998). I will thus examine, for my own data set, whether there are statistical variations between male and female levels of approval of male dominance in the couple. Secondly, I will test whether the global indexes of ethnic and religious identity are statistically related to respondents' level of agreement with the statement under discussion. Thirdly, given that traditional attitudes toward gender relations are commonly associated with lower education, it will be interesting to verify whether "father's level of education" has an impact on the respondents' endorsement of female obedience. It is expected that individuals coming from families with high educational capital are more likely to challenge traditional gender role models. Finally, the bulk of research into patterns of social control exerted by some ethnic communities on their female members focused on Muslim groups. It is therefore relevant to examine the extent to which Christian and Muslim Arabs' positions coincide on this topic.

As seen in Table 27, Muslims are as likely as Christians to endorse the notion of female obedience. This finding is interesting since, as mentioned, most studies calling attention to gender-based inequalities among ethnic groups have focused on Muslim communities. The present data indicate that Muslim and Christian Arabs support gender equality in the same proportions (around 60 percent). Hence one must be careful not to single out Islam when attempting to explain gender-based power differentials within Arab communities.

Interestingly, "religious identity strength" is statistically related to the dependent variable, and the relationship is very strong ($p<0.01$). This means that the stronger one's religious identity, the more likely one is to support female submission in the household. The variable "ethnic identity strength" is also positively correlated with levels of agreement with female obedience in the household, though to a lesser extent. It thus appears that the more one retains one's religious and ethnic identities, the more likely one is to approve of gender inequalities between mates. This suggests that a traditional approach to gender politics in the household may be a vector of ethnoreligious identity retention among Arab communities.

The variable "father's level of education" has an almost insignificant effect on one's level of agreement with female obedience. Also, quite expectedly, the most recent migrants (those who have been in

Table 27: Percentages of Agreement with the Statement "A Woman Should Obey Her Husband," with Selected Variables

| | | "A Woman Should Obey her Husband" | | |
		I Agree	I Disagree	Total
Respondents' level of agreement	TOTAL	38.8	61.2	100
Respondents' estimated level of agreement of their parents	TOTAL	44.8	55.2	100
By gender**	Females	21.2	78.3	100
	Males	54.5	45.5	100
By time spent in Canada	Less than 10 years	42.9	57.1	100
	10 to 15 years	40.0	60.0	100
	More than 15 years	34.1	65.9	100
By religious affiliation	Christians	38.3	61.7	100
	Muslims	39.8	60.2	100
By ethnic identity score*	Weak	28.1	71.9	100
	Strong	42.9	57.1	100
By religious identity score**	Weak	32.9	67.1	100
	Strong	50.6	49.4	100
By father's level of education	Low	42.9	57.1	100
	High	38.5	61.5	100

* = $p < 0.05$
** = $p < 0.01$

Canada for ten years or less) and those who have been in Canada for ten to fifteen years, are six percent to eight percent more likely to approve of female submission than those who have spent the longest period of time in Canada (more than fifteen years). However, this relationship is not significant.

Finally, the most striking feature of Table 27 is undoubtedly the large discrepancy between male and female levels of agreement with the statement that a wife should obey her husband. Furthermore, this strong relationship is statistically significant at the 0.01 level. Whereas a majority of males (54.5 percent) agree with the statement, a much larger majority of females (78.3 percent) disagree with it. This observation lends support to the notion, put forward by many authors, that females are more inclined than males to critically engage the gendered double standards to which they are potentially exposed in the course of their socialization within Arab communities.

Table 28: Percentages of Agreement with the Statement "A Woman Should Obey Her Husband" by "Gender" and "Religious Affiliation"

		I agree	I disagree	TOTAL
Christians*	Females	25.7	74.3	100
	Males	48.9	51.1	100
Muslims*	Females	13.6	86.4	100
	Males	65.9	34.1	100

* = p < 0.01

Now could it be that males and females have different attitudes toward this issue depending on their religious affiliation? Table 28 displays respondents' level of approval of male dominance in the household according to gender, when controlling for religious affiliation.

Some fascinating variations can be observed in Table 28. Whereas 65.9 percent of Muslim males approve of the statement under discussion, Christian males are almost equally split over the issue of gender equality in the private sphere (48.9 percent pro, 51.1 percent con). Thus, Muslim males seem to be more comfortable than Christian males with the notion that women should obey their husbands. However, among both Christians and Muslims, the overwhelming majority of women oppose the statement, though the majority is stronger among Muslim (86.4 percent) than among Christian females (74.3 percent).

This suggests that Muslim women are more likely than Christian women to resist, and disapprove of, their male religious peers' endorsement of patriarchal models of gender relationships. It also points to acute divergences between Muslim males and females on this issue; the majority of Muslim males (65.9 percent) endorse the notion of male dominance, while an even stronger majority of Muslim females (86.4 percent) strongly oppose it. Given that the Muslim youths of this sample attach much importance to marrying inside their religious group (62.8 percent), such a large attitudinal discrepancy suggests that these male and female Muslims will have to adjust, later in life, to each other's very different expectations regarding the sexual division of power within the household.

PREMARITAL VIRGINITY

This section explores the issue of premarital virginity as a potential ethnic or religious identity marker among second-generation Arabs. According to several authors in North America and Europe (Barazangi 1989; Lacoste-Dujardins 1994; Raissiguier 1995; Morck 1998; Ajrouch 1999, 2004), the value placed on premarital virginity – especially that of females – is often regarded by Arab and Muslim migrants as an important cultural difference between the majority group(s) and their own ethnoreligious groups. As a result, second-generation Arabs end up also construing premarital virginity as an important aspect of what makes their ethnocultural group of belonging distinct from the majority group(s).

Because they are enmeshed in majority group institutions and networks where premarital virginity is regarded, at best, as outdated, these young Arab-Canadian adults are led to engage with the normative value of this model. But in so doing, they are forced to reflect on their ethnocultural identity, because whether they decide to abide by this rule or not tells the public something about the ethnocultural "camp" they have chosen, so to speak. In this section I examine, in turn, the quantitative and qualitative data pertaining to levels of agreement with compulsory premarital virginity.

As shown in Table 29, respondents' positions vary drastically depending on whether the question is about female or male premarital virginity. While 40.8 percent of the whole sample "completely agree" that a female should remain a virgin before marriage, about the same proportion (41.6 percent) "completely disagree" with premarital virginity as an obligation for males. Thus respondents' views on this issue are acutely informed by gendered double standards. More specifically, premarital virginity tends to be considered as a gender-specific obligation applying mostly to females.

As seen in Table 30, a majority in all three "time-spent-in-Canada" categories support compulsory premarital virginity for females, though this majority decreases significantly as time spent in Canada increases. However, time spent in Canada is not statistically correlated with one's attitude toward compulsory premarital male virginity. Religious affiliation is significantly correlated with levels of agreement with both male and female premarital virginity (Table 30). More specifically, the proportion of female virginity advocates is much higher among Muslim respondents (78.4 per-

Table 29: Percentages of Agreement with the Statement "A Girl/Boy Should Remain a Virgin Before Marriage"

	Level of Agreement	Respondents (%)	Parents (respondents' estimation) (%)
Girls' virginity	Completely agree	40.8	75.6
	Somewhat agree	24.8	11.6
	Somewhat disagree	18.0	7.4
	Completely disagree	16.4	5.4
	TOTAL	100	100
Boys' virginity	Completely agree	13.2	30.6
	Somewhat agree	24.0	29.3
	Somewhat disagree	21.2	17.8
	Completely disagree	41.6	22.3
	TOTAL	100	100

cent) than it is among Christians (58.6 percent). Also, while Muslims are almost equally split over the issue of male premarital virginity, a strong majority of Christians (70.4 percent) oppose premarital male virginity as an obligation. Interestingly, strong ethnic and religious identity holders are significantly more likely (at the 0.01 level) to embrace the notion of compulsory premarital female virginity than weak ethnic and religious identity holders (Table 30). However, if a majority among both weak and strong religious identity holders approve of chastity as an obligation for unmarried women, only a majority of strong ethnic identity holders endorse the same principle, while most weak ethnic identity holders are against it. Overall, these results suggest that the notion of compulsory premarital female virginity is central to the process of religiosity and ethnicity building.

I shall now examine whether the attitudes toward male and female premarital virginity in my sample vary according to gender. As seen in Table 30, there is a remarkable consensus between both gender groups on the issue of premarital female virginity. Indeed, compulsory premarital female virginity is fostered by both sexes in almost the exact same proportions (around 65 percent).

Justifications for the pro-female virginity stance tend to be similar for both males and females. Compared to their male ethnic peers, however, most female informants who believe in premarital female chastity do so on more nuanced and complex grounds. Thus, female informants K, H, and I stated that the prospect of losing their virginity before marriage was conceivable, although very

Table 30: Percentages of Agreement with "A Girl/Boy Should Remain a Virgin before Marriage," with Selected Independent Variables

Level of Agreement		Girl should be a virgin before marriage			Boy should be a virgin before marriage		
		Agree	Disagree	Total	Agree	Disagree	Total
For the whole sample	TOTAL	65.6	34.4	100%	37.2	62.8	100%
By gender	Females	66.1	33.9	100%	44.9	55.1	100%
	Males	65.2	34.8	100%	30.3	69.7	100%
By time spent in Canada*	< 10 years	75.0	25.0	100%	38.1	61.9	100%
	10 to 15 years	68.0	32.0	100%	34.7	65.3	100%
By religious affiliation** ††	Christians	58.6	41.4	100%	29.6	70.4	100%
	Muslims	78.4	21.6	100%	51.1	48.9	100%
By ethnic identity's strength**	Strong	73.5	26.5	100%	37.1	62.9	100%
	Weak	43.9	56.1	100%	36.8	63.2	100%
By religious identity's strength**	Strong	76.4	23.6	100%	43.8	56.2	100%
	Weak	59.7	40.3	100%	33.6	66.4	100%

* = $p < 0.05$ (for "Girl should be a virgin before marriage") †† = $p < 0.01$ (for "Boy should be a virgin before marriage")

** = $p < 0.01$

unlikely. They consider that losing their virginity over a fleeting romance would be unworthy, given the importance they attach to premarital virginity. Informant I, a Canadian-born Muslim female of Moroccan descent, explains: "Yeah! Personally, I say it's important [premarital virginity]. Except if it happens, well, there is nothing you can do about it! But if you're able to wait, well, you better wait, you see. There is no hurry! Why ruin everything because of one night? Besides, chances are that, after this one night, you won't even do it again until you get married ... Me, I am a virgin, you know. But I am twenty years old, so I tell myself ... '*If I was able to wait up to now, why can't I still wait until I reach twenty-two, twenty-three years old, when I get married?*' You know, it depends on the person. For me, it's like an objective. It's part of my life. Except if something happens, well so be it."

According to informants H and K, two Muslim females of Algerian descent, if they were involved in a relationship with someone they loved, they would consider transgressing their self-imposed rule. Informant K put it as follows: "My parents are really strict about that [premarital virginity]. It's really important to preserve it until marriage. So, for me to go as far as changing my values, it would have to be someone really important to me."

Of all the female informants who were attempting to retain their virginity before marriage, only informant K did so mainly to obey her parents' rule. The others stressed they were refraining from getting involved in premarital sex primarily for themselves. Some referred to their choice as a form of self-imposed objective or challenge. Many reported avoiding premarital sex on the ground that, for them, sexuality had to be coupled with love, which in turn is associated with marriage. Interestingly, several male informants put forward the same argument to justify their view that women should preserve their virginity until marriage. Thus, for informant B, a Christian male of Lebanese origin, sex and love need to go hand in hand as far as women are concerned: "When a man makes love for the first time, he doesn't need to be in love. It's done mechanically, only for pleasure. But I consider that a woman who loses her virginity [before marriage] is giving away something to a man without really knowing whether he really deserves it." In other words, according to this male informant, female virginity is a sort of gift that should only be offered to a male suitor who proved himself to be worthy of it by making the ultimate commitment: marriage. Finally, informant F (a Muslim male of Algerian descent) mentioned that preserving family honour is the primary reason why he insists on both marrying a virgin and also making sure his sister retains her virginity before marriage.

If there is a quasi-consensus between men and women on the issue of female premarital virginity, the same cannot be said about the topic of male premarital virginity. As shown in Table 30, while 55.1 percent of female respondents disagree with compulsory premarital virginity for males, as many as 69.7 percent of males oppose the notion, a 15 percent difference. Thus, although a majority among both gender groups approve of premarital sex for males, female respondents are more deeply split over this issue. These figures offer support to studies arguing that female Arab youths in a migratory context are more likely than their male counterparts to oppose gendered double standards. The young Arab-Canadian women surveyed here tend to embrace these double standards,[2] but just not as much as males do.

However, female opposition to gendered double standards over sexuality issues would be ill measured if one were to rely exclusively on statistics. In this respect, informants' narratives disclosed precious information that quantitative data failed to flag. Thus, at least three female informants (K, I, and L) who had subscribed to these gendered double standards in the questionnaire engaged critically with them during their interviews. It turned out that these informants, while opposing gendered double standards with regard to premarital virginity, are putting up with them for various reasons. Informant I, for instance, resents the double standards but is nonetheless resigned to accepting them because of parental pressure and a feeling that it is beyond her power to change well-entrenched traditions: "Personally, I don't see why guys should have the right [to engage in premarital sex], and not girls ... But that's the way we [Arabs] have always thought. You know, if I speak to my mother, she's gonna tell me *be careful, don't do these kinds of things*, while perfectly knowing that my brother has been with this girl for two years now. And I go *It's not fair, why do you let him*, they answer *Ha! But he's a guy!* When you come to think of it, it's the same thing. We are both human beings, except guys can do it, and girl cannot. Just because that's the way it is!" Informant L (a Christian woman of Lebanese origin) expresses similar feelings of powerlessness in the face of tradition: "As far as boys are concerned, I am completely in agreement with this statement ["*boys should remain a virgin until marriage*"]. I'd prefer that they ... I completely agree with it. But unfortunately, I think that 99.9 percent of them are not virgins. And you've got to accept it because that's the way society is, and you can't change things."

The sharpest and most lucid criticisms came from informant K who is preserving her chastity in the name of tradition while questioning the fact that the observance of tradition represents an extra burden only for women, not for men: "I think here in Quebec, guys of Arab origin kept a lot the traditional mentality. I would say that they kept it more than girls. Because we, girls, are more receptive to changes, and we seek more to adapt. Also, because guys have so much power, and because they can do whatever they want, they can allow themselves to have the [traditional] mentality; They do whatever they want regardless."

Informant K underlines the fact that it is easier for men to respect tradition since doing so requires far less self-sacrifice from them than it does from women. This comment calls attention to the fact that, within Arab families, tradition is enforced primarily at the expense of girls, who are expected to give up much of their liberty in the process. Informant K points to some of the costly implications of these double standards for Arab girls: "They [boys] want their future wife to be a virgin, but they fool around here and there with girls. And if they sleep with an Arab girl just for fun, they'll judge her. If they see that the girl has no values, they are gonna say, like, *She's an Arab and she's got no values*, and they will have no respect for you. That's why people need to respect you. That's why I manage to be respected."

These remarks highlight an important contradiction resulting from gendered double standards. On the one hand, they allow Arab male teenagers to experience sexuality with few restrictions; on the other, they make premarital virginity an obligation for females. Thus, sexually active Arab males having sex with their female ethnic peers inevitably help to deplete the pool of virgin Arab girls, who are considered by these same males to be the only marriageable women. This in turn puts a great deal of pressure on Arab females, who are expected to preserve their virginity, upon which the public acknowledgment of their respectability depends. The issue of reputation lies at the core of the ethnic identity building process experienced by young Arab females. More specifically, for Arab-origin females, leading a chaste and morally virtuous life is often a precondition for being considered worthy of respect by ethnic peers, whether male or female. As reported by informant K, the normative gaze originating from the ethnic community carries a permanent threat that weighs heavily on girls: that they may be seen as "having no values."

The expression "having no values" was often mentioned during the interviews in reference to the perceived moral laxity of Canadian women, whose "sexually unbridled behaviour" was harshly condemned by male and female informants alike. Several interviewees conceive of the behaviour of Canadian women as the exact opposite of the "honourable" behaviour expected from a "decent" Arab women. Their representations of Canadian women – whether based on first-hand observations or media portrayals – conjure up images of a sexually and morally unrestricted lifestyle. The following statement made by informant H, a Muslim female, is a case in point: "My Canadian friends often go *Ha! We went clubbing and I drank and woke up in his bed. Ha! Ha! Ha!* And they really think it's funny! I really don't find it funny. You know what I mean?" Informant F, a Muslim male, is even more specific: "Sometimes people think that if it's an Algerian, it's a good girl, and if it's a Canadian, it's a tart. Well, it's not exactly that. It's just … Well, actually, it's not too far from the truth [laughter]."

Therefore, for Arab females enmeshed in traditional ethnic networks, gaining full recognition as a legitimate and respectable ingroup member is largely contingent upon the public acknowledgment of their chastity. For them, the consequence of acquiring a "bad reputation" is to be brought into social disrepute for having adopted a behaviour associated with the outgroup, the behaviour of the "depraved Western girl" (read "easy women with no values"). This is a premium illustration of how female sexuality can play a crucial role in the formation of ethnic boundaries, thus helping to crystallize the group's collective identity. This parallels Ajrouch's finding that, for Arab Americans of the second generation, being American is signified, in a quite negative fashion, by the figure of the American girl whose sexual conduct is morally suspect (Ajrouch 2004, 382).

It also follows that Arab females who wish to marry an ethnic peer (and, as seen above, most of them do) are forced to monitor their own sexuality or at least offer an asexual image to the public in order not to incur a bad reputation, which would seriously decrease their symbolic value on the market of marriageable women. Informant K reports: "They [men] force me to keep tradition and all, but they do whatever they want. But if I want to marry an Arab, I am a little bit forced to respect traditions. And personally, I think that traditions are important, the values and all."

Informant K's relationship to "traditions" reveals an ambivalent position characterized by an identification with traditional values ("traditions are important, the values and all"), and overt criticism of the gendered double standards informing these traditions ("They [men] force me to keep tradition and all, but they do whatever they want"). Such mixed feelings, shared by most other female informants, offer much support to Raissiguier's observation (1995) that Arab girls living in a Western context are often critical both of the host society's dominant standards with regard to female sexuality and of the power effects resulting from Arab males' controlling attitudes and behaviours in the name of tradition.

As highlighted earlier, second-generation Arab males, more so than their female counterparts, seem to cultivate gendered double standards when it comes to defining proper sexual behaviour. Indeed, if Arab females tend to criticize these double standards, Arab males tend to accept them unquestioningly. The following exchange with informant A, a Christian male of Lebanese origin (who otherwise provided answers favourable to gender equality), is eloquent in this regard:

INFORMANT A: Both girls and boys should be allowed to gain some experience before marriage, I mean sexual experience. Well, I got to say that I wouldn't like that ... you know ... that the girl I am gonna marry turned out to have had sexual relationships before she met me. I mean not sexual relationships per se. As I said before, it doesn't matter. But I wouldn't marry a girl who had, like, four hundred guys before me ... Well, if it's clear that she was having sexual relationships because she was in love, that's fine. But if she does it just for pleasure, then that's different. 'Cause there are two ways to go about it [for girls]: I call it being either a whore or just normal. If she's a whore, she does it only to have fun.

INTERVIEWER: OK. I understand. And is it the same thing for a boy?

INFORMANT A: A guy? Hell no! As far as I am concerned, my boy won't have the right to come back home before three o'clock in the morning [laughter].

Upon surveying the qualitative data, it appears that the gendered double standards prevailing among young Arab-Canadian males can be accounted for, in part, by the quasi-absence of any parental and social pressure to prevent them from indulging in premarital sex. This finding stands in contrast to the quantitative data, which could lead one to believe that male sexuality is also subject to parental surveillance and control. Indeed, as highlighted in Table 29, a majority of parents (59.9 percent) are thought by their children to either completely agree, or somewhat agree, with compulsory premarital virginity for males. This figure, though much smaller than the proportion of parents who reportedly believe in compulsory premarital virginity for females (87.2 percent), nonetheless suggests that parents are less imbued with gendered double standards than their children.

However, although a majority of parents are thought to con-
demn both male and female premarital sex, the qualitative materials suggest that, in the case of Arab-origin sons, parental
condemnation is not accompanied by strict control and surveillance. Also, because non-compliant males are not at risk of incur-
ring social disrepute and disapproval, parental pressure aimed at
regulating their sexual behaviour is generally rather soft and symbolic. For instance, when asked whether the Canadian part of his
identity could be held responsible for conflicts between him and
his parents, informant F reported: "Well, there is also the question
of sex. She [his mother] is not against it. But she'd prefer me to
avoid it. And this is because of religion. She goes *It's not because
you're a boy that you have more rights than your sister.* But, in
practice, for sure, it [virginity] is more important as far as my sister is concerned. She [his mother] says that our culture, our traditions, do not allow us to do such things. But she more or less turns
a blind eye, because, in Algerian culture, in Arab culture in general, when it's a boy, we let go … That's the mentality. According
to religion, I should preserve my virginity until I get married as
well. But as I told you, because I am a guy, I am not bothered. I can
fool around left, right, and centre."

PREMARITAL DATING

I shall now turn to the issue of premarital dating, which is closely
related to that of premarital virginity. Premarital dating – a common and generally straightforward practice for most young Canadians and Quebecois – is often viewed by Arab parents with, if not
moral disapproval, at least distrust. This parental interdiction is
again mostly directed at daughters in order to preserve not only
their virginity but also their reputation and, by extension, their
family's reputation. Because it opens the door to sexual activities
without the sanction of marriage, dating is condemned by many
Arab parents on moral and religious grounds. Furthermore, dating
(like premarital virginity) tends to be deployed by Arab migrant
parents as an ethnocultural marker feeding ethnoreligious consciousness. In this section the data are surveyed with a view to finding out whether second-generation Arabs (critically) engage with
this norm, and whether they see in it a source of ethnocultural
demarcation between them and their majority group age peers.

Table 31: Percentages of Agreement with the Statement "Girls/Boys Can Have a Boy/Girlfriend," by "Gender"

Level of Agreement		Girls are allowed to have a boyfriend before marriage			Boys are allowed to have a girlfriend before marriage		
		Agree (%)	Disagree (%)	Total	Agree (%)	Disagree (%)	Total
For the whole sample	Total	78.4	21.6	100	88.0	12.0	100
By gender	Females	86.4	13.6	100	86.4	13.6	100
	Males	70.5	29.5	100	89.4	10.6	100

Based on both qualitative and quantitative data, there appears to be a consensus between males and females on the issue of male dating. As seen in Table 31, the right of men to date women before marriage is largely taken for granted by a strong majority of respondents, be they male (89.4 percent) or female (86.4 percent). There is no need to expand on the rationales underlying this trend since they do not differ, in essence, from those put forward by informants who condone premarital sex for men.

The picture is not that different when we look at respondents' views on female dating (Table 31). Interestingly, a large majority of respondents (78.4 percent) either completely agree or somewhat agree with the statement "Girls should be allowed to have a boyfriend before marriage if they want to." Among women only, as many as 86.4 percent approve of premarital dating for women. Since women approve of premarital dating for men in the same proportions (86.4 percent), it can be said that the great majority of them consider dating to be an equal right for both gender groups. Similarly, a majority of male respondents consider dating to be acceptable for both sexes. However, male respondents are more likely to deem dating acceptable for men (89.4 percent) than for women (70.5 percent).

These findings are surprising on the whole since, as seen in the previous section (see Table 30), a large majority of both males and females oppose female premarital sex. Even more surprising is that among those respondents advocating premarital female virginity, a majority (72 percent) believe that women should be allowed to have a boyfriend if they wish (note that this majority is much larger among females – 82.1 percent – than among males – 62.8 percent).

It thus appears that, although female premarital sex is harshly disapprove of and even regulated through subtle yet omnipresent forms of social control, female dating is widely accepted by both gender groups. This suggests that a majority of both males and females do not oppose female dating as long as it does not involve sexual intercourse. Consistent with this principle, two male informants (B and C) reported that they go out with Arab girls as long as it is understood between them that the girls' virginity has to be preserved. This self-imposed rule, however, only applies to Arab or Muslim women. As Christian informant B reports:

INFORMANT B: I allow myself to have girlfriends. But if I have one, she's a virgin. I'll never be the one who'll make her lose her virginity. I consider that I don't have the right to do that.
INTERVIEWER: "Even if she is Quebecoise?"
INFORMANT B: [Long hesitation and mumbling] I was about to say *there ain't much virgin Quebecoises* [laughs]. No, I think it's only good for a Lebanese or an Arab ... A *Quebecoise*, on the other hand, I wouldn't mind. But I would never marry her.

Similarly, Muslim informant F sets himself a rule to date only non-Arab women when he knows the relationship is purely flirtatious. This is a common strategy that allows second-generation men to resolve the contradiction resulting from wanting to avail themselves of the sexual liberty at their disposal, while expecting their future wives to be virgins. The following exchange with informant F was very interesting in that regard:

INTERVIEWER: You give yourself the right to have girlfriends. But on the other hand, you think it is important for girls to preserve their virginity. So I wonder whether your girlfriends are Algerians.
INFORMANT F: Personally no. I wouldn't want it. I am the one who don't want to. Well, I'll give you an example: just last week, I went out on a date with this Algerian girl I met a month ago, and we only kissed in the movie theatre, you see. But then I told her *I can't go any further because when I see you, I see my own sister* ... So I told her *I am a guy who likes very much having sex, going out a lot, having fun. And I couldn't do that with you.* And she thinks the same thing, you see?

INTERVIEWER: So your girlfriends are Quebecoises or Canadians?
INFORMANT F: Yes, or Brazilian, Italian. But not with Muslims ...
If I go out with an Algerian, she's like my sister. So, because I
wouldn't like someone to do this to my sister, I am sure that the
boy – because she's got brothers – I am sure that her brother
wouldn't like to see me with his sister.

All of these narratives convey a dichotomous representation of
women split along ethnic lines. This type of rationalization presup-
poses a distinction between, on the one hand, the chaste, respectable, "sister-like" (ingroup) Arab woman and, on the other, the
non-Arab woman who, not being bound by the same cultural
expectations, is therefore made sexually available, which makes her
somewhat less respectable.

According to this dual image, the respectability of Arab females
rests upon the maintenance of impenetrable frontiers between two
opposite representations of women: the pure, virgin, and marriageable woman (i.e., the Arab woman), as opposed to the sexually and
morally depraved woman (i.e., the Western woman). The implication
of such a framework is that young Arab-origin women who choose
to have a sexual life before marriage run the risk of being associated
with the latter category, which would not only bring them into social
disrepute but also single them out as culturally "deviant." Therefore,
female premarital virginity acts as a strong ethnoreligious identity
marker that helps to reinforce group boundaries.

Although, as reported above, some Arab males take it upon
themselves to preserve the virginity of their girlfriends or dates, the
majority of Arab women believe it is incumbent mainly upon them
to ensure that they remain "pure" before marriage. This puts young
Arab females – those who value premarital virginity – in a position
where they have to carefully assess the seriousness of any boys
whom they date. Furthermore, it makes many of them reluctant to
date non-Arab males, who are more likely to expect an active sexual life as part of a "normal" relationship. Hence some female
informants reported a preference for dating Arab males exclusively,
on the ground that they are less likely to tarnish their reputation.
Informant K, for example, clings to her virginity but nonetheless
allows herself to date Arab boys because, she argues, they are more
accepting of such sexual restrictions: "I went out with a Muslim
Moroccan and he broke up with me because of that [his respecting

female virginity], because he didn't want to ... Because he has the
same mentality, he said to me: *I don't want to be the one who's
gonna make you lose it* [your virginity]. He said *I respect you too
much to do this to you* ... Guys understand that! Well, it depends on
the person you're with. But any Arab who doesn't understand that
is ... toying with you."

FEMALE VIRGINITY AND FAMILY REPUTATION

Thus far the issue of family reputation has been addressed on the sur-
face when dealing with premarital virginity and dating issues. It was
shown that family reputation and honour are central concerns to
Arab parents, and that the responsibility of maintaining family honour lies more heavily upon daughters than sons. In other words,
female sexuality is at the heart of the process whereby Arab families
come to secure for themselves a good name and reputation. But even
more relevant to the present inquiry is that upholding family reputation proved to be an important contributing factor in ethnoreligious
identity building. This section further explores the notion that in
Arab communities, family reputation and, by extension, group
boundary maintenance is mediated by the chastity of female family
members.

As seen in Table 32, respondents are split almost evenly with
respect to the importance they attach to female virginity in the
building of family reputation. However, according to respondents,
a large majority of their parents (72.7 percent) would endorse such
reasoning.

One resounding finding in Table 32 is the extremely strong correlation between gender and levels of agreement with the statement
linking female chastity to family reputation. Whereas a majority of
women (63.6 percent) oppose this statement, an almost equal
majority of men (61 percent) agree with it. It should be noted that,
during the interview process, informants were not asked specifically
to comment on their answers to this question, which makes it
harder to account qualitatively for the large gender discrepancy.
However, when addressing related issues, two male informants
clearly articulated that female chastity, in their family as well as in
their culture, is closely connected to family reputation. For
instance, when asked whether it was important for him that his sister remained a virgin until marriage, Muslim informant F answered

Table 32: Percentages of Agreement with "A Girl's Virginity Should be Protected by Male Kin for Family Reputation," with Selected Independent Variables

Level of Agreement		Family reputation is dependent on female premarital virginity		
		I AGREE	I DISAGREE	TOTAL
For respondents	Total	52.0	48.0	100
For parents (as reported by respondents)	Total	72.7	27.3	100
By gender*	Females	39.0	61.0	100
	Males	63.6	36.4	100
By religious affiliation	Christians	50.6	49.4	100
	Muslims	54.5	45.5	100
By father's education	Low	52.9	47.1	100
	High	51.5	48.5	100
By ethnic identity's strength*	Strong	57.6	42.4	100
	Weak	35.1	64.9	100
By religious identity strength*	Strong	62.9	37.1	100
	Weak	45.0	55.0	100
By time spent in Canada	Less than 10 years	58.3	41.7	100
	10 to 15 years	53.3	46.7	100
	More than 15 years	45.1	54.9	100

* = $p < 0.01$

thus: "Yes! It's quite mean of me. Sometimes, when I think about it, I think it's unfair that I have the right to deflower girls, to have sex, whereas I want my sister to be always ... It's about family honour. Perhaps I am being selfish, perhaps it's mean. But we are all like that. But it's about family honour."

It is interesting to recall that, as shown earlier in Table 30, males and females agree that women should remain virgins until marriage in approximately the same proportions (66.1 percent vs. 65.2 percent, respectively). However, this common agreement does not hold when it comes to justifying premarital female virginity. As opposed to males, females seem to reject the family reputation argument. Based on both quantitative and qualitative data, it appears that most men tend to be comfortable with the use of female virtue as a core mainstay of family honour, whereas a majority of women refuse to see their sexual conduct subjected to strict male surveillance for the sake of preserving the family name. The data gathered from the interviews suggest that most Arab women wish to preserve their virginity for themselves, that is, out of personal motivation. Christian Informant N is an example:

INFORMANT N: Well, I think it is important that I preserve my virginity, but I do it for myself. It is a choice that I've made, and I want to stick to this principle because ... It's not as if it was a challenge but, I don't know, it's something special."

INTERVIEWER: "Do you think that this choice has anything to do with your culture or religion?

INFORMANT N: It has something to do with my culture and my religion. But if I'd want to do as I please [have sex], I don't think anybody could ever find out. I think I would be the only one to know. And if I'd do it [have sex], I wouldn't be hurting anyone ... What I mean is that I choose to preserve my virginity for myself, not for others. It's your life, your body, it's your choice."

Thus, these Arab-origin women do not want their sexual life to be put under scrutiny, though they are personally committed to preserving their virginity until marriage. A majority of female respondents and interviewees are uncomfortable with the notion that family honour is contingent upon the chastity of female family members. The data indeed suggest that these young women oppose, to varying degrees, any attempts to make the upholding of family reputation dependent on the preservation of their chastity. Many of them consider their sexuality to be a private matter as opposed to a collective property that warrants public attention and protection.

In a Western context, as Ajrouch (1999) pertinently remarked, when Arab parents think their daughter's virginity is under threat, they clamp down on their female children far more harshly than they would have done in the home country. The issue of female chastity can thus become particularly salient within Arab migrant families, especially those integrated into traditional ethnic networks. As previously reported, a large majority of respondents (72.7 percent) think that their parents would agree that their daughters' virginity should be preserved for the sake of family reputation. It follows that the normative gap between Arab-Canadian female youths and their parents on this issue is likely to be particularly wide, especially in a culturally liberal society such as Canada.

As seen in Table 32, time spent in Canada does not have a significant impact on one's belief that female chastity is linked to family honour, although predictably, the more time respondents spent in Canada, the more likely they were to disagree with this notion. Christian and Muslim respondents endorsed the statement in almost the same proportions (50.6 percent versus 54.5 percent, respectively). This suggests, once again, that Muslim and Christian Arabs are to a large extent enmeshed in a common frame of traditions, whose maintenance depends largely on female family members. It also appears that the respondents with the better-educated fathers are not more likely than the others to see in female chastity a moral safeguard against social disrepute.

Finally, Table 32 shows that both ethnic and religious identity strengths are positively correlated with levels of agreement with this statement. This observation lends further support to the hypothesis that female conduct, and especially female sexual conduct, acts as a crucial contributing factor to ethnoreligious identity maintenance among Arab communities.

This whole section dealing with gender-related traditions highlighted the weight of certain cultural models inherited from the homeland on ethnoreligious identity building strategies. On the one hand, gender-related traditions constitute, for second-generation Arabs, an ethnic identity marker drawn from the ethnic group's cultural repertoire. On the other, the young people in my study, especially women, engage critically with these traditions, transforming them in the process.

The next and last section dwells on two other external factors, namely, perceived prejudice and discrimination, which also mediate ethnoreligious identity building processes among Arab communities of the diaspora. This is not to argue that these second-generation Arabs' relationship to the majority group(s) is structured exclusively through prejudice and discrimination. However, as they attempt to negotiate their ethnoreligious identity in a Western context, Arab-origin Canadians can hardly remain immune to the damaging effect of these factors.

7

Perceived Prejudice and Discrimination

Up to now, I have focused essentially on ethnic identity defined in general terms, as opposed to Arab identity specifically. As stressed in the introduction, the reason behind this choice was to avoid ascribing to the group under study the Arab category as the primary frame shaping their ethnic consciousness. The Arab label encompasses a wide variety of national, religious, and ethnic groups, each giving rise to distinct communal allegiances that, while intersecting, are nonetheless perceived by the actors as incommensurable. Arab identity is thus one of many collective identities made socially available to individuals within both the Arab world and the Arab diaspora. Therefore, ethnic consciousness can take on multiple, multidimensional, and "creolised" forms, which are of course contingent upon the social context of interaction. It follows – this cannot be overstressed – that neither Arabness, national membership, nor any other form of collective identity can exhaust the multifarious forms that Arab-Canadian ethnicity can assume.

In a migratory context, however, the remarkable heterogeneity of ethnicity can be seriously compromised when minority groups attempt to have their identity choices validated by the majority group. As previously underscored, the majority group tends to view the Other through its own categorizing lenses, reducing any differences to a series of stereotypical and easily decipherable characteristics. Furthermore, the majority group's interpretive frame is very often impervious to the "identity proposals" originating from minority groups. As a result, it can be extremely difficult for ethnic minorities to successfully challenge the categorizing framework through which they are represented.

In the dominant Western system of representations, individuals of Arab origin tend to be construed and labelled as "Arabs." Of course, in the Arab world, individuals and groups have at their disposal a wide range of less globalizing and unidimensional categories to choose from when performing identity choices. Actors can indeed mobilize and combine various forms of belonging (e.g., national, ethnic, or religious). However, in the Western world in general, and in North America in particular, the importance of the Arab category among Arab-origin minorities tends to be disproportionately magnified. This is in part due to the fact that these minorities are locked into an externally assigned "Arabness," which they can hardly ignore since it constitutes the primary referential frame through which their ethnicity is "imagined" by the majority group.

Moreover, in the West, the Arab and Muslim categories convey a collection of prejudicial stereotypes that are not only integrated into a common symbolic system but are also self-referentially reproduced, each of them mirroring and reinforcing the others (Said 1979). These categories are played up in Western representations as the antitheses of Judaeo-Christian values. Each time the Western Us is pitted against the Muslim/Arab Them in popular imagery and discourses – think of the rhetoric after September 11, 2001 – it helps to reinforce rigid "civilizational" boundaries differentiating between *our* "free," "secular," "democratic," and "rational" world and *their* "intolerant," "fanatical," "terrorist," and "irrational" world (Antonius 2002).

It was argued that this process of categorization and stigmatization ought to be taken into account to understand why the Arab label has turned out to be such a popular source of self-designation among second-generation Arabs.[1] Because these young people are all subsumed into the same Arab category by the majority group, they are forced to engage critically with the figure of the Arab that Canadians reflect back at them through categorization. It was shown earlier that, in the process, a majority of them attempt to neutralize the derogatory meanings attached to this externally produced Arabness by turning it into a source of pride. Others, however, preferred downplaying this socially compromised category by emphasizing alternative ethnocultural identities instead.

In any case, Arab-Canadian youths can hardly remain neutral toward the Arab category since it is the cornerstone of the representational frame through which their otherness is constructed by the majority group. This section analyzes the data with a view to high-lighting precisely how these second-generation Arabs think they are perceived by the majority group. If, as hypothesized, they perceive themselves to be subjected to anti-Arab stereotyping and prejudice, it could be taken as evidence that their strong identification as Arabs emerges in conflictual conditions, perhaps even in reaction to such adverse conditions.

It will also be interesting to see whether the reception of anti-Arab stereotypes by young Arab Canadians varies along religious lines. In Western representations, Arab and Muslim categories are frequently amalgamated to a point where they are sometimes used interchangeably, especially in the mass media.[2] Indeed, the Arab category as framed by the majority group is to a large extent imbued with Islamic symbols and images. In other words, Islam serves as a primary signifier giving shape and content to the Western notion of Arabness (Antonius and Bendris 1998). As a result, Christian Arab Canadians are ascribed an Arabness that is not only severed from a central component of their collective identity, namely, their Christianity, but that also locks them into an Islamized, and thus largely distorted, image of themselves. Furthermore, it must be re-emphasized that, in the post-1970 Arab world, Arab nationalism became increasingly intertwined with Islam, thus excluding Christian minorities from the space of enunciation from which the notion of Arabness emerged. These factors help to make the Arab category less appealing as a source of identification among Christian Arabs of the diaspora.

However, because the majority group's standardizing gaze tends to crush the ethnocultural and religious diversity permeating the Arab-Canadian community, both Christians and Muslims are being categorized under a single all-encompassing and derogatory Arab label. In other words, as Mary Waters demonstrated (1990, 1996) for non-white minorities in the US, ethnicity does not always amount to an "optional card" that one can freely choose to play or downplay at will; it can sometimes be imposed from the outside. This section thus explores the various modes of resistance offered to Christian and Muslim Christian Arabs in the face of such "symbolic violence."

The section also looks at how second-generation Arabs consider their religious group to be perceived by the majority group. For evident reasons, religion-based stereotyping and prejudice affect more

Muslim than Christian Arabs. Moreover, Arab Muslims in Canada are likely to experience both anti-Arab and anti-Muslim stigmatization, which, as mentioned, largely feed each other. As for Christian Arabs, they are less likely to endure religious prejudice since they share the majority group's dominant religion. Nevertheless, they also tend to be regarded by Westerners as a religious outgroup, although to a lesser extent than their Muslim counterparts. In addition, Christian Arab religious consciousness is itself loosely connected to Western Christianity and draws upon very different rites, traditions, beliefs, and cultural heritages. It can thus be said that the relationship of Christian Arabs with the religious majority is characterized by both sameness and difference, which makes it all the more interesting to see how this group think their ethnoreligious identity and community are perceived by Canadians.

In addressing the issue of ethnic and religious biases, I pay special attention to the role played by the mass media, since there is now a great deal of evidence, accumulated over recent decades, that the North American media help to portray Arab and Muslim cultures in a prejudicial manner (see for example Antonius and Bendris 1998; B. Abu-Laban and S.M. Abu-Laban 1999, 150; Shaheen 2001; Antonius 2002; Karim 2003). I survey the data with a view to assessing how Arab-origin youth consider their ethnoreligious communities to be portrayed in the media.

The issue of discrimination is addressed separately from that of stereotyping and prejudice since it is an analytically distinct phenomenon. Whereas a stereotype is a preconceived notion based on generalizations, a prejudice refers to adverse attitudes, judgments, or discourses directed against a targeted group. It could be said that prejudice is generally fuelled by negative stereotypes. Therefore, in what follows, the expressions negative stereotyping and prejudicial stereotyping are used interchangeably to refer to derogatory attitudes and discourses directed against a minority group. Discrimination, on the other hand, refers to an unfair and prejudicial treatment based on one or more minority group characteristics (socially constructed as distinctive). It should thus be clear that prejudices and stereotypes relate to the realm of representations, whereas discrimination pertains to social practice. What's more, while prejudicial stereotyping does not necessarily lead to discrimination, the latter always involves some form of prejudicial stereotyping. The second part of this chapter examines the extent to

Table 33: Percentages of Agreement with the Statment "There Are Negative Stereotypes against Arabs," and "There Are Negative Stereotypes against my Religious Group"

Level of Agreement	Statements	
	"There are negative stereotypes against Arabs prevailing among Canadians"	*"There are negative stereotypes against my religious group in Canada"*
I completely agree	28.1	21.3
I somewhat agree	49.8	23.7
I somewhat disagree	15.7	22.1
I completely disagree	6.4	32.9
TOTAL	100	100

which Arab-origin youths feel discriminated against by majority group members in their daily lives.

PERCEIVED NEGATIVE STEREOTYPING

Stereotypes in the Canadian Population

As Table 33 shows, a majority of respondents either completely agree (28.1 percent) or somewhat agree (49.8 percent) with the statement "There are negative stereotypes against Arabs prevailing among Canadians." Only a minority of respondents are either somewhat in disagreement (15.7 percent) or in complete disagreement (6.4 percent) with the statement.

Table 33 also indicates that a majority of respondents (55 percent) either somewhat or completely disagree with the statement "There are negative stereotypes against my religious group prevailing among Canadians." However, these results are influenced by the fact that 65 percent of the sample are Christians. Drastically different patterns of response are obtained when controlling for religious affiliation. Thus, while only 30.2 percent of Christian respondents agree that Canadians are negatively biased against their religious group, 72.4 percent of Muslim respondents hold the same view. The qualitative materials reviewed below will shed further light on how Arab-origin Muslims consider the media to misportray the religious component of their identity.

Interviewees were asked whether in their opinion Canadians portray Arabs in an accurate or unfair manner. All but one informant stated that Canadian images of Arabs are generally distorted. The most commonly reported (prejudicial) stereotype is that all Arabs are terrorists or have a predisposition to violence. Note that the interviews were completed around April 2001, namely, five months before the September 11 terrorist attacks on US soil. Yet eleven informants considered that Canadians tend to associate Arabs with terrorism.

When asked, for instance, whether Canadians perceive Arabs in a favourable light, informant G, a Muslim female of Egyptian origin, answered, "As a bunch of terrorists. A bunch of terrorists. Personally, I don't see that. I mean of course there are fanatics, but as in any culture, any religion, anything." Similarly, when asked how Canadians perceive Arabs, informant K, a Muslim female of Algerian descent, replied, "For them [Canadians], hmm ... Personally, I am often being called the terrorist. For them [Canadians], we are a bit aggressive."

Some respondents stated that Arabs are regarded by Canadians as cunning crooks. As informant D, a Christian male, reports: "I know a guy who told me 'You Arabs are all a bunch of crooks and you are all terrorists.'"

Gender issues were also frequently reported as a chief source of stereotyping. According to several interviewees, both male and female, Canadians tend to perceive gender relationships in Arab culture as bearing the hallmark of domination. Interestingly, informants addressing this issue often did so from the perspective of the gender group to which they belonged. Thus, men tended to report the stereotype of the Arab male as dominating wife abuser, whereas women mentioned the stereotype of the submissive and dominated Arab wife. Informant I, a Canadian-born woman of Moroccan descent, said: "They think that in every Arab country, women are obliged to wear the veil, and that they can't talk to a man on the street, or that they can only go out accompanied by their husband. But it depends on which country you're talking about. Like in Saudi Arabia or in Palestine it's kind of true. But Quebecois lump together all the nationalities, but it's not an accurate picture!" Informant C, a Christian male, provided the following example of anti-Arab stereotypes: "We are all violent terrorist, and we beat our women."

Some informants lamented the fact that Canadians make no distinction between the various national groups that comprise the Arab community. As informant A (a Christian male of Lebanese origin) put it: "For Canadians, it's like, anyone who speaks Arabic is ... whether you're Egyptian, Moroccan, Algerian, it's all in Africa. As a matter of fact, they [North African Arabs] are not even Arabs, they're Berbers."

Another commonly reported stereotype has to do with the economic, cultural, and technological level of development of Arab countries. Several informants consider that the mental image Canadians have of Arabs amounts – more out of ignorance than racism – to a series of clichés about, for example, villages built in the desert, camels as the chief means of transportation, and a cultural incompatibility with modern technology. Thus, Informant M: "They still picture us on our camels. And what do we know of the outside world? We know nothing! We know nothing of liberal societies, and of liberal ideas. For example, computers, anything related to technology, we don't know that!" Similarly, informant F said: "I knew this Canadian girl. We were talking and I mentioned I was Algerian. She told me: *Ha! Do you go to school on a camel? Are your streets made of sand?* And she was a student!"

Thus, in general, these young adults of Arab origin consider that Canadians and Quebecois hold preconceived notions about Arabs. They also think that such misrepresentations often convey prejudicial and disparaging stereotypes. However, as reported earlier, most participants regard such prejudicial stereotyping as a form of ignorance, rather than as bold racism. These findings are fully consistent with Hayani's (1999, 299), which also showed that a large majority of Canadian-born Arabs consider that Canadians have a very low regard for their ethnic group(s).

According to quantitative data, a large majority among both Christian and Muslim respondents consider that Canadian representations of Arabs are biased. However, this majority is stronger among Muslims (83.9 percent) than Christians (74.7 percent). The slight discrepancy may be due in part to the fact that, as shown in chapter 4, Muslim respondents are more likely than their Christian counterparts to identify themselves as Arabs. More specifically, Muslims' greater level of identification with the Arab community could largely account for their greater awareness of, and sensitivity to, anti-Arab stereotyping. Also, because Canadians tend to merge Arab culture and Islam, as if the two formed a single entity, Muslim Arabs are perhaps more likely to feel specifically targeted by anti-Arab stereotypes. This conjunction between anti-Arab and anti-Islamic prejudices was also highlighted in a study based on a sample of 152 Christian students at a private university in the southwestern United States, in which Rowatt and colleagues (2005, 40) found a positive and strong correlation between self-reported anti-Arab racism and negative attitudes toward Muslims.

Nonetheless, a large majority of Christian respondents (74.7 percent) also agree with the statement "There are negative stereotypes against Arabs prevailing among Canadians." Most importantly, both quantitative and qualitative data suggest that Christian Arabs are affected by anti-Arab prejudice as well. First, as highlighted in Table 4, the "Arab" label turned out to be the most popular source of self-designation among Christian respondents. Second, several Christian informants reported falling victim to anti-Arab stereotyping even though the stereotypes were directed against Islam; after all, Canadians tend to lump all Arab individuals together, regardless of religious differences. When informant P, a Christian female, was asked why she "completely agreed" with the statement that Canadians held negative stereotypes against Arabs, she said, "Well for one thing, to them [Canadians], Arab equals Muslim. Secondly, for them, Muslim equals violent, terrorist." Informant N, another Christian female, made a similar observation when she was asked whether she thought that the image Canadians have of Arabs is accurate or distorted: "I think it is biased because, right away, whenever they [Canadians] speak of the Arab people, they associate them with peoples of the Middle East, they associate them with the Islamic religion, with submission, with domination, murders, and all that sort of things. And they think it's horrific, and the veil, and all that."

That being said, because anti-Arab and anti-Muslim prejudices are indeed largely coterminous with each other, Christian Arabs, as opposed to their Muslim counterparts, have more power to mitigate some of the negative connotations attached to their Arab identity. They can do so by emphasizing their Christianity – as many of them did during the interviews – so as to detach the Arab label they embrace from its most socially compromising component: Islam. Several Christian informants are thus aware that anti-Arab prejudice is to a large extent informed by anti-Islam prejudice. This gives them even more reason to want to be recognized by Canadians as both Arab and Christian. Nabeel Abraham (1989, 21) made a similar argument when he stressed that Arab-American Christians often overemphasize their denominational allegiances in order not to be associated with Muslim communities, which would jeopardize their chances of being accepted by Americans. It is ironic that whereas Christian minorities in Arab countries suffer from not being recognized by majority groups as "authentic" compatriots and Arabs because of their religious difference, Christian Arabs in North America suffer from the majority groups' tendency to lump them together with Muslim Arabs while overlooking their religious difference. In any case, the various ways that Arab Christians combine their Arab and Christian identities, depending on the majority group they interact with, constitute a prime illustration of the influential power of outside labelling on minority groups' self-definitions.

Interestingly, Muslim informants were more inclined than their Christian counterparts to report stereotypes portraying Arab males as dominating and controlling, and Arab females as dominated and submissive. Furthermore, while acknowledging that Canadians associate male domination with Arab culture in general, several Muslim informants stressed that Islam was targeted more specifically by such gender-related generalizations. As informant F put it: "In general, when I say I am Algerian, they say *terrorist*. And when I mention Muslim, they go *wife beater*, or *you guys have three or four wives*."

According to other Muslim informants, another common gender-related stereotype about Muslims is that "their" women all wear the Islamic veil (hijab in Arabic). Indeed, many Muslims identified the hijab as an issue highly loaded with stereotypes, most notably because Canadians are thought to equate this form of veil wearing with female submissiveness.

Regarding the hijab, the case of informant J, though clearly not representative, is particularly interesting. Informant J, a Canadian-born Muslim female who scored very low on both the ethnic and religious identity scales, first stated that Canadians often make incorrect generalizations about the hijab, assuming for instance that all Arab women have to wear it. Then, unexpectedly, she said that some of the generalizations were accurate, and even started to take issue with hijab wearers:

INTERVIEWER: What kind of image of Arabs and Muslims do you think Canadians have? Do you think this image is biased, or does it match reality?

INFORMANT J: Maybe they [Canadians] generalize. Like, they think every Muslim woman has to wear the djihab.

INTERVIEWER: You mean the hijab?

INFORMANT J: Yeah yeah! Sorry, I feel so embarrassed [about not knowing the proper term]. And yeah, sometimes, I guess they [Canadians] generalize right!

INTERVIEWER: What do you mean by that? What's right about what other people think of Arabs?

INFORMANT J: Hmmm ... Hypocrite maybe. I see some girls in the metro, they wear the scarf. But then they wear, like, flashy make-up and blue jeans. It's like, *what are you doing?* I mean you are either gonna [follow the rules] one hundred percent, or you are gonna be zero percent. You are not gonna be fifty-fifty.

This narrative points to the cognitive distance separating informant J from her ethnoreligious culture. Take the sentence "They [Canadians] think that every Muslim woman has to wear the *djihab*" (my emphasis). In this phrase, the informant's poor knowledge of her religious culture is denoted by the phoneme inversion she performed in attempting to pronounce the word "hijab," which she mistakenly turned into "djihab." Also revealing is that whereas all other participants but one[3] saw in this question an opportunity to deconstruct negative outside stereotyping, informant J validates what she considers to be a Canadian-endorsed yet accurate generalization about hijab wearers. Indeed, instead of criticizing derogatory stereotyping, she criticized the "hypocrisy" of veiled women whose Western lifestyle seems to be inconsistent with their outwardly religious devotion. Being herself a Muslim, at least nominally, informant J has a certain latitude in subscribing publicly to what she calls accurate generalizations about veiled women's behaviours and attitude. In this respect, her statement could more accurately be described as a critique from the inside than as an endorsement of outside stereotypes.

In any case, this example shows how different members of a minority might have divergent views on what constitutes prejudicial stereotyping against their group depending on each person's understanding of which practices or norms qualify as legitimate expressions of their ethnoreligious culture. What can appear to certain minority group members as derogatory stereotyping by outsiders may be considered as legitimate criticism by others.

Some Muslim informants stressed the Islam-specific character of the Arab terrorist stereotype. Informant G reported: "I do believe that being labelled as a terrorist is really hard for certain Arab people, especially for Muslim people."[4] Once again, many Muslims considered that anti-Arab and anti-Muslim stereotypes largely overlap. In other words, they recognize that religion and ethnicity intersect in the construction of derogatory stereotypes directed at their community.

According to the quantitative data, men are more likely than women to perceive anti-Arab stereotyping among Canadians (81.7 percent versus 73.7 percent), though this relationship is not statistically significant. The slight discrepancy is not surprising given that males tend more than females to identify themselves as Arabs. This may explain in part why Arab males are more sensitive to anti-Arab stereotyping than their female ethnic peers. One must also bear in mind that the vilification of Arabs is mediated mainly through the male figure. Arab women, on the other hand, tend to be portrayed as disempowered and unaware victims exploited by their own men. As a result, because Arab men are demonized by Westerners more than Arab women, they are perhaps more likely to consider Western representations of their ethnocultural community as biased and distorted.

Neither perceived anti-Arab prejudices nor perceived religion-based prejudices are statistically correlated with time spent in Canada, though the likelihood of reporting either form of prejudicial stereotyping rises slightly as time spent in Canada increases. Finally, the strength of one's religious or ethnic identity has practically no effect on one's likelihood of perceiving Canadians as being biased against either Arabs or their religious group.

Stereotypes in the Media

In the following, the data are surveyed with a view to highlighting the role the subjects attribute to the media when accounting for prejudicial stereotypes directed against their communities. As seen in table 34, a large majority of respondents endorse the notion that Western media help to generate a biased picture of Arabs. Indeed, more than 82 percent of the sample either completely (44.2 percent) or somewhat (38.2 percent) agreed with the statement "The media contribute to propagate a biased picture of Arabs." Also, whereas 53.4 percent of all respondents are either in complete or partial

Table 34: Percentages of Agreement with the Statements "Media Propagate a Biased Picture of Arabs," and "Media Propagate a Biased Picture of My Religious Group"

	Statements	
Level of Agreement	"The media help to propagate a biased picture of Arabs"	"The media help to propagate a biased picture of my religious group"
I completely agree	44.2	28.1
I somewhat agree	38.2	25.3
I somewhat disagree	12.4	20.5
I completely disagree	5.2	26.1
TOTAL	100	100

agreement with the notion that the media misrepresent their religious group, this proportion rises to 85.1 percent among Muslims only and drops off to 36.4 percent among Christians only.

During the interviewing process, the majority of informants blamed the media for the fact that Canadians have such a low opinion of Arabs. Furthermore, many of them did so before they were asked any media-related questions. In the informants' view, the two media that have most contributed to the negative stereotyping of Arabs are television and cinema, particularly the Hollywood film industry. Three informants consider that Canadians have a stereotypical and negative image of Arabs because of television. According to informant H, a Muslim female: "There are a lot of stereotypes, but it's not their [Canadians'] fault, it's more because of the media, of what they show on TV." Informant A, a Christian male, agrees: "Their image of Arabs is biased because, as we all know, it's all propaganda. That's what happens on TV especially. And as we all know, every one has a TV set at home, which explains why, in the end, Canadians and Quebecois have an opinion of Arabs that doesn't match reality."

Even more than television, Hollywood movies were the most frequently blamed for prejudicial stereotypes against Arabs in the media. Indeed, Hollywood was often held responsible for fostering stereotypes about gender relations in the Arab world. One movie in particular was considered by informants to have been extremely damaging in this regard: *Not Without My Daughter*. This 1991 movie directed by Brian Gilbert is about an American woman who manages to escape from Iran with her daughter after her Iranian husband attempted to turn their two-week vacation into a permanent relocation and a life of subservience for her and her daughter. As least six informants mentioned that this film was a major contributor to the demonization of Arabs in the Western mind. At first this seemed surprising, given the plethora of Hollywood movies made since 1991 that have matched, if not surpassed, Gilbert's film in stereotyping Middle Eastern groups in a prejudicial manner. Perhaps the fact that the movie was based on an autobiographical book written by an average American woman contributed to greater viewer identification. Even more importantly, at the time of the interviews it was still easier for North American viewers to relate to the suffering of a mother whose child had been kidnapped and sent to a country that was unfriendly to women, than to the improbable danger of mass-scale terrorist attacks on US soil such as those carried out by Arab villains in so many Hollywood movies since the nineties. It may reasonably be assumed, however, that the events of September 11, 2001, heralded a shift in Western (mis)representations of Arabs and Muslims. Since then these groups have been more at risk than ever of being portrayed by the media, and perceived by viewers, as religious fanatics and violent terrorists committed to the destruction of the (Western) free world.

In any case, it cannot be overstressed that stereotypes of Arabs, far from being disconnected from one another, are forged relationally, caught up in a complex reciprocity where each one helps to legitimate the others. It could be said, following Edward Said (1979), that they are integrated into a unified system of self-referential representations. Thus, the figures of the violent Arab man and the exploited Arab woman feed and reinforce each other.

It is noteworthy that, even though the informants were fully aware that *Not Without My Daughter* was set in a non-Arab country (Iran), they nonetheless identified it as a major contributor to anti-Arab stereotyping in Canada. This paradox illustrates how the categories manufactured by the majority group can reproduce themselves while disregarding the identity proposals articulated by the minority groups that are being categorized. Stereotypical categories are geared toward the reproduction of their own cognitive and normative criteria for the mapping and creating of minority groups' otherness. The self-referential character of categorization explains why a film about Iran can end up reinforcing prejudicial stereotyping against Arabs, even though neither Iranians nor Arabs consider Iran to be part of the Arab world.

It is also worth mentioning that of the six informants who linked the film *Not Without My Daughter* to anti-Arab stereotyping, four were Christians identifying themselves as Arabs. In the following narratives, two Christian males of Lebanese origin (informants B and D) explain how the movie helped to shape Canadian representations of Arabs:

INTERVIEWER: In the questionnaire, you circled "*I somewhat agree*" for the statement "*Canadians have negative stereotypes against Arabs.*"

INFORMANT B: Yes. I would even say "*Completely agree.*" Because when I see ... When a Canadian tells you *Ho! You're Arab* sure enough the next comment is *Ho! Not Without My Daughter*".

INFORMANT D: For sure there are stereotypes! Like for instance, I have a friend who was going out with this Quebecoise girl from Lac-St-Jean. She called her family in Lac-St-Jean to tell them she was going out with a Lebanese. The first thing they told her is *Ha! Did you see Not Without My Daughter?*

The fact that so many informants who self-identified as Christian Arabs saw *Not Without My Daughter* as a major contributor to anti-Arab stereotyping is startling, since the vilification of Islam and Muslims is central to both the explicit message and subtext of the movie. This is another reminder that anti-Muslim prejudice tends to rebound on Christian Arabs since, once again, Arab culture and Islam are interchangeable in the minds of a great many Canadians. It also highlights, on a more theoretical level, how the simple binary logic informing ethnic categorization is inadequate for tapping into the symbolic complexity of the social world (e.g., not all Arabs are Muslims and not all Muslims are Arabs). Two Hollywood action movies were also criticized by informants – *The Siege* (1998), with Denzel Washington, and *Passenger 57* (1992), with Wesley Snipes. These movies, which portray Arabs as violent hate-mongering anti-Western terrorists, were often mentioned as examples of Hollywood's detrimental influence on the majority group's perception of Arabs.

Television and Hollywood movies were thus particularly, though not exclusively, identified by Arab-Canadian youths as major contributors to anti-Arab prejudice in Canada. These results are in agreement with Jack Shaheen's discourse analysis of Hollywood's portrayal of Arabs. Shaheen (2001, 2003) provided a comprehensive mapping of Arab culture vilification in Hollywood movies over the span of a century.

Two informants stressed that media coverage of the Israeli-Palestinian conflict was highly instrumental in bringing about the stereotype of the violent Arab terrorist. Informant C, a Christian man who is himself half-Palestinian, put it this way: "CNN is the worst TV channel I've ever seen. It's terrible. It's them who sell their footages to a lot of other companies. So these images are transmitted everywhere. You always see Arabs, Palestinians, who throw stones at Israeli soldiers ... But on CNN, you only hear *Poor Jews, stones are thrown at them, poor Jews!* And people end up saying *It's their country, why aren't Palestinians leaving?*"

These remarks are in line with observations by B. Abu- Laban (1988, 111) and Karim (2003, 104–20) that, for many Arab Canadians, the Arab-Israeli conflict as portrayed by North American media bring an added dimension to anti-Arab prejudice. According to these authors, it is widely agreed within the Arab diaspora that the interpretive lenses through which these conflicts are filtered in Western media have helped enormously in bringing about the stereotypical figure of the Arab terrorist committed to violence that is perpetrated, most of the time, in the name of God.

Male respondents are significantly more likely than female respondents to believe that the media are biased against both the Arab community (89.3 percent of males, 74.6 percent of females) and their religious group (59.5 percent of males, 46.6 percent of females). A similar gender discrepancy was detected and discussed earlier when looking at prejudicial stereotyping attributed to Canadians in general. The same arguments hold when explaining the greater propensity of males to single out the media as a major contributor to prejudicial stereotyping. As a reminder, Arab and Muslim men are often portrayed in the mass media as violent, hate-mongering individuals in both the public and private domains. Inversely, Arab and Muslim women are portrayed as submissive victims enduring exploitation at the hands of their own husbands or fathers. Therefore, Arab males, who are portrayed as aggressors, tend perhaps to feel more directly targeted by anti-Arab stereotyping in the media. It bears reiterating that the nature of the anti-Arab stereotypes reported by informants was contingent upon the informant's sex; while males underscored the Arab terrorist and wife abuser clichés, females stressed the stereotype of the submissive and dominated Arab wife.

Time spent in Canada is not statistically related to one's assessment of media representations of Arabs. However, there are slight variations: the proportion of respondents who consider that the media portray Arabs in a biased manner is 82 percent among those who have spent the shortest period of time in Canada (less than ten years), and 78 percent among those who have spent the longest period of time in this country (more than fifteen years). Surprisingly, those respondents belonging to the intermediate category (ten to fifteen years in Canada) are the most likely to agree that the media are biased against Arabs (88 percent). Similarly, the proportion of respondents who believe that the media are biased in portraying their religious group varies insignificantly across all three "time spent in Canada" brackets, from 52 percent to 54 percent. Thus, in spite of minor variations, time spent in Canada does not make one significantly more likely to single out the media as a chief contributor to prejudicial stereotyping.

As reported earlier, and quite predictably, Muslims (85.1 percent) are significantly more likely than Christians (36.4 percent) to regard the media as being prejudiced against their religious group. More interesting, however, is that Muslims are also 13 percent more likely than Christians to hold the media responsible for propagating anti-Arab prejudice (90.8 percent versus 77.8 percent). How can we account for this (statistically significant) discrepancy? As previously stressed, anti-Arab and anti-Muslim prejudices largely intersect to form a common system of (mis)representations. Thus, films such as *Not without My Daughter*, *Passenger 57*, or *True Lies*, seldom feature an areligious Arab character. Instead, in most cases, the Arab villain conspicuously displays his Muslim faith in a generally radical and fanatical manner. As pertinently argued by Antonius and Bendris (1998), such a representation is consistent with a typically "Orientalist" framework, in which Islam becomes the primary source of meaning for every action and attitude associated with the archetypical figure of the Arab. This could partly explain why Muslims were more inclined than Christian respondents to detect anti-Arab prejudice in the media.

It must be kept in mind, however, that a large majority of Christian Arabs (77.8 percent) also consider that the media provide a biased picture of Arabs. Most importantly, the remarks examined above showed that Christian Arabs were quite sensitive to, and affected by, misrepresentations of Arabs in the media, in spite of being aware that Islam constitutes the pivotal axis around which the stereotypical figure of the Arab revolves. This is because media representations of Christian and Muslim Arabs are encoded with the same Islam-centred references, which in turn causes both groups to share the same Islam-centred *external* boundaries. However, as shown earlier, Christians have more power than Muslims to mitigate anti-Arab prejudice by asserting a specifically Christian Arab identity. As for Muslim Arabs, their power to resist anti-Arab stereotypes lies in their capacity to confront anti-Muslim stereotypes at the same time, since the two are inextricably entangled. Needless to say, this struggle is fundamentally unequal since neocolonial representations of the Other are self-referential and thus remain largely unaltered by the subalterns' attempts at challenging them (Said 1979). Inversely, Christian Arabs can more easily, though never entirely, rehabilitate the Arab label they embrace by dissociating themselves from Muslim Arabs, especially when the anti-Arab stereotypes they face rest explicitly on Islamophobia.

Finally, neither ethnic nor religious identity strength has a significant impact on perceived prejudice in the media. Indeed, the proportion of respondents who consider that the media misrepresent Arabs or their religious group varies negligibly according to ethnic and religious identity strengths.

SELF-EXPERIENCED ANTI-ARAB DISCRIMINATION

This section taps into Arab-Canadian youth's personal experiences of anti-Arab discrimination. It must be remembered that, while the notion of prejudice relates to the realm of (negative) representations, the concept of discrimination refers to exclusionary behaviours. Discrimination can take the form of either open rejection or unwarranted differential treatment based on a distinctive group characteristic. A discriminatory act generally results in putting the targeted individual or group at a disadvantage. Conversely, in a non-discriminatory environment, minority groups do not see their

Table 35: Percentages of Agreement with the Statement "In My Personal Life, I Feel Accepted as an Arab by Canadians

	Statement
Level of Agreement	"Personally, I feel accepted as an Arab by Canadians"
I completely disagree	0.4
I somewhat disagree	9.2
I somewhat agree	32.5
I completely agree	57.9
TOTAL	100

distinctive characteristic turned into a social stigma justifying their exclusion.[5]

As stressed in the preceding section, whereas discrimination generally entails prejudicial representations, the latter do not necessarily lead to discrimination. However, depending on such factors as the economic conjuncture, international politics, or social class dynamics, majority group members can always draw on a vast pool of prejudicial representations to socially legitimize discrimination against a given minority group. In other words, there is no mechanical relationship between prejudice and discrimination, though the former is generally necessary if the latter is to blossom.

It is thus interesting to examine whether the strong levels of perceived anti-Arab stereotyping reported by my sample of second-generation Arabs are coupled with corresponding levels of self-reported discrimination. To this end, respondents were asked in the questionnaire to report the extent to which they agreed with the statement "In my personal life, I feel accepted as an Arab by Canadians." As shown in Table 35, while a large majority of respondents agreed either completely (57.9 percent) or somewhat (32.5 percent) with the statement, only a small minority disagreed either somewhat (9.2 percent) or completely (0.4 percent). It thus appears, on the basis of these partial results, that the great majority of these second-generation Arabs experience very little ethnic discrimination in their personal lives.

Let us contrast these results with those yielded by two studies in which self-reported discrimination against Arab Canadians was also investigated. First, the above finding is consistent with B. Abu-Laban and S.M. Abu-Laban's research results (1999). Using survey methods and interviews, these authors measured the level and type

of discrimination experienced by a sample of Arab-Canadian youth
in Edmonton. It was found that self-reported levels of discrimination
were surprisingly low. As the authors report (1999, 150): "Contrary
to classic accounts of the marginal position that the second generation occupies in American society, the results from the Edmonton
survey do not seem to reflect the marginality of Arab-Canadian
youths despite the difficult situation that they experience."

The authors warn readers against generalizing, however, on the
basis of their sample, to the whole population of second-generation
Arab Canadians. Their results are in part attributable, they say, to
the relatively high socioeconomic status of their Edmonton sample.
Such a warning is equally relevant to the present study. Indeed, the
cegep students sampled here belong for the most part to the middle
and upper-middle classes. Ethnic prejudice and discrimination are
generally more virulent within lower socioeconomic milieus, where
right-wing discourses portraying foreigners as cultural and economic threats find fertile ground for their large-scale propagation
(Dubet and Lapeyronnie 1992).

Likewise, Ibrahim Hayani (1999), analyzing a 1993 Ontario data
set, also concluded that self-reported levels of discrimination among
Arab Canadians were relatively low. According to Hayani, "the
Ontario study respondents did feel that there was discrimination
directed against their group, but not as much as one would have
expected given their perceptions of how poorly Canadians regarded
Arabs, their culture, their way of life' (1999, 300). Furthermore,
Hayani added, compared to self-reported levels of discrimination
among other minority groups in Canada (as measured by the 1992
Toronto Star/Goldfarb Minorities Report),[6] those reported by the
Arab Canadians sampled for the Ontario study are among the lowest.

As opposed to the Ontario study quoted by Hayani, I resorted
to an indicator of self-reported discrimination that is frequency-
sensitive (agree/disagree on a scale of four), thus providing a more
accurate and nuanced picture of the phenomenon. Still, only a small
minority of these second-generation Arabs feel either completely
(0.4 percent) or somewhat excluded (9.2 percent) by their fellow
Canadians in their personal lives. However, it could be speculated
that, had these respondents been full-time wage earners instead of
students, much higher levels of discrimination would have been
reported since, according to the 2002 *Ethnic Diversity Survey*, visible minorities in Canada identify the workplace as the institutional

setting where they are most likely to face ethnoracial discrimination. Thus, among those who reported having experienced discrimination "sometimes" or "often," 64 percent said that it occurred in the workplace, 40 percent in stores and banks, 29 percent in the street, and 17 percent when dealing with courts and the police (Statistics Canada 2003).

Finally, it cannot be overstressed that the post-September 11 era may have marked a radical shift in terms of anti-Arab and anti-Muslim discrimination in the public sphere. As reported earlier (see Table 1), the number of discrimination complaints filed by Arab Quebecois with Quebec's Human Rights Commission increased by 130 percent from 2000 to 2001 and has never gone back to its pre-2001 levels. One can thus hypothesize that had my fieldwork been conducted after September 11, the Arab-origin youths surveyed for this research would have been less likely to "feel accepted as Arabs by Canadians in their personal lives." I will now turn to the issue of self-reported discrimination in light of the qualitative data.

The interviews tend to support the statistically backed observation that second-generation Arabs are largely shielded from discrimination. Most informants consider themselves generally well accepted by Canadians in their personal lives. Some of them reported having encountered discriminatory behaviours or attitudes at one point or another in their lives but added that such experiences were isolated cases attributable to a minority of close-minded individuals. Thus, when informant N was asked whether she felt accepted in her personal life as an Arab and a Syrian by Canadians and Quebecois, she replied: "Hmm, by most of them yes. Because the only real racists are the extremists. I haven't met too many of them, and it doesn't interest me. But usually, everywhere I go, whether in school, in the workplace, in my personal life, I haven't been affected by discrimination as far as I can remember."

Upon closer examination of the data, this picture of a tolerant and inclusive Canadian society ought to be qualified. On the one hand, the informants' narratives indicate that second-generation Arabs are indeed fairly well sheltered from discrimination. This seems to be the case, however, only insofar as they avoid publicly displaying their ethnicity. Many of these Arab-origin Canadians gave me to understand that they were spared discrimination mainly because in a social context they stripped themselves of any distinguishable signs that would give away their ethnocultural background. Female informant H felt accepted as an Arab and Muslim by Canadians because, she said, "most of them don't know that I am Arab. They don't think ... I don't look like an Arab ... Sometimes at work ... I work with Quebecois, and they'll often say stereotypical comments about Arabs. But they never realize that I am Algerian, that I am Arab too. You know, for them, it's really the stereotype of the Arab: it's the woman wearing the hijab with twelve kids who comes to the store. ... And often, they'll say something, and I'll go *Hey, I am Arab too. Me too* ... and then they'll go *No no, you, you're different*. But I still take it as an insult."

INTERVIEWER: Why do they say *Well, you, you're different* [from other Arabs]?

INFORMANT H: I don't know. Perhaps because I've adapted to this country. I was born here. I speak like them, I dress like them. That's why they'll say *Ha but you, it's not the same*. Because they have their prefabricated image [of what an Arab should be].

Informant G, a Canadian-born Muslim female of Egyptian origin, made a similar statement:

INFORMANT G: They [Canadians] have pre-notions about Arabs, and that's why I don't like to introduce myself as an Arab. I say *Hi my name is* [censored], because I don't want them to put a stereotype or an opinion on me, when they didn't have a chance to really get to know me.

INTERVIEWER: Right. You want to stay away from prefabricated labels, eh?

INFORMANT G: Labels, yeah! That's why I don't emphasize much my Arab origins in the first place. I think it's more my humanity after all. I am a human just like any other Canadian.

Similarly, informant B, a Canadian-born Christian male of Lebanese origin, says that he downplays his ethnic identity when interacting with Canadians, with a view to warding off exclusion or, as he euphemistically put it, to "avoid conflicts":

INTERVIEWER: Could you tell me whether you agree with the statement "In my personal life, I feel accepted as an Arab and a Lebanese by Canadians?" Could you also explain to me why?

INFORMANT B: Yes. I agree completely. Well, since I was born here, I have never felt that I was discriminated against as a Lebanese. But in any case, I avoid this type of conflicts. I mean, I don't introduce myself as a Lebanese in front of Canadians, just to show them I am Lebanese. I avoid this type of conflicts in order to develop harmonious relationships with them.

These remarks exhibit certain commonalities that deserve special attention. As mentioned, the informants all suggest that their acceptance by Canadians is contingent upon their "de-ethnicizing" themselves in a social context. In other words, for many subjects, being accepted by Canadians requires that they keep a low ethnic profile, so to speak. This implies that they have the ability to adopt, or drop at will, selected ethnocultural traits depending on the reaction they anticipate from the majority group. It thus points to the optional character of their shifting ethnic identities, which can be activated or downplayed depending on the context of interaction.

It thus clearly appears that these second-generation Arabs are somewhat reluctant to exhibit their Arab identity publicly because they expect a negative response from their conversational partner(s) or from the public in general. In other words, given the perceived prevalence of anti-Arab prejudice, many informants prefer not to be identified as Arabs by members of the majority group. To this end, they need to conceal as far as possible any distinctive cultural signs, whether linguistic, attitudinal, or behavioural, that could betray their ethnic origins. Such "ethnic camouflage" can only take place if these second-generation Arabs have been incorporated into the dominant culture sufficiently for them to be familiar with the majority group's sociocultural and linguistic codes. The following comments by informant K (a Muslim female of Algerian descent) exemplify this phenomenon whereby one's ethnic self is voluntarily confined to ethnic networks in order to ward off ethnic prejudice and discrimination:

INFORMANT K: There is no such things here [in Canada] as *Hey! We don't want you!* It's more subtle. They say *Ha! You guys* [Arabs] *are different* ... But when you're being told repeatedly that you're different, that you're not like them, you prefer to stay with those who are like you ... Anyway, personally, I don't feel that I am so different from them. Our differences are things that

stay in the family. We keep them for ourselves, when we're
⌊ among ourselves, among Arabs.
INTERVIEWER: So you change your behaviours and attitudes when
   you're with Quebecois?
INFORMANT K: Yes. I change completely. But everybody does that.
⎧ Whenever you're among Quebecois, you don't act the same as if
⎩ you were with Arabs ... You got to learn to adapt ... quick! I think
   that this is the real difference."

This sort of strategy is captured by the notion of optional ethnicity, as brilliantly theorized by Mary Waters (1990) and Alba (1990)
⎛ in their research on second- and third-generation "ethnic Whites"
   of European descent in the United States. Just like these "ethnic
Whites," the young Arab Canadians making up this sample tend to
⎛ deploy a contextual ethnicity that can be selectively activated
⎝ depending on the return on (symbolic) capital they can expect from
doing so. However, there is one fundamental difference between the
"ethnic Whites" researched by Waters and Alba and second-generation Arabs. "Ethnic Whites" are socially encouraged to emphasize
publicly their European origin, which has a high symbolic value on
the North American market of "hyphenated" ethnic identities. For
instance, Irish Canadians, Italian Canadians, Portuguese Canadians
all tend to exhibit their ethnicity proudly, knowing that European
culture is highly regarded in North America. In contrast, North
Americans tend to hold Arab cultures and peoples in much lower
esteem,[7] while members of Arab minorities consider that North
Americans, particularly thanks to the mass media, are extremely
prejudiced against them.

Thus, both "ethnic Europeans" and second-generation Arabs
have the same range of ethnic options at their disposal. When the
former play their ethnic card, however, they help to enhance their
social status, whereas when the latter play theirs, they may be invit-
ing stigmatization or exclusion. This largely explains why so many
informants reported that they felt almost compelled to avoid displaying any attitudes or behaviours that could give away their Arab
origin when interacting with other Canadians.

In addition, it must be kept in mind that, as opposed to most
"ethnic Whites," racialized minorities are very limited in their ability to choose when and where to advertise their ethnic differences
(Waters 1990, 1996). Indeed, members of racialized minorities are

restrained in their ethnic options since the majority group tends to impose on them outside definitions that reduce their group identity to phenotypical characteristics. In other words, while white North Americans of European descent can celebrate "individualistic symbolic ethnic identities," racialized groups are faced with a "socially enforced and imposed racial identity" (Waters 1996, 449). Skin colour is of course the main factor in the racialization of certain minorities.

Racial assignment can affect Arab Canadians, though not as acutely as African Canadians, Caribbean Canadians, or any of the other more "visible" minorities. Within the Arab community, there are almost infinite variations in skin colour. The fact that most participants in my research have a light complexion allows them to decide more freely when and where they wish their ethnicity to be made salient. However, the following example, reported by informant C, reminds us that Arab Canadians with a swarthier complexion don't always have that choice:

INTERVIEWER: In your personal life, do you feel accepted as an Arab by Canadians? In the questionnaire, you checked "I completely agree." Does that mean you haven't been affected too much by discrimination and stigmatization?

INFORMANT C: Yes. It wasn't too bad for me ... But I remember that my cousin who has a darker complexion, hmm. For him, it was a bombardment! My cousin really got the worst of it! But me, I have always been accepted, and I've never got any problems with that!

Feelings of being accepted by Canadians on a personal level may vary according to certain social factors, such as gender, religious affiliation, or ethnocultural retention. In my sample, all of these variables have a slight impact on self-reported levels of discrimination, though no correlation turned out to be statistically significant. More precisely, females, Christians, and those with a strong sense of high ethnic and religious identity are slightly more likely to feel accepted as Arabs by Canadians than males, Muslims, and those with a weaker sense of ethnic and religious identity. The same variations were detected and explained in the section on perceived stereotyping, and it is reasonable to assume that these explanations are equally relevant here.

However, there is one correlation that, while statistically insignificant, varies in a counterintuitive direction. The respondents most
likely to feel accepted as Arabs are those who have lived in Canada
for the shortest period of time, that is, for less than ten years (94
percent feel accepted). Comparatively, respondents who have spent
the longest period of time in Canada, that is, more than ten years,
are the least likely to feel accepted as Arabs by Canadians (89 percent feel accepted). At first sight, it is difficult to understand why
Canadian-born respondents and those who arrived at an early age
would be more likely to feel rejected by the majority group than
the most recent migrants. Interestingly, the 1993 study of Arab
Ontarians cited by Hayani yielded similar results. It was found that
Canadian-born Arab Ontarians had higher rates of self-reported
discrimination than Arab Ontarian immigrants (Hayani 1999,
301). Hayani explained this surprising variation by suggesting that
Canadian-born respondents are more likely to recognize, and
object to, discriminatory behaviour, compared with more recent
immigrants. Another possible explanation is that identity politics
and equity issues as framed by Canadian multiculturalism are
deeply entrenched in North America's political culture. This may
make young Canadian-born Arabs as well as those who migrated at
an early age more sensitive to, and indignant at, the most subtle
manifestations of discrimination.

A COMPARISON WITH FRANCE

Before closing this chapter, I shall offer some general reflections on
a question that deserves consideration. As mentioned, the perception of second-generation Arabs that anti-Arab stereotyping is
prominent stands in stark contrast to their professed feeling of
being well accepted by Canadians on a personal level. How can we
account sociologically for this puzzling discrepancy? It was argued
that part of the answer lies in the ability of second-generation Arabs
to ward off discrimination by downplaying in public any distinctive
signs of their Arab or Muslim backgrounds. However, the case of
second-generation North Africans in France (also called "Beurs")
suggests that a situational and flexible ethnicity is not the only
factor to consider.

The majority of French Beurs of the second and third generations
are very much culturally incorporated into their "host" society

(Begag 1990; Roy 1994; Leveau 1997; Venel 2004). Yet several studies demonstrate that they still endure significant socioeconomic discrimination in the public sphere and consider themselves to be rejected by the majority group in their daily lives (Dubet and Lapeyronnie 1992; Jazouli 1995; Duprez 1997; Santelli forthcoming). Furthermore, this perception is coupled with feelings of humiliation and anger that, in France's impoverished suburbs ("les banlieues"), periodically spark social unrest and confrontations with the police. Think of the violent suburban riots in the fall of 2005, which were driven mainly by children of Arab and African immigrants as a means of protest against police harassment, exclusion, and discrimination. These riots – the worst in the country's recent history – are a reminder of France's tense racial relations.

Thus, in the case of second-generation Arabs in France, their extended familiarity with the majority group culture as well as their ability to perform cultural code switching at will does not seem to spare them discrimination, quite the reverse. It follows that other factors must be considered when attempting to understand why, and under which conditions, perceived ethnoracial prejudice comes to be converted into perceived discrimination. In the following, the French and Canadian sociohistorical contexts are briefly examined with a view to drawing inferences about the complex relation between prejudice and discrimination among children of immigrants.

First, one cannot adequately grasp France's current relationship with its Arab minorities without taking into account the country's recent colonial past. During the colonial era, native and migrant North African populations were categorized – at the representational and juridical levels – as inferior subjects of the French colonial empire, as opposed to full-fledged citizens of the French Republic. Today, this colonial category has evolved into a more subtle one, in which the irreducible otherness (as opposed to inferiority) of the *immigré* confines the targeted individuals to the status of perpetual strangers from within (Blancel 1997; Lorcerie 1997). The current socioeconomic marginalization experienced by the Beurs is related in part to the neocolonized status they occupy in French society. Indeed, in spite of their thorough cultural integration, they continue to be regarded by the majority group as an eternal outgroup, which helps to confine them to the periphery of the labour market. Thus, the French Beurs are left on the margins of mainstream institutions even though they blend in culturally with the majority group.

By contrast, Arab Canadians have never been historically caught up in a colonialist/colonized relationship with their host society. This certainly explains in part why, by comparison with French Beurs, Arab-Canadian youths are less affected by structural discrimination, and why their integration into mainstream institutions is less resisted by the majority group(s). As a result, ethnic mobilization against anti-Arab discrimination may be much stronger in France, compared with Canada, simply because structural discrimination against Arab communities is more virulent in the former country for reasons that, once again, cannot be understood without taking into account the history of French colonialism.

However, there is another factor that could account for variations in levels of self-experienced discrimination among Arab-Canadian youths and French Beurs, a factor that may be unrelated to the actual magnitude of anti-Arab discrimination in each country. These cross-national variations may also be related to France's and Canada's very different models for integrating immigrants. Whereas Canada's multiculturalism policy actively encourages minority groups to preserve their ethnocultural differences (Kymlicka 1998), France's official policies and discourse foster an assimilationist model of integration (known as the "republican model") requiring that minorities be absorbed into the hegemonic French culture (Schnapper 1997).

If things were simple, one could conclude that Canadian multiculturalism's greater openness to ethnocultural differences ensures that Canada is relatively free of discrimination; hence the tendency of Arab-Canadian youth to report extremely low levels of discrimination. Unfortunately, things are more complex. Upon reviewing the literature, it seems there is no correlation between the value placed by government policies on ethnocultural diversity and actual levels of discrimination experienced by ethnic minorities. Most notably, Jeff Reitz (1988) compared discrimination rates in Canada with those found in Great Britain, where ethnicity retention is not purposely fostered by immigration policies, or at least not to the same extent as in Canada. Reitz observed that, even though cross-national comparisons suggest that rates of ethnoracial employment and housing discrimination are largely similar in Canada and Britain, there are far more ethnic and racial conflicts and protests in the UK.

To explain this anomaly Reitz argues that Canada's brand of multiculturalism mitigates ethnic tensions through its ideological and political promotion of ethnocultural diversity, rather than by actually reducing discriminatory behaviours on the part of Canadian individuals and institutions. More specifically, multiculturalism appeases ethnic communities by advocating the preservation of minority group cultures but neglects to address the actual manifestations of ethnoracial intolerance and inequality that, in effect, permeate civil society (Reitz 1988). Himani Bannerji (2000), going one step further, argues that Canadian multiculturalism operates as an ideological screen masking discrimination against racialized minorities. Once it was filtered through multiculturalism's ideological lenses, "the concept of race lost its hard edges of criticality, class disappeared entirely, and color gave a feeling of brightness, brilliance, or vividness, of a celebration of a difference which was disconnected from social relations of power, but instead perceived as diversity, as existing socio-cultural ontologies or facts" (Bannerji 2000, 545).

This argument could be put to use when accounting for the extremely low levels of discrimination reported by the Arab-Canadian subjects sampled for this research. Although Reitz's study has yet to be duplicated so as to make rigorous comparisons between French Beurs and Arab-Canadian youths, the existing literature strongly suggests, as mentioned, that the former undergo greater structural exclusion and discrimination. Nonetheless, research also suggests that racialized minorities in Canada suffer from discrimination in the labour and housing markets (Lian and Matthews 1998; Renaud et al. 2003). Moreover, Raymond Breton's study (1983, 431–3) unveiled very low levels of racial discrimination awareness among visible minorities in Canada; rates of self-reported discrimination among Canada's racialized minorities are abnormally low, according to Breton, when measured against the actual magnitude of the problem.

Could it be that the low propensity of Arab-Canadian youths to report self-experienced discrimination in part reflects the tendency of visible minorities to overestimate ethnoracial tolerance on the part of Canadians? The positive image of an inclusive Canadian society harboured by my respondents may be a by-product of Canada's multiculturalism policy, which could help to deflect minority groups' responses to actual discrimination. In other words, perhaps the Canadian politics of recognition acts as the "opium" of visible minorities in Canada, numbing their capacity to detect and resist discrimination. It may perpetuate the illusion, both among ethnic minorities and the majority group, that Canadian people and institutions are more tolerant of ethnic and racial differences than they really are.

That being said, it should be reiterated that these youths' low levels of self-experienced ethnic discrimination are also due to the very nature of the sample: middle-class, pre-university students who enjoy a relatively "sheltered" environment compared with their ethnic peers who face more pervasive discrimination in the labour market. And once again, all of the cegeps sampled for recruitment purposes had multiethnic student populations, which certainly helps to foster more tolerant attitudes toward ethnocultural diversity within the school environment.

Conclusion

In this final chapter I would like to summarize the findings of this study of ethnic and religious identity maintenance among second-generation Arab Canadians and reflect on their significance for understanding the social and political conditions under which children of immigrants can come to build a sense of citizenship as Canadians or Quebecois.

The second-generation Arabs in my sample harbour a strong sense of identification with their ethnic culture (i.e., the subjective/cultural dimension). In other words, their ethnocultural background acts as a strong marker differentiating the ingroup from the outgroup, which helps to accentuate ethnic consciousness. However, this "hypertrophied" ethnic self-concept stands in sharp contrast to the other aspects of their ethnic identity, which tend not to be as developed. This confirms the observation by Raymond Breton and his colleagues (1990) that ethnic identification is not necessarily dependent on communal socialization into ethnic culture and community to be maintained over time.

However, my findings only partially support the symbolic ethnicity hypothesis. The objective/cultural aspect of young Arab Canadians' ethnic identity turned out to be sufficiently salient to conclude that their self-definitions are not only structured along ethnic lines but also minimally buttressed by a knowledge of, and familiarity with, their ethnic culture. For instance, a majority of respondents, regardless of time spent in Canada, reported having a good command of their ethnic language, though proficiency in Arabic clearly decreases as time spent in Canada increases. Also, the most widely retained ethnic pattern of behaviour is eating ethnic food, a finding commonly yielded by case studies on ethnic identity retention among the second generation. Listening to ethnic music was also fairly popular and seemed to be part of a process of ethnic rediscovery that takes place during adolescence. Thus, their relative familiarity with, and exposure to, their ethnic culture suggests that the ethnic identity of these youths means more than mere subjective strategies of self-identification.

The notion of "costless community" (Waters 1990) is nonetheless relevant in accounting for the fact that the respondents retain their ethnic identity more at the cultural than at the social level. It was suggested that by retaining their ethnic identity in the cultural realm, these youngsters are spared many of the social obligations that usually result from being tightly enmeshed in ethnic-based socialization groups. However, the data showed that their ethnic identity tends to be anchored in the social realm in some respects. In particular, their preference for ingroup marriage and friendship points to a tendency to sustain their ethnic culture through integration into primary groups of like-minded ethnic peers.

It should be noted that the informants were more staunchly committed to ingroup marriage than ingroup friendship. Both parental and self-imposed pressures are responsible for the great importance they placed on marital endogamy. The most common rationale for favouring ingroup marriage was cultural connectedness between spouses, especially with regard to gender relations. Interestingly, many female informants were adamant in wanting to marry an ethnic peer who was born in Canada as opposed to one who had recently migrated, mainly because they deemed the former more likely to be committed to gender equality. This was taken as a sign that the ethnic identity of these children of immigrants is hybrid; hence the young women's tendency to stay away from recently arrived ethnic peers who, in their minds, epitomize cultural purity (as opposed to plurality). Paradoxically, while the informants' self-definitions frequently draw upon essentialized notions of identity, culture, and community, their narratives often give away their preference for creolized forms of cultural models.

This study also explored what the notion of Arab identity meant to these second-generation Arabs. It is significant that a majority of respondents favoured the "Arab" label (whether taken alone or in a hyphenated form) over other sources of group identification. The narratives suggested, however, that the Arab category, far from superseding national or parochial allegiances, was understood as an overarching form of group identity. Furthermore, the meaning these subjects attach to their Arab identity is forged differently depending on the subgroups to which they belong. Most notably, Christian Arabs were more hesitant than their Muslim ethnic peers about using the Arab label as a source of self-identification. Some Christian Arabs embraced the Arab label but expressed frustration at Canadians' failure to acknowledge the religious plurality encompassed by the Arab "community." This is a reminder that identity building among minority groups is often driven by what Taylor (1994) referred to as the "politics of recognition." It was also suggested that the reluctance of some Christian Arabs to identify themselves as Arab may be exacerbated by their desire to dissociate themselves from a label that, in the West, is often synonymous with Islam, that is, a socially compromised identity.

But despite these hesitations, the Arab category turned out to be the most popular self-defining label among Christian respondents as well, even if to a lesser extent than among Muslims. The data thus suggest that both Christian and Muslim ethnic identities are extensively enmeshed in pan-Arab consciousness. It was argued that the considerable salience of Arab identity is largely due to the fact that majority groups tend to ascribe an undifferentiated "Arabness" to all Canadians of Arab origin, regardless of religious or national differences. The Arab label as externally defined by Canadians tends to exert "symbolic violence" on the individuals so labelled. Symbolic violence results not only from the suppression of the plurality of identities lumped together under this umbrella term but also from the prejudicial connotations conveyed by the Arab category in Western imagery.

Because of prejudicial categorization, the adoption of Arab identity by Arab-Canadian youth involves the subversion of the dominant significations attached to the reappropriated label, that is, turning a derogatory notion into a source of pride. To this end, second-generation Arabs can draw on a rich pool of symbols and references sustained by a collective memory rooted in history. Overall, the data show that the Arab label constitutes a significant identity provider, though certainly not the only one.

The qualitative data were also richly informative about attitudinal discrepancies between Arab parents and their children. Many informants, especially women, felt that their parents were holding on to an outdated ethnic identity that they deemed incompatible with their own more dynamic and fluid ethnicity. Predictably, most of the interviewees stressed that their parents were too restrictive regarding such issues as permissions, curfews, dating, etc.

Interestingly, women were far more likely than men to mention restrictions as examples of cultural features their parents want them to retain. This lends much support to the notion that, for a great many Arab parents, ethnic identity transmission is closely connected to female conduct. More specifically, Arab parents often implicitly identify their daughters as the repositories of the ethnic traditions they wish to preserve in a Western context. Consequently, many female informants tried to avoid conflict with their parents by keeping certain behaviours secret (especially dating). In general, however, female informants are hardly in favour of a wholesale rejection of their parents' normative framework. In fact, they were often equally critical of Western culture, which they perceive to be excessively lax with regard to child-rearing practices and expression of sexuality.

Religion also proved to be a pivotal axis around which the identity structure of second-generation Arabs, whether Muslim or Christian, revolved. The strong religious self-concept of my subjects could be accounted for largely by the fact that in their home country their parents experienced the refocusing of national narratives along religious lines. In this respect, they differ starkly from previous cohorts of second-generation Arab-Canadians, who were typically raised by secular parents whose own religious self-concept was only loosely connected to national identity.

But the importance these Arab-Canadian youths attach to religion should not be understood exclusively as a sign of religious devotion and piety. In fact, it seems that the development of a symbolic form of religiosity is well underway among this sample of second-generation Arab Canadians. The data suggest that their religious identity is significantly more developed at the subjective than at the objective level. In this respect, second-generation Arabs tend to mirror Canadians' more private relation to religion; their religious identity has lost much of its driving force as a structuring element in social interactions and is more confined to personal beliefs and self-consciousness. A majority of respondents nonetheless reported that they prayed fairly often. This is not surprising since prayer is particularly well suited to a privatized approach to religion. On the other hand, religious practices requiring more communal involvement, such as religious service attendance and participation in religious affairs, were shown to be limited to special holidays or occasional events. This disengagement from formally organized religion on the part of young people is a phenomenon that, far from being unique to Arab communities, is common to most religious communities in Canada and in the West in general.

In some cases, the high value placed on religion reflects a desire to find general spiritual guidance in life. At the same time, many subjects tend to frame religion as a group identity provider, thus stressing close ties between their religious and ethnic identities. Even Christian Arabs tended to use their specific denominational allegiances as identity markers differentiating their group from mainstream (Canadian) Christians. Also, the normative content of these second-generation Arabs' ethnoreligious identity differs in fundamental ways from that of their parents. It tends to be structured in relation to more Westernized, secular, and liberal cultural models. In the process, their ethnoreligious identity is partially divested of the restrictive and binding communal basis upon which their parents' ethnoreligious identity rests. Once again, this can be taken as evidence that these young people are not different from other Canadians of the same age group; for they too prefer to tailor their religious beliefs and practices to fit their personal needs.

Both Muslims and Christians, however, place a high value on religious endogamy. But marrying a religious peer was often explicitly perceived as necessary to ensure cultural connectedness between spouses. Revealingly, none of the informants justified their preference for religious endogamy by stressing the importance of sharing with their future spouse the same God, the same religious beliefs, or the same religious rituals and prescriptions. The fact that religion is widely perceived as culturally binding by these young Arab Canadians can be taken as evidence of an ethnoreligious identity delineating distinct group boundaries.

Furthermore, for most subjects (more so for Muslims than Christians), religious identity is weakly linked to social networks organized along religious lines. Tabular analysis examining the attendance of religious social affairs provided further evidence of the strong connections between religion and ethnicity among these second-generation Arabs. It appeared that the majority of the sample only occasionally attend religious social functions. But what is interest-

ing is that the vast majority of these occasional participants in religious social events hold an "average" religious identity while
holding a "strong" ethnic identity. Thus, attending religious social
events should be understood to contribute as much, if not more, to
ethnic identity maintenance as to religious identity building.

It was also shown that Christian Arabs observe rituals far more
than their Muslim ethnic counterparts. Prayers, for instance, was
more frequently practised by Christian than Muslim respondents,
and Muslims attended religious services far less often. In the Arab
world, Eastern Christianity and its myriad subrites became historically interwoven with group identity building among Christian
minorities. This could explain in part why these Christian Arab-
Canadians are more dependent on religion to maintain a distinct
ethnic identity than their Muslim ethnic peers. In the case of Muslims of Arab descent, succumbing to North American secularism is
not as likely to compromise their distinct ethnicity within Canada's
multicultural landscape. Thus, in spite of the Islamization undergone by national self-narratives in the post-1970s Arab world,
these Muslim youths rely less on religious practice than Christians
to maintain distinct ethnoreligious group boundaries. It was
pointed out, however, that because Muslims and Christians confer
upon their respective religious rituals different meanings, these variations should be interpreted with caution.

Special attention was also paid to the role played by gender issues
in ethnoreligious identity maintenance. Within Arab migrant families, gender relations come to be highly problematized in the process of ethnic boundary maintenance. This stems from the fact that,
for many Arab parents, the excessive moral laxity of Canadian society with regard to female conduct calls for the strict gendering of
child-rearing practices. More specifically, because the moral virtue
of female family members, embodied primarily in their chastity, is
considered by many Arab parents as a key element in the preservation of family honour and reputation, second-generation Arab
females come to be subjected to stricter parental surveillance and
control.

These double standards cultivated by parents and by the ethnic
community in general beget, among male and female Arab youth, a
sense that there is a profound normative and cultural gap between
their ethnic group (Us) and the host society (Them). Such a perception helps to produce clear-cut distinctions between two antagonis-

tic representations of women, each epitomizing a different pole of this us/them dialectic: the pure virgin Arab woman versus the depraved Canadian/Western woman. It would be interesting to explore the underlying symbolism of their image of the licentious Western woman. How did they come to internalize such an image? Could it be the magnified reflection of the objectified female body and sexuality as portrayed in Western media, and as promoted through the increasingly globalized sex industry? Perhaps the figure of the "liberated woman" pioneered by the West appears specious in the eyes of many Muslims, for whom this so-called liberation amounts to women's confinement to their physical and sexual being. Although the notion that Western women are more sexually unbridled is of course largely stereotypical, it is true that women in the West are subjected to the dictates of a hypersexualized model of femininity that, in effect, helps to shape gendered relations of domination. In this context, it becomes easy to understand how migrant parents – who are already destabilized by the migratory process – come to mobilize tradition as a protective shield against the risk that their daughters might become "morally corrupted" in a Western environment.

Still, the hypothesis that second-generation Arab women, more than their male counterparts, oppose the recycling of traditional gender roles into ethnoreligious identity markers was *partially* confirmed. Framed this way, such a hypothesis – which is given wide currency in the literature – is perhaps too simplistic a view because it overlooks the complexity of the contradictory gender patterns in which these young women are enmeshed. They are still considered by their community as the bearers of tradition and culture, while at the same time being expected by the host society to engage with more liberal Western-based cultural models. As a result, on the one hand, these young Arab-Canadian women tend to resign themselves to the restrictions imposed on their freedom in the name of tradition. In fact, many regard such restrictions as necessary to meet their group's expectations – which have also become their own – about proper female conduct. On the other hand, they oppose the controlling gaze of males who act as self-proclaimed guardians of their purity and virtue while considering themselves exempt from the same normative constraints. In particular, young Arab females strongly resent the view that the preservation of their virginity constitutes a matter of collective interest linked to family honour and reputation. Thus, it is not tradition per se that is resisted by these young women but rather the paternalistic double standards informing the traditions.

My research also provided insights into the relation between perceived stereotyping, self-experienced discrimination, and ethno-religious identity building. The data indicate that a strong majority among young Arab-Canadian adults are under the impression that Canadians portray Arabs in a stereotypical and prejudicial manner. In the past, many authors have argued that the emergence of pan-Arab consciousness in North America was primarily fuelled by perceived biases in the coverage of Middle Eastern conflicts by Western media. The present data do not support this argument. The film industry, and Hollywood movies in particular, were identified by a large majority of informants as the most important catalyst for the production of anti-Arab and anti-Muslim prejudices. It is telling, for example, that the Arab youths in my sample were far more inclined to blame Hollywood than the media coverage of Middle Eastern conflicts when accounting for the stereotyping of Arabs and Muslims as terrorists. Ironically, the strong emphasis placed on the American film industry as a vector of anti-Arab prejudice is perhaps reflective of the centrality of American culture in these young people's system of cultural references. However, since the interviews were conducted prior to the events of Semptember 11 and the ensuing wars against Afghanistan and Iraq, it can be hypothesized that, today, these same individuals would place far greater emphasis on international politics as a contributing factor in anti-Arab stereotyping.

Several informants stressed that Canadian representations of Arabs are closely connected to gender-related stereotypes. Males referred mainly to the stereotype of the Arab wife abuser and females to that of the submissive Arab wife as being at the core of North American images of Arabs.

The great majority of Muslim Arabs consider that, in addition to being the target of anti-Arab prejudice, they also have to face anti-Muslim prejudice. Predictably, only a minority of Christian respondents believe that their religious group is the target of prejudicial stereotyping. During the interviews, however, many Christians said that they resented Canadians for lumping them together indiscriminately with Arab Muslims. The general effect of this undifferentiated view is that it suppresses a fundamental part of their group identity: their denominational allegiances. In North American culture, after all, images of Arabs and Muslims are often conflated into a single Islam-centred representational system. For this reason, it is more difficult for Muslim Arabs to fight anti-Arab prejudicial stereotypes because, to do so, they also need to critically engage derogatory representations of Islam. In comparison, Christian Arabs have the power, though limited, to increase the symbolic value of the Arab label they embrace by severing it from its Islamic component, that is, by stressing instead their Christian Arab identity, which many of them did during the interviews. But this strategy often fails because, once again, Christian and Muslim Arabs are socially *made* to share the same Islam-centred Arab boundaries.

Surprisingly, the data revealed that a large majority of respondents feel personally well accepted by their fellow Canadians. However, several informants preferred to downplay their ethnic differences when interacting with majority group members, hinting that they did so to avoid ethnic profiling and stigmatization. It thus seems that anti-Arab prejudice deters many of these second-generation Arabs from making their ethnicity salient in social interactions with other Canadians. Such a situational ethnicity is made possible by their command of mainstream cultural codes, which allows them, when needed, to keep a low "ethnic profile" so as to ward off ethnic prejudice and discrimination.

It thus appears that, while Arab-Canadian youth are acutely aware of being disparaged as a group, they do not feel rejected as Arabs in their personal lives. How can these two apparently opposite opinions coexist without contradiction? Part of the answer emerged by making cross-national comparisons. As briefly sketched out – but this calls for further investigation – research in France and Britain suggests that structural discrimination, and even more so the awareness of it, is a more important catalyst for ethnic conflict and resistance than ethnic prejudice per se.[1] In particular, the case of French Beurs indicates that ethnic prejudice tends to translate into ethnic protest only when members of the targeted group realize they are prevented from reaping the socioeconomic benefits of cultural integration and remain marginalized regardless of how many "ethnic features" they have dropped in the process.

Because anti-Arab exclusion in Canada is not as overt and virulent as in France, Arab Canadians are perhaps not as likely as French Beurs to become aware of, and mobilize against, ethnic discrimination. Nonetheless, research shows that actual levels of ethnoracial discrimination in Canada are sufficiently high to be considered starkly at odds with visible minorities' rather positive assessment of ethnoracial inclusiveness in this country. I have suggested that the discordance between representation and reality may be due in part to the ideological impact of Canada's multiculturalism policy, which may lead visible minorities to underestimate ethnoracial exclusion and, inversely, to overestimate Canadian tolerance of ethnoracial diversity.

In contrast, France's rigid universalistic model of citizenship helps to make excluded minorities more aware and resentful of their socioeconomic marginalization. Indeed, this assimilationist model can exacerbate frustration among minorities suffering from discrimination because it seeks overtly to flatten ethnocultural differences in the public domain. More specifically, when racialized minorities in France are subjected to structural discrimination and racism, they are being denied the equality they have been promised (on paper) as their sole compensation for giving up ethnic identity in the public sphere. In such cases, all the conditions are ripe for ignition of the sort of ethnic conflict that shook France in the fall of 2005. These dramatic events reflected the profound disillusion of France's racialized youth with the French Republican model, which efficiently enforces universalism through cultural integration but fails to fully extend its equalizing scope to the socioeconomic domain. In this respect, second-generation Arab Canadians largely depart from French Beurs; for their ethnoreligious identity is maintained on a far less confrontational basis. Although this is due in part to the very different demographic strengths of the Arab communities in Paris and Montreal, further comparative research is needed to get a better understanding of how France's and Canada's respective approaches to integration and diversity affect their Arab minorities' responses to discrimination and stereotyping.

In any case, the fact that the ethnicity of these young Arab Canadians is not bolstered by exclusion and discrimination – at least at this stage in their lives – does not say much about the extent to which they identify with majority groups and integrate into mainstream social institutions. It is nonetheless possible, drawing on this case study, to formulate hypotheses for further research about the impact of ethnic prejudice on the ways ethnic minorities conceive their relation to majority groups.

Because the overwhelming majority of these second-generation Arabs consider that Canadians and Quebecois have a very low regard for their Arab or Muslim culture, they could be inclined to develop *insular* patterns of ethnoreligious identity retention. More specifically, high levels of perceived anti-Arab/Muslim prejudice are likely to impede the integration of members of the targeted groups into mainstream primary social networks. Members of stigmatized ethnic minorities might also be deterred from identifying themselves as Quebecois or Canadian if they perceive the latter as being hostile to the ethnocultural heritage they claim as their own.

That being said, could it be that because they feel well accepted in their personal lives by the majority group, young Arab Canadians, despite perceiving themselves to be stigmatized as a group, end up nonetheless showing involvement in, and identification with, Canadian and Quebecois societies? Possibly. But the stigmatization factor, whether real or perceived, could severely limit the scope of such participation and identification. The best case for stigmatized minorities could be a "functional" integration into public institutions and the labour market coupled, however, with a civic identity devoid of symbolic attachment to the political community, that is, a "desubstantialized" citizenship. Thus, in the case of young Arab-origin Canadians, the strong anti-Arab prejudices to which they are generally exposed could put a damper on their desire to incorporate socially, culturally, and symbolically into majority group structures, institutions, and networks, that is, to become part of the Canadian or Quebecois Us.[2] Given that Canada's multiculturalism policy is not aimed solely at preserving ethnic identities in mutual isolation but also at fostering sociocultural rapprochement between majority and minority groups, prejudicial stereotyping targeting "vulnerable" ethnic groups, such as the Arabs, constitutes a problem that begs for immediate government attention.

Moreover, whereas Canadian multiculturalism pursues a politics of recognition of cultural differences, Quebec's politics of immigration attempts to achieve a difficult balance between two objectives that sometimes conflict with each other: accommodating cultural diversity while integrating ethnic minorities into the French-speaking community. It is axiomatic that, in Quebec, French culture and language are regarded by the majority group as collective goods to be preserved through political and legal means. Indeed, for the past thirty years, most Quebec governments, be they federalist or sovereigntist, have considered the "Frenchification" of immigrants and their offspring as a vital necessity for Franco-Quebecois political and cultural survival in a North American context. Moreover, from the majority group's standpoint, this "Frenchification" process amounts to more than mere language acquisition; it also entails, in keeping with a Republican ideology *à la Française*, that immigrants eventually blend in, identify with, and participate in, Quebec's dominant French-speaking culture. The chance that such a political agenda will succeed is seriously compromised, to say the least, as long as certain ethnic and racialized groups remain subjected to cultural denigration at the representational level. Fortunately, my research indicates that stigmatization is not as yet coupled with exclusion in the case of these Montreal students of Arab origin. Eventually, however, when they leave their sheltered multiethnic schools to look for jobs, these young people's Arabness, whether self-proclaimed or externally ascribed, could turn into a serious obstacle to their integration into the labour market, where ethnic and racial prejudices are more likely not only to be outwardly expressed but also to translate into actual discriminatory and exclusionary behaviours.

In conclusion, the creative ways in which second-generation Arabs negotiate their ethnic and religious identity show that, in effect, cultural integration need not be synonymous with cultural assimilation. In this respect, young Arab Canadians, like any other children of immigrants, are emblematic products of the Canadian model of integration, which rests upon the promotion of a plural and culturally multifaceted form of civic identity. Some critics in Canada – and especially in Quebec – have singled out multiculturalism as the main contributor to the crystallization of fragmented ethnocultural communities undermining social cohesion. First, with or without multiculturalism, children of immigrants, no matter how strongly committed they are to preserving their ethnic background, do not mechanically duplicate their parents' culture, which they profoundly transform through cultural borrowings and innovation. Second, rather than splitting up the nation, which has never been homogeneous in any case, multiculturalism contributes to its diversification in ways that change and enrich majority group cultures without posing any serious threat to their dominant position in the public sphere.

Therefore, the large space given to cultural diversity in this country rests upon a flexible brand of citizenship whose most remarkable feature is its capacity to accommodate multiple identity projects at its very core. However, let us be clear: multiculturalism policies and ideology per se neither ensure nor hinder intercultural dialogue, national unity, social cohesion, or the holding of meanings and values in common. But perhaps these challenging and ongoing political objectives require, *as a precondition*, that the multicultural ideals of tolerance, openness, and respect for cultural otherness come to shape the behaviours, attitudes, and representations of Canadians of every origin, both in the private and the public sphere.

APPENDICES

Variable and Index Measurement

A.1 ETHNIC IDENTITY (GLOBAL SCALE)

Isajiw, Sev'er, and Driedger's ethnic identity scale (1993) offers a nuanced and exhaustive measuring device, one that both expresses and reflects the conceptual distinctions between 1) the subjective and objective aspects of ethnic identity, and 2) its social and cultural expressions. The result is a four-by-four matrix formed by the objective/subjective and cultural/social dimensions of ethnic identity. The matrix below, with its four sets of indicators, is a simplified version of Isajiw and colleagues' scale.

Measurement of the four types of ethnic identities
Objective/Cultural (EC)
- How would you qualify your knowledge of spoken Arabic? (var. 1 in appendix B)
- Which language do you mostly use when speaking to your parents? (var. 2 in appendix B)
- Which language do you mostly use when speaking to your brother(s) and sister(s)? (var. 3 in appendix B)
- Which language do you use when speaking to your friends of Arab background? (var. 4 in appendix B)
- Do you eat any food that is associated with your ethnic group? (var. 5 in appendix B)
- Do you listen to ethnic group's radio broadcasts, or watch television ethnic group's television programs? (var. 6 in appendix B)
- Do you read any of your ethnic group's newspapers, magazines, or other periodicals (var. 7 in appendix B)

– Do you listen to music associated with your ethnic group? (var. 8 in appendix B)

Subjective/Cultural

– How do you usually think of yourself? As an Arab, a (national group), an (Arab or national group)-Canadian, or a Canadian, or other? (var. 9 in appendix B)

– If you had to assign a percentage to the two following parts of your identity, what would it look like (it must add up to 100%) (var. 10 in appendix B) :

    a) The ethnic group(s) you belong to:_____

    b) Canadian or Quebecois_____

– How important is your ethnic or cultural background to you? (var. 11 in appendix B)

Objective/Social

– How often do you attend ethnic group' s dances, parties, or informal social affairs? (var. 12 in appendix B)

– How often do you go to your ethnic group's vacation resorts or summer camps located in Canada ? (var. 13 in appendix B)

– Think about your three closest friends who are not relatives. Of these friends, how many belong to your ethnic group? (var. 14 in appendix B)

Subjective/Social

– Is it important for you to have a job that will benefit your ethnic group as well as yourself? (var. 15 in appendix B)

– Is it important for you to marry within your own ethnic group? (var. 16 in appendix B)

This matrix resulted in the computation of four new numerical continuous variables, objective/cultural, objective/social, subjective/cultural, and subjective/social. These new variables were computed by adding up the numerical values assigned to each one of the respondents' answers used as indicators (where the lowest value indicates a strong ethnic identity). Then each respondent's score was divided by the maximum one could get on the scale. This yielded a coefficient ranging from zero to one, where zero corresponds to the strongest ethnic identity, and one to the weakest. Finally, the variable "ethnic identity strength" (global index) was generated by computing the average of the four coefficients resulting from the four-by-four matrix. For descriptive purposes (percentage analysis), the variable "ethnic identity strength" was converted into a categorical ordinal variable ("ethnic identity strength–2") with five categories, namely, "very strong," "strong," "moderate," "weak," and "very weak." Then, the variable "ethnic identity strength–2" was recoded to produce "ethnic identity strength–3," including two categories, "strong" and "weak," with a view to getting larger cells when performing tabular analysis.

A.2 ESTIMATED PARENTAL COMMITMENT TO ETHNIC IDENTITY TRANSMISSION (GLOBAL SCALE):

In order to measure the influence of family socialization on the youth's ethnic identity structure, respondents were asked another set of questions. These questions were meant to measure the extent to which parents have actively attempted to transmit their ethnic identity in its various forms to their children. The transmission process is measured by a set of questions aimed at understanding the extent to which, in the respondent's estimation, his or her parents have attempted to instil into them practices, norms, and values associated with their ethnic group:

Measurement of the Ethnic Identity Transmission Process:
- Which language do your parents speak most often to you? (var. 17 in appendix B)
- How important is it for your parents that you know Arabic? (var. 18 in appendix B)
- Is it important for your parents that you attend activities/events offered by your national ethnic group or by the Arab community? (var. 19 in appendix B)
- How important is it for your parents that you retain your ethnic culture and traditions (at least those traditions they deem relevant)? (var. 20 in appendix B)
- How important is it for your mother that you marry someone within your own ethnic group? (var. 21 in appendix B)
- How important is it for your father that you marry someone within your own ethnic group? (var. 22 in appendix B)

The variable "Parental Commitment to Ethnic Identity Transmission" was computed, first, by adding up the values assigned to the respondent's answers used as indicators, and, second, by dividing the respondent's score by the maximum one could get on the scale. This yielded a coefficient ranging from zero to one, where zero indicates active parental commitment to the ethnic identity transmission process, and one a low commitment. For descriptive purposes (percentage analysis), the variable "parental commitment to ethnic identity transmission" has been converted into a categorical ordinal variable ("parental commitment to ethnic identity transmission–2") with five categories, namely, "very strong commitment," "strong," "average," "weak," and "very weak." Then, the variable "parental commitment to ethnic identity transmission–2" was broken down into two categories, "strong," and "weak," with a view to getting larger cells when performing tabular analyses. The latter variable was named "parental commitment to ethnic identity transmission –3."

A.3 RELIGIOUS IDENTITY (GLOBAL SCALE)

The concept of religious identity is measured according to the same theoretical premises used to measure the notion of ethnic identity. As mentioned above, the scale taps primarily into the sociocultural uses that are made of religion in order to consolidate group identity and solidarity. Thus, religious identity was subdivided into the four following components: subjective/cultural, subjective/social, objective/social, objective/cultural. The subjective dimension is related to the importance of religion to one's self-concept. The objective aspect of religious identity refers to the behavioural expression of one's religious self-concept, that is, the sociocultural practices that actors legitimate by drawing on religion, or at least religious symbols. In the scale, the items measuring the subjective/cultural, subjective/social, and objective/social dimensions of religious identity are, for the most part, adapted from Isajiw and Driedger's ethnic identity matrix (1993). The items measuring the objective/cultural aspect of religious identity pertain to the observance of religious rituals.

Subjective/Cultural
– How important is religion in your life? (var. 23 in appendix B)
Subjective/Social
– How important is it for you to have a job that will benefit your religious group as well as yourself? (var. 24 in appendix B)
– Is it important for you to marry within your own religious group? (var. 25 in appendix B)

- Do you personally feel that you should support the special causes and needs of your religious group in Canada and abroad? (var. 26 in appendix B)

Objective/Cultural (Observance of Rituals)

- On average, in a year, how often do you go to either the mosque or to the church (or any other temple)? (var. 27 in appendix B)
- How often do you pray on average? (var. 28 in appendix B)
- In general, do you try to fast during religious holidays during which fasting is prescribed? (var. 29 in appendix B)

Objective/Social

- How often do you attend religious events, activities, or social affairs (formal or informal)? (var. 30 in appendix B)
- Are you a member of a religious movement or organization? (var. 31 in appendix B)

This four-by-four matrix resulted in the computation of three new numerical continuous variables, namely "objective/cultural," "objective/social," and "subjective." Note that the subjective/cultural and the subjective/social dimensions of religious identity were merged to generate a single coefficient measuring the subjective aspect of religious identity. This manoeuvre was necessary because the subdimension subjective/cultural was measured by means of only one indicator (namely, "How important is religion in your life?"). Because a sole indicator is hardly sufficient to qualify as a sensitive statistical measurement tool, this variable could not be treated as a separate component of the religious identity matrix. For this reason, the indicator "How important is religion in your life?" was added to the three indicators measuring the variable subjective/social, so as to yield a single coefficient corresponding to the subjective aspect of religious identity. This latter coefficient helps along with the two others (objective/cultural and objective/social), to compute the global index measuring religious identity strength. However, the indicator "How important is religion in your life?" is considered as a variable of its own for percentage analysis purposes only.

The variables objective/cultural, objective/social, and subjective were computed, first by adding up the numerical values assigned to each of the respondents' answers used as indicators (where the lowest value indicates a strong religious identity, and the highest value a weak one). Then each respondent's score was divided by the maximum one could get on the scale. This yielded, for each dimension of religious identity, a coefficient ranging from zero to one, where zero corresponds to the strongest religious identity, and one to the weakest. Finally, the variable "religious identity strength" was generated by computing the average of the three coefficients resulting from the three-by-three religious identity matrix. For descriptive purposes (percentage analysis), the variable "religious identity strength" was converted into a categorical ordinal variable ("religious identity strength–2") with five categories, namely "very strong," "strong," "moderate," "weak," and "very weak." Then the variable "religious identity strength–2" was recoded to produce "religious identity strength–3," which includes only two categories, "strong," and "weak," with a view to getting larger cells when performing cross-table analysis.

A.4 RESPONDENTS' ESTIMATION OF THEIR PARENTS' RELIGIOUS IDENTITY STRENGTH (GLOBAL SCALE)

As seen above, the role of parental influence on ethnic identity retention was measured through a set of questions tapping exclusively into perceived parental commitment to ethnic identity transmission. Parental influence on religious identity retention, on the other hand, was measured differently. This decision was taken on the basis of a pretest run on fifteen respondents, and five exploratory interviews. It appears that most of the late adolescents in my sample reported or remarked that, throughout their socialization processes, their incorporation into their religious culture had little to do with their parents' active commitment to passing on their religious heritage to their offspring.

It rather seems that exposing children to their parents' religious attitudes and behaviours influences their decision either to reject or embrace religion as a defining element of their identity. However, such an influence rarely takes the form of active teaching and application of pressure to force the familial religious culture and its corresponding system of beliefs on the children. In other words, parents' religious identity strength is more likely than parental commitment to religious identity transmission to influence children's relationship to religion later in life.

It was therefore considered a priority to tap into parental levels of religious identity retention. Thus, through a series of four questions, respondents were asked to assess the intensity of their parent's religiosity. Only two questions were added to assess how much parents wish their children to perpetuate their religious heritage.

Finally, it was deemed that "perceived parents' religiosity" could not be adequately measured using the same questions as those aimed at measuring the respondents' religiosity. Two questions in particular relating to the subjective/social dimension of religious identity, referred to attitudes and opinions that could hardly be measured by relying on second-hand sources (i.e., the respondents). Thus, variables 18 ("How important is it for you that your job benefit your religious group?") and 20 ("Do you feel that you should support the special causes and needs of your religious group?") are attitudes that can only be reliably measured by questioning the parents directly. In addition, item 19 ("Is it important for you to marry within your ethnic group?") does not apply to respondents' parents, who are all married to a religious peer.

Because of these limitations, another scale was created, allowing us to tap into parental religious attitudes and behaviours that are more easily accessible to respondents. This scale is made up of one item measuring the subjective/cultural aspect of religious identity, one item measuring the objective/cultural aspect, and one item measuring perceived parental attempts at transmitting their religious identity to their children. Each of these selected items was duplicated in order to get separate information about mothers' and fathers' respective religious attitudes and behaviours; according to the literature, while mothers are often more committed to ethnic identity transmission, fathers are often more pious and devout (Vertovec 1998). It is then possible to examine, in the analytical section, the extent to which the respondents' relation to religion is conditioned by, most importantly, their parents' level of religiosity, and secondarily, by parental commitment to religious identity transmission. The following chart sums up the composition of the scale:

Subjective/Cultural
- Does religion play an important role in your father's life? (var.32 in appendix B)
- Does religion play an important role in your mother's life? (var.33 in appendix B)

Objective/Cultural
- In your estimation, is your father a practising person? (var. 34 in appendix B)

- In your estimation, is your mother a practising person? (var. 35 in appendix B)

Parental Attempt at Transmitting their Religious Identity to their Children

- How important is it for your father that you retain your religious heritage? (var. 36 in appendix B)
- How important is it for your mother that you retain your religious heritage? (var. 37 in appendix B)

Based on the respondents' assessment, a score measuring parents' religious identity strength was computed, first by adding up the numerical values assigned to each answer given to the questions used as indicators (where the lowest value indicates a strong religious identity). Then, each individual score was divided by the maximum the parents of each respondent could get on the scale. This yielded a coefficient ranging from zero to one, where zero denotes a strong religious identity and one a weak one. This new variable was named "parents' estimated religious identity strength." For descriptive purposes (percentage analysis), this latter variable has been converted into a categorical ordinal variable ("parents' estimated religious identity strength–2") with five categories – "very strong," "strong," "moderate," "weak," and "very weak." Then, the variable "parents' estimated religious identity strength–2" was recoded to generate "parents' estimated religious identity strength–3," including two categories, "strong" and "weak," with a view to getting larger cells when performing tabular analysis.

A.5 GENDER-RELATED TRADITIONALISM (GLOBAL SCALE)

An attitudinal scale measuring respondents' level of gender-related traditionalism was crafted. The subjects were asked to report the extent to which they agreed or disagreed with a series of nine statements (see variables 38 to 46 in appendix B). In order to examine the relationship between their own normative frame and that of their parents, the respondents were asked to report what they thought their parents' level of agreement would be with the same nine statements (see variables 47 to 55 in appendix B). This tradition scale is partially informed by the one crafted by Rooijackers (1992) and used subsequently by Nijsten (1996), but it also contains a few items either taken from or inspired by Kucukcan's questionnaire (1998). The items included in the scale are the following:

Arabo-Islamic Tradition Scale (Youths):
- Women should essentially be housewives. (var. 38 in appendix B)
- In general, a woman should obey her husband. (var. 39 in appendix B)
- Girls should compulsorily remain virgins before marriage. (var. 40 in appendix B)
- Boys should compulsorily remain virgins before marriage. (var. 41 in appendix B)
- A girl's virginity should be "protected" by her male kin in order for family reputation and honour to be preserved. (var. 42 in appendix B)
- Male teenagers should be allowed to have a girlfriend before marriage if they want to. (var. 43 in appendix B)
- Female teenagers should be allowed to have a boyfriend before marriage if they want to. (var. 44 in appendix B)
- Premarital sexual relationships are acceptable for boys. (var. 45 in appendix B)
- Premarital sexual relationships are acceptable for girls. (var.46 in appendix B)

Arabo-Islamic Tradition Scale (Parents):
The items making up the parents' scale are exactly the same as those found in the above children's scale (see variables 47 to 55 in appendix B)

The respondent's score on this scale was computed, first, by adding up the numerical values assigned to each answer given to the questions used as indicators (where the lowest possible value reflects strong traditional attitudes toward gender roles). Then, each respondent's total score was divided by the maximum score one could get on the scale. This yielded a coefficient ranging from zero to one, where zero denotes pronounced traditional attitudes and one liberal ones. Another coefficient was also generated for parents' reported attitudes, using the exact same method.

These two recoded variables were named, respectively, "gender-related traditionalism/youth," and "gender-related traditionalism/parents." For descriptive purposes, each of these two latter variables was converted into a categorical ordinal variable ("gender-related traditionalism/youth–2" and "gender-related traditionalism/parents–2"), with five categories, "very traditional," "somewhat traditional," "borderline," "somewhat liberal," and "very liberal." Then, these

recoded variables were themselves converted into "gender-related tra-
ditionalism/youth–3," and "gender-related traditionalism/parents–3,"
each being reduced to only two categories, "strong level of traditionalism" and "low level of traditionalism," with a view to getting larger
cells when performing bi- or trivariate cross-table analysis.

A.6 PERCEIVED PREJUDICIAL STEREOTYPING

The respondents were asked to express the degree to which they
agree with the following statements:

- There are negative stereotypes against Arabs prevailing among Canadians, (var. 57 in appendix B)
- There are negative stereotypes against my religious group prevailing
  among Canadians (var. 58 in appendix B)
- The media help to propagate a biased picture of the Arabs. (var. 59 in
  appendix B)
- The media help to propagate a biased picture of my religious group.
  (var. 60 in appendix B)

A.7 PERCEIVED DISCRIMINATION

The respondents were asked to express the degree to which they
agree with the following statement:

- Personally, I feel accepted as an Arab by Canadians (var. 56 in appendix
  B)

A.8 GENDER

The independent variable "gender" (variable 61 in appendix B) was
measured through an open-ended question and treated as a categorical nominal variable with two categories (male and female). No
recoding was required.

A.9 RELIGIOUS AFFILIATION

The independent variable "religious affiliation" (variable 62 in
appendix B) was measured through an open-ended question asking
respondents to report their father's religion. This parameter may

appear at the outset as an incomplete tool; for it only provides an indirect measure of the respondents' religious affiliation, which, theoretically, could depart from their father's. However, the purpose served by this question was to identify the respondents' religious cultural background, or the religious banner under which they were raised (in any case, it is extremely uncommon among Arab youth to adopt a religion other than their parents'). Nonetheless, the question could be regarded as problematic in other respects. One potential shortcoming is that it overlooks the possibility that respondents raised in religiously mixed families may have been socialized into their mother's religious culture, rather than into their father's. With this in view, respondents were also asked to identify their mother's religion, but not a single case of mixed religious background was reported. One last shortcoming is that the question does not detect cases where the respondent's father is himself agnostic or atheist. It must be said, however, that such cases are extremely unlikely to be found among Arab parents of this migratory cohort. The variable "father's religious affiliation" was treated as a categorical nominal variable with two categories, Christian and Muslim. No recoding was required.

A.10 CONTROL VARIABLES

The variable "father's level of education" (see variable 63 in appendix B) is meant to provide an indicator of the respondent's sociocultural capital. It was measured using an open-ended question, and was then recoded twice so as to facilitate cross-tabular analysis. The first recoding yielded an ordinal categorical variable ("father's level of education–2) with four categories: primary school years, high school years, college years, and university years. Then, this latter variable was itself recoded so as to obtain "father's level of education–3," with two categories, namely, "low education" (merging of primary and high school), and "high education" (merging of college and university).

The second control variable is "self-estimated ethnic residential segregation" (variable 64 in appendix B). It must be said that the measurement of this variable is rather imprecise, as it was done by asking respondents whether, in their estimation, ethnic concentration in their neighbourhood was high, normal, low, or insignificant. Then, this latter variable was collapsed into "ethnic residential segregation–2," with the categories "high" and "normal" merged together to form the "above average" category, and the categories "low" and "insignificant" merged to form the "below average" category.

Finally, the dichotomous variable "canadian-born vs. foreignborn" was measured through an open-ended question (see variable 65 in appendix B). The variable "time spent in Canada" was measured by subtracting the respondent's age at arrival in Canada from his or her current age. The resulting variable, "time spent in Canada," was then recoded in order to generate "Time spent in Canada–2," including three categories: "less than 10 years," "between 10 and 15 years," and "more than 10 years."

Coding of Variables

Variable 1: "How would you qualify your knowledge of spoken Arabic?"
Categories of the variable:
a) good = 1
b) average = 2
c) poor = 3
d) I don't speak it = 4

Variable 2: "Which language do you mostly speak with parents?"
Variable 3: "Which language do you mostly speak with brothers and sisters?"
Variable 4: "Which language do you mostly speak with friends of Arab background?"
Original categories of the 3 variables:
a) Arab
b) French
c) English
d) Other _____

These variables were recoded respectively into "language spoken to parents," "language spoken to brother," and "language spoken to Arab friends," in order to assign a value of one to respondents who chose Arab (category a), and a value of two to respondents who chose either French or English (categories b and c). The self-reported languages written under the category "other" were not considered for analysis purposes. Note that, even though respondents were asked not to choose more than one answer, a minority of them chose two languages. Whenever either French, English, or Arabic were chosen simultaneously, the respondent's dual answer was assigned a value of 1.5 to mark the hybrid character of his or her relationship to language.

Variable 5: "How often do you eat ethnic food?"
Categories of the variable:
a) often (e.g., once a week or more) = 1
b) occasionally (e.g., once a month or so) = 2
c) rarely (e.g., on special holidays) = 3

Variable 6: "How often do you listen or watch ethnic radio broadcasts or TV programs?"
Variable 7: "How often do you read ethnic newspapers, magazines, or other periodicals?"
Variable 8: "How often do you listen to ethnic music?"
Categories and values of these variables:
a) often (once a week or more) = 1
b) occasionally (e.g., once a month or so) = 2
c) rarely (e.g., five times a year or so) = 3
d) never = 4

Variable 9: "How do you usually think of yourself first and foremost?"
Original categories of the variable:
a) Arab
b) As a member of a national group (e.g., Egyptian, Moroccan)
c) as an Arab Canadian (or Quebecois)
d) as a (national group)-Canadian (or Quebecois)
e) as either a Canadian or a Quebecois
f) Other _____

   This variable was recoded into "self-labelling–2," in order to assign a value of one (strong ethnic identity) to respondents who identify with either the Arabs or their national group (categories a and b), a value of two (hybrid identity) to respondents who identify with both the majority group and any of their ethnic groups (categories c and d), and a value of three (weak ethnic identity) to respondents who identify themselves as either Canadians or Quebecois (category e). Finally, the self-reported identities written under the category "other" were assigned a value of either one, two or three depending on the answer given.

Variable 10: "Percentage assigned to the ethnic side of you"
Original categories of the variable:
a)   The ethnic group(s) you belong to _____
b)   Canadian or Quebecois _____
   This variable was recoded in order to assign a value from one to
ten to each respondent, where each unit covers ten percent (one corresponding to the lowest percentage bracket and ten to the highest):
(90% through 100%=1) (80% through 89.99%=2) (70% through
79.99%=3) (60% through 69.99%=4) (50% through 59.99%=5)
(40% through 49.99%=6) (30% through 39.99%=7) (20%
through 29.99%=8) (10% through 19.99%=9) (0% through
9.99%=10).

Variable 11: "Importance of cultural background"
Categories of the variable:
a)   very important = 1
b)   important = 2
c)   somehow important = 3
d)   not important = 4

---

*Variable 12: "How often do you attend your ethnic group's dances,
parties, or informal social affairs?"*
Categories of the variable:
a)   often =1
b)   occasionally= 2
c)   never= 3

---

*Variable 13: "How often do you or did you use to attend ethnic
summer camps or resorts located in Canada?"*
Categories of the variable:
a)   almost every summer = 1
b)   I have been there once = 2
c)   I have been there more than once = 3
d)   never = 5

---

*Variable 14: "Of your three best friends who are not relatives, how
many belong to your ethnic group?"*
Categories of the variable:
a)   three = 1
b)   two = 2

c) one = 3
d) none = 4

Variable 15: "Job should benefit ethnic peers as well as yourself"
Categories of the variable:
a) very important = 1
b) important = 2
c) ideally but not necessarily = 3
d) not important = 4

Variable 16: "Importance of marrying within your ethnic group"
Categories of the variable:
a) important = 1
b) ideally but not necessarily = 2
c) not important = 3
d) I do not want to marry within my own ethnic group = 4

Variable 17: " Which language do your parents most often speak to you?"
Categories of the original variable:
a) Arabic
b) French
c) English
d) Other _____

This variable was recoded into "language spoken by parents to children–2," in order to assign a value of one to respondents who chose Arab (category a), and a value of two to respondents who chose either French or English (categories b and c). Once again, whenever French, English, and any ethnic language were chosen simultaneously, the respondent's dual answer was assigned a value of 1.5 to mark the hybrid character of the linguistic transmission process in which his or her parents were engaged.

Variable 18: "How important is it for your parents that you know Arabic?"
Categories of the variable:
a) very important = 1
b) important = 2
c) ideally but not necessarily = 3

d) not important = 4

Variable 19: *"Is it important for your parents that you attend activities offered by your ethnic group"*
Categories of the variables:
a) important = 1
b) ideally but not necessarily = 2
c) not important = 3

Variable 20: *" How important is it for your parents that you retain your ethnic culture and traditions?"*
Variable 21: *"How important is it for your mother that you marry within your ethnic group?"*
Variable 22: *"How important is it for your father that you marry within your ethnic group?"*
Categories of the variables:
a) very important = 1
b) important = 2
c) ideally but not necessarily = 3
d) not important = 4

Variable 23: *"How important is religion in your life?"*
Categories of the variable:
a) very important = 1
b) important = 2
c) not very important = 3
d) not important = 4

Variable 24: *"Is it important that your job benefits your religious group as well as yourself?"*
Categories of the variable:
a) very important = 1
b) important = 2
c) ideally but not necessarily = 3
d) not important = 4

Variable 25: *"Is it important for you to marry within your religious group?"*
Categories of the variable:

a)   very important = 1
b)   important = 2
c)   ideally but not necessarily = 3
d)   I don't want to marry within my religious group = 4

Variable 26: "Is it important to support the causes and needs of members of your religious group?"
Categories of the variable:
a)   very much so = 1
b)   ideally but not necessarily = 2
c)   not at all = 3

Variable 27: "How often do you go to either the mosque or the church?"
Categories of the variable:
a)   at least once a week = 1
b)   once a month = 2
c)   only on religious holidays = 3
d)   never or rarely = 4

Variable 28: "How often do you pray on average".
Categories of the variable:
a)   at least once a day = 1
b)   once a week = 2
c)   once a month = 3
d)   never or rarely = 4

Variable 29: "Do you try to fast during appropriate religious holidays?"
Categories of the variable:
a)   yes = 1
b)   no = 2

Variable 30: "How often do you attend religious events, activities, or religious social affairs?"
Categories of the variable:
a)   often = 1
b)   occasionally = 2
c)   never = 3

Variable 31: "*Are you a member of a religious movement or organization?*"
Categories of the variable:
a) yes = 1
b) no = 2

Variable 32: "*Does religion play an important role in your father's life?*"
Variable 33: "*Does religion play an important role in your mother's life?*"
Categories of the variables:
a) very important = 1
b) important = 2
c) not very important = 3
d) not important = 4

Variable 34: "*In your estimation, is your father a practising person?*"
Variable 35: "*In your estimation, is your mother a practising person?*"
Categories of the variables:
a) a very practising person
b) a fairly practising person
c) a not very practising person
d) a non-practising person

Variable 36: "*How important is it for your father that you retain your religious heritage?*"
Variable 37: "*How important is it for your mother that you retain your religious heritage?*"
Categories of the variables:
a) very important = 1
b) important = 2
c) not very important = 3
d) not important = 4

Variable 38: "*Women should essentially be housewives*"
Variable 39: "*Women should obey their husband*"
Variable 40: "*Girls should compulsorily remain a virgin before marriage*"

Variable 41: "*Boys should compulsorily remain a virgin before marriage*"

Variable 42: "*A girl's virginity should be protected by her male kin for family reputation and honour to be preserved*"

Categories of these variables:
a)   I completely agree = 1
b)   I somewhat agree = 2
c)   I somewhat disagree = 3
d)   I disagree completely = 4

Variable 43: "*Male teenagers are allowed to have a girlfriend before marriage*"

Variable 44: "*Female teenagers are allowed to have a boyfriend before marriage*"

Variable 45: "*Premarital sex is acceptable for boys*"

Variable 46: "*Premarital sex is acceptable for girls*"

Categories of these variables:
a)   I completely disagree = 1
b)   I somewhat disagree = 2
c)   I somewhat agree = 3
d)   I completely agree = 4

Variable 47: "*Women should be housewives – PARENTS*"

Variable 48: "*A woman should obey her husband – PARENTS*"

Variable 49: "*Girls should remain virgins before marriage – PARENTS*"

Variable 50: "*Boys should remain virgins before marriage – PARENTS*"

Variable 51: "*A girl's virginity should be protected by her male kin for family reputation and honour to be preserved – PARENTS*"

Categories of these variables:
a)   I completely agree = 1
b)   I somewhat agree = 2
c)   I somewhat disagree = 3
d)   I disagree completely = 4

Variable 52: "*Male teenagers can have a girlfriend before marriage – PARENTS*"

Variable 53: "*Female teenagers can have a boyfriend before marriage – PARENTS*"

Variable 54: "Premarital sex is acceptable for boys – PARENTS"
Variable 55: "Premarital sex is acceptable for girls – PARENTS"
Categories of these variables:
a) I completely disagree = 1
b) I somewhat disagree = 2
c) I somewhat agree = 3
d) I completely agree = 4

Variable 56: "Personally, I feel accepted as an Arab by Canadians"
Variable 57: "There are negative stereotypes against Arabs prevailing among Canadians"
Variable 58: "There are negative stereotypes against my religious group prevailing among Canadians"
Variable 59: "The media help to propagate a biased picture of the Arabs"
Variable 60: "The media help to propagate a biased picture of my religious group"
Categories of these variables:
a) I completely disagree = 1
b) I somewhat disagree = 2
c) I somewhat agree = 3
d) I completely agree = 4

Variable 61: "Sex" _____

Variable 62: "Religion of your Father" _____

Variable 63: "Level of education of your father" _____
   This variable, originally measured through an open question, was converted into an ordinal categorical variable (father's level of education–2) with four categories.
a) primary school degree or less = 1
b) high school years = 2
c) college years = 3
d) university years = 4

Variable 64: "All things being equal, in your estimation, the concentration of individuals belonging to your ethnic group who live in your neighbourhood is ..."
a) high = 1

b)   normal = 2
c)   low = 3
d)   insignificant = 4

Variable 65: "Were you born in Canada?"
a)   yes
b)   no. In which country were you born? _____

Variable 66: "How old were you when you arrived in Canada?"

_____

Variable 67: "Do you eat halal meat?"
a)   almost all the time = 1
b)   ideally but not compulsorily = 2
c)   only for religious holidays = 3
d)   I don't eat halal meat = 4

Variable 68: "Do you drink alcohol?"
a)   yes = 1
b)   no = 2

Questionnaire

GENERAL INFORMATION

1) Sex: _____

2) Age:_____

3) In which programme are you enrolled? _____

4) How far are you in your programme? _____

5) Level of education of your father? _____

6) Level of education of your mother? _____

7) What is your father's occupation? _____

8) What is your mother's occupation? _____

9) All things being equal, in your estimation, the concentration of individuals belonging to your ethnic group who live in your neighbourhood is ...
   a) high
   b) average
   c) low
   d) insignificant _____

10) What is your father's country of origin? _____

11) What is your mother's country of origin? _____

12) Religion of your father?_____

13) Religion of your mother?_____

14) Were you born in Canada?
   a) Yes_____
   b) No. In which country were you born? _____
      How old were you when you arrived in Canada? _____

15) In which country have you lived for the longest period of time between 0 and 15 years old?_____

QUESTIONNAIRE

1) How would you qualify your knowledge of spoken Arabic?
   a) good
   b) average
   c) poor
   d) I don't speak it

2) Which language do you **mostly** use when speaking to your parents? (only one answer)
   a) Arabic
   b) French
   c) English
   d) Other_____

3) Which language do you **mostly** use when speaking to your brother(s) or sister(s) (only one answer)?
   a) Arabic
   b) French
   c) English
   d) Other_____

4) Which language do you **mostly** use when speaking to your friends originating from an Arab-speaking country (skip the question if you have no Arab friends)?
   a) Arabic
   b) French
   c) English
   d) Other _____

5) Do you eat any food that is associated with your ethnic group?
   a) rarely (e.g., only on special holidays)
   b) occasionally (e.g., once a month or so)
   c) often (e.g., once a week or more)

6) Do you listen to your ethnic group's radio broadcasts, or watch ethnic group's television programs?
   a) never
   b) rarely (5 times a year or so)
   c) occasionally (once a month or so)
   d) often (once a week or more)

7) Do you read any of your ethnic group's newspapers, magazines, or other periodicals?
   a) never

    b) rarely (5 times a year or so)

    c) occasionally (once a month or so)

    d) often (once a week or more)

8) Do you listen to music associated with your ethnic group?

    a) never

    b) rarely (5 times a year or so)

    c) occasionally (once a month or so)

    d) often (once a week or more)

9) How do you usually think of yourself **first and foremost**? (only one answer)

    a) as an Arab

    b) as a member of a national Arab group (e.g., Egyptian, Moroccan)

       If so, which one: _____

    c) as an Arab-Canadian (or Quebecois)

    d) as a (national group)-Canadian (or Quebecois)

    e) as either a Canadian or a Quebecois

    f) other _____

10) If you had to assign a percentage to the two following parts of your identity, what would it look like? (it must add up to 100%):

    a) The ethnic group(s) you belong to: _____

    b) Canadian or Quebecois: _____

11) How important is your ethnic or cultural background to you?

    a) very important

    b) important

    c) somewhat important

    d) not important

12) How close are the ties that you maintain, **on a personal level,** with member of other ethnic groups in Canada?

    a) very close

    b) close

    c) rather loose

    d) no ties at all

13) How often do you attend your ethnic group' s dances, parties, or social affairs (formal or informal)?

    a) often

    b) occasionally

    c) never

14) Do you or did you use to spend your summer in vacation resorts or summer camps located in Canada but attended mainly by your ethnic group?
   a) almost every summer
   b) I have been there once
   c) I have been there more than once
   d) never

15) I would like you to think about your three closest friends who are not relatives. Of these friends, how many belong to your ethnic group (or to any another Arab group)?
   a) one
   b) two
   c) three
   d) none

16) Is it important for you to have a job that will benefit your ethnic group as well as yourself?
   a) very important
   b) important
   c) ideally but not necessarily
   d) not important at all

17) Is it important for you to marry within your own ethnic group?
   a) important
   b) ideally but not necessarily
   c) not important at all
   d) I do not want to marry within my own ethnic group

18) Which language do your parents speak **most often** to you (only one answer)?
   a) Arabic
   b) French
   c) English
   d) other _____

19) How important is it for your parents that you know Arabic?
   a) very important
   b) important
   c) ideally but not necessarily
   d) not important at all

20) Have you ever attended Arabic classes here in Canada?
   a) yes
   b) no

21) If so, whose idea was it?
  a) your own
  b) your parents'
22) How important is it for your parents that you attend activities and events offered by your national ethnic group or by the broader Arab community?
  a) important
  b) ideally but not necessarily
  c) not important
23) How important is it for your parents that you retain your ethnic culture and traditions (at least those traditions they deem relevant)?
  a) very important
  b) important
  c) ideally but not necessarily
  d) not important
24) How important is it for your mother that you marry someone within your own ethnic group?
  a) very important
  b) important
  c) ideally but not necessarily
  d) not important
25) How important is it for your father that you marry someone within your own ethnic group?
  a) very important
  b) important
  c) ideally but not necessarily
  d) not important
26) How important is religion in your life?
  a) very important
  b) important
  c) not very important
  d) not important
27) Here in Canada, how close are the ties which you maintain, **in your personal life**, with persons whose religious background is different than yours.
  a) very close
  b) close
  c) rather loose
  d) no ties

28) How important is it for you to have a job that will benefit your religious group as well as yourself?
   a) very important
   b) important
   c) ideally but not necessarily
   d) not important

29) Is it important for you to marry within your own religious group?
   a) important
   b) ideally but not necessarily
   c) not important
   d) I don't want to marry someone within my own religious group

30) Do you personally feel that you should support the special causes and needs of members of your religious group in Canada and abroad?
   a) very much so
   b) ideally but not necessarily
   c) not at all

31) On average, in a year, how often do you go to either the mosque or the church (or any other temple)?
   a) at least once a week
   b) once a month
   c) only for religious holidays
   d) never or rarely

32) How often do you pray on average?
   a) at least once a day
   b) once a week
   c) once a month
   d) never or rarely

(The following question should only be answered by Muslim respondents)

33) Do you eat halal?
   a) almost all the times
   b) ideally but not necessarily
   c) only during religious holidays
   d) I do not observe this prescription

34) In general, do you try to fast during religious holidays during which fasting is prescribed?
   a) yes

b) no

(The following question should only be answered by Muslim respondents)

35) In everyday life, do you try not to drink alcohol as prescribed in the Koran?
   a) yes
   b) no

36) How often do you attend religious events, activities, or social affairs (formal or informal)?
   a) often
   b) occasionally
   c) never

37) Are you member of a religious movement or organization?
   a) yes
   b) no

38) I would like you to think about your three closest friends who are not relatives. Of these friends, how many share your religious background?
   a) one
   b) two
   c) three
   d) none

39) Does religion play an important role in your father's life?
   a) very important
   b) important
   c) not very important
   d) not important

40) Does religion play an important role in your mother's life?
   a) very important
   b) important
   c) not very important
   d) not important

41) In your estimation, is your father ...
   a) a very practising person
   b) a fairly practising person
   c) a not very practising person
   d) a non-practising person
   e) an atheist or agnostic

42) In your estimation, is your mother ...
   a) a very practising person

    b) a fairly practising person

    c) a not very practising person

    d) a non-practising person

    e) an atheist or agnostic

43) How important is it for your father that you retain your religious heritage?

    a) very important

    b) important

    c) not very important

    d) not important

44) How important is it for your mother that you retain your religious heritage?

    a) very important

    b) important

    c) not very important

    d) not important

45) Have you ever attended a religious school in Canada?

    a) yes. If so, for how long:

    b) yes, but in addition to regular school (weekends or evenings)

    c) no

Instructions for questions 46 to 56:

Under each of the following statements, you will find two columns. In the left one, please indicate your level of agreement with the statement. In the right one, indicate what in your opinion would be your parent's level of agreement with the same statement (except for statement 56)

(N.B. Statement 46 concerns only Muslim respondents)

46) Women should **NOT** be obliged to wear the hijab (the veil) outside the home.

    a) I agree completely   a) They would completely agree

    b) I somewhat agree   b) They would somewhat agree

    c) I somewhat disagree   c) They would somewhat disagree

    d) I disagree completely   d) They would completely disagree

47) Women should essentially be housewives.

    a) I agree completely   a) They would completely agree

    b) I somewhat agree   b) They would somewhat agree

    c) I somewhat disagree   c) They would somewhat disagree

    d) I disagree completely   d) They would completely disagree

48) In general, a woman should obey her husband.

a) I agree completely   a) They would completely agree
b) I somewhat agree   b) They would somewhat agree
c) I somewhat disagree c) They would somewhat disagree
d) I disagree completely d) They would completely disagree

49) Girls should compulsorily remain virgin before marriage.

a) I agree completely   a) They would completely agree
b) I somewhat agree   b) They would somewhat agree
c) I somewhat disagree c) They would somewhat disagree
d) I disagree completely d) They would completely disagree

50) Boys should compulsorily remain virgin before marriage.

a) I agree completely   a) They would completely agree
b) I somewhat agree   b) They would somewhat agree
c) I somewhat disagree c) They would somewhat disagree
d) I disagree completely d) They would completely disagree

51) A girl's virginity should be "protected" until marriage by her male kin in order for the family's reputation and honour to be preserved.

a) I agree completely   a) They would completely agree
b) I somewhat agree   b) They would somewhat agree
c) I somewhat disagree c) They would somewhat disagree
d) I disagree completely d) They would completely disagree

52) Male teenagers should be allowed to have a girlfriend before marriage if they want to.

a) I agree completely   a) They would completely agree
b) I somewhat agree   b) They would somewhat agree
c) I somewhat disagree c) They would somewhat disagree
d) I disagree completely d) They would completely disagree

53) Female teenagers should be allowed to have a boyfriend before marriage if they want to.

a) I agree completely   a) They would completely agree
b) I somewhat agree   b) They would somewhat agree
c) I somewhat disagree c) They would somewhat disagree
d) I disagree completely d) They would completely disagree

54) Premarital sexual relationships are acceptable for boys.

a) I agree completely   a) They would completely agree
b) I somewhat agree   b) They would somewhat agree
c) I somewhat disagree c) They would somewhat disagree
d) I disagree completely d) They would completely disagree

55) Premarital sexual relationships are acceptable for girls.

a) I agree completely   a) They would completely agree

b) I somewhat agree   b) They would somewhat agree
c) I somewhat disagree   c) They would somewhat disagree
d) I disagree completely d) They would completely disagree

56) In my home, parental control is (or was) excessive.
    a) I agree completely
    b) I somewhat agree
    c) I somewhat disagree
    d) I disagree completely

Instructions for questions 57 to 61:

Please indicate your level of agreement with each of the following statements:

57) I feel accepted as an Arab by Canadians in my personal life.
    a) I agree completely
    b) I somewhat agree
    c) I somewhat disagree
    d) I disagree completely

58) There are negative stereotypes against Arabs prevailing among Canadians.
    a) I agree completely
    b) I somewhat agree
    c) I somewhat disagree
    d) I disagree completely

59) There are negative stereotypes against my religious group prevailing among Canadians.
    a) I agree completely
    b) I somewhat agree
    c) I somewhat disagree
    d) I disagree completely

60) The media help to propagate a biased picture of my religious group.
    a) I agree completely
    b) I somewhat agree
    c) I somewhat disagree
    d) I disagree completely

61) The media help to propagate a biased picture of Arabs.
    a) I agree completely
    b) I somewhat agree
    c) I somewhat disagree
    d) I disagree completely

———— End of the questionnaire————

Thank you very much!

Would you be interested in eventually participating in a 30-minute interview during which you would be asked to elaborate on some of the responses you wrote down in this questionnaire?

a) Yes

b) No

If you answered yes, please write down below your name and phone number, so I can contact you subsequently:

Name: _____

Tel.: _____

Interview Question Sheet

1) Do you identify first and foremost as an Arab, a "national origin," an Arab Canadian, a National-origin Canadian, or a Canadian? Could you explain your answer?
2) Do you identify at all as an Arab? Why?
3) Do you think there are many differences between your ethnic group and Canadians in general? In which respects is your ethnic group different?
4) Is it important for you to maintain your ethnic culture? Which aspects of this culture do you want to retain the most and why?
5) Is it important for you to maintain your religious culture? Which aspects of this culture do you want to retain the most and why?
6) Is it important for your parents that you retain your ethnic culture? Which aspects of it do they want you to retain in particular, and how do they let you know about it ?
7) Is it important for your parents that you retain your religious culture? Which aspects of it do they want you to retain in particular, and how do they let you know about it ?
8) Do you find sometimes that the Canadian component of your identity can lead to arguments or even conflicts between you and your parents? If so, could you give examples?
9) Is ethnicity important in your choice of friends? Why?
10) Is religion important in your choice of friends? Why?
11) Will ethnicity be important in your choice of a future life partner?
12) Will religion be important in your choice of a future life partner?

13) Do you agree with the statement "A woman should obey her husband?" Why?

14) Do you agree with the statement "A girl's virginity should be preserved until marriage?" Could you please justify your answer?

15) Do you agree with the statement "A boy's virginity should be preserved until marriage?" Could you please justify your answer?

16) In your personal life, do you feel well accepted as an Arab by Canadians?

17) In general, do you think that there are negative stereotypes of Arabs prevailing among Canadians? Could you give examples?

18) In general do you think that there are negative stereotypes of your religious group prevailing among Canadians? Could you give examples?

19) Do you think that the media help to propagate a biased, or an accurate picture of the Arabs? Why?

20) Do you think that the media help to propagate a biased, or an accurate picture of your religious group? Why?

Notes

INTRODUCTION

1 In Quebec, for example, one can safely contend that the French language has replaced religion as a primary collective identity marker and vehicle (see Meintel 1998).

2 During the same period, many migrants came from South Asian countries such as India, Sri Lanka, Bangladesh, and Pakistan, where nationalist awakening and religious revivalism were also coterminous.

3 Harvard professor Samuel Huntington's book *The Clash of Civilizations* (1996) reminds us that scholarly representations of the "Arabs" are by no means devoid of such reductive and simplistic dichotomies.

4 It should be noted, however, that the data for this study were collected between January 2000, and May 2001, prior to the terrorist attacks of September 11.

CHAPTER ONE

1 When Syria became an independent state, these early migrants started to call themselves Syrians, only to find later that the "Lebanese" among them resented that appellation once Lebanon also became a free and separate entity.

2 Although the first mosque in Canada was founded in Edmonton in 1938 (Abu-Laban 1995, 209), the Canadian Muslim population was so marginal in size until World War II (only 645 Muslim residents were recorded in Canada in 1931) that its organizational infrastructure remained extremely limited throughout this entire period.

3 More specifically, 64,147 Arab migrants came during the 1970s, 75,899 during the 1980s, and 133,489 from 1990 to 1997 (Hayani 1999, 286).

4 However, it should be stressed that this pan-Arab solidarity structured around the Palestinian issue was also undermined by political conflicts between Arab nations, most notably between the Lebanese Maronites and the Palestinians.

5 Note that pan-Arabism, the ideology calling for the creation of a unitary Arab state, did not originate with Nasser. Its emergence goes back to the end of the nineteenth century (Farah 1987).

6 Tunisia remains a noteworthy exception in this respect (though Islamist movements have recently been gaining considerable political influence). President Habib Bourguiba is known for having successfully fostered the secularization of both the state apparatus and civil society during his years in office (1957–87).

7 It should be stressed that census data are bound to overestimate the number of Arab-origin individual in Canada since they include respondents who declared multiple ethnic origins. Consequently, double counts may occur as respondents who declared more than one ethnic origin related to the Arab world will be counted twice.

8 Even more interesting is that, both in Quebec and in Canada, "Arab" is the most commonly reported single ethnic origin response among immigrants who migrated from the Arab world between 1996 and 2001.

9 The following figures include only those Arab-origin Canadians who reported one of the six most reported ethnic origins pertaining to the Arab world.

CHAPTER TWO

1 Authors who share Hall's understanding include Homi Bhabha (1990), Jonathan Rutherford (1990), Gerd Baumann (1996, 1997), Pina Werbner (1997), Alberto Melluci (1997), Caglar (1997), and Steven Vertovec and Alisdair Rogers (1998).

2 The survey was sponsored by Gallup, Le Monde, and IFOP.

3 The next section, dedicated to methods, provides further details regarding the parameters used to measure each of religious identity's subdimensions.

4 That being said, it must be kept in mind that, in many other Western societies such as Canada, France, Germany, and Holland, religious institutions remain relatively disempowered in the political arena.

5 This is due in part to the fact that the proportion of foreign-born Jews is much higher in Canada (31 percent) than in the United States (10 percent).

6 However, it should be mentioned that some studies have shown that there is a small minority of second-generation Muslims born in Europe for whom the use of Islam in the construction of ethnic identity is more than purely symbolic. This group comprises young orthodox "Islamists" who are extremely pious and strict in their observance of religious rules of conduct. Contrary to the trajectory typically followed by children of immigrants in general, that followed by the "Islamists" does not intersect with mainstream institutional and cultural systems. Whereas the former group tends to pick ethnoreligious cultural items that are compatible with the Western sociocultural models they have internalized, the latter attempts to conform rigorously to a rigid "quasi-mythical" body of behavioural and normative religious prescriptions (Bastenier 1992, 212–13; Cesari 1997, 31; Venel 2004). Whereas this minority of ultra-orthodox Muslim youths generally foster the creation of separate institutions where their Islam-based ethnicity can be completely shielded from Western influences, their more culturally and structurally incorporated peers are trying to carve out a space in the public arena where their civic allegiance to the political community and their identification with their ethnic and religious communities can be made to coexist harmoniously.

7 The following nations were considered as Arab countries: Algeria, Bahrain, Democratic Yemen, Djibouti, Egypt, Iraq, Jordan, Kuwait, Lebanon, Libya, Mauritania, Morocco, Oman, Palestine, Qatar, Saudi Arabia, Somalia, Sudan, Syria, Tunisia, United Arab Emirates, and Yemen.

8 As previously reported, among the active population, 24,5 percent of Arab-Canadian females and 33 percent of Arab-Canadian males aged 15 years and older hold a university degree, whereas the national average is 14.9 percent for women, and 16 percent for men (Statistics Canada 2001).

9 In the following, any census data referring to "Arab-Canadians" or "Arab-Quebecois" is understood to include only the six most commonly reported ethnic origins relating to the Arab world, in Canada and Quebec respectively. These top six categories account together for 86 percent of Arab migration to Canada as a whole, and 89 percent of Arab migration to Quebec specifically.

10 Note that in Quebec as in Canada, Arab immigrants, like many other immigrant groups, have on average a much higher level of education

than the rest of the population. As a comparison, in Quebec only 19 percent of women and 20 percent of men hold a university degree among the adult population aged twenty-five and over.

CHAPTER THREE

1 In this book, notions of "visible minorities" and "racialized groups" are used interchangeably. While the former is commonly used by the general population, the latter tends to be preferred by social scientists, since it underlines the socially constructed character of the notion of "race," which by now has proven to be without any scientific value as far as biology and genetics are concerned. It also conveys that these so-called "races" are in fact ascribed to human populations on the basis of superficial phenotypic variations that are made socially relevant through categorization.

2 Cited in Antonius 2002, 259 (my emphasis).

3 *Ottawa Citizen*, 11 November 2000. Cited in Antonius 2002, 261.

4 Gil Courtemanche, *Le Devoir*, 30 July 2005, my translation.

5 Quebec turned out to be the province with the highest percentage of people (48 percent) wanting Muslim immigration to be reduced.

6 The above surveys provide a good overview of the extent of prejudicial representations of Arabs and Muslims among Canadians. For a critical account of prejudicial attitudes against Muslims and Arabs occurring more specifically in Canadian media, see Antonius (2002). Similarly, see McAndrew (1985, 2002) for more detailed case-study analyses of anti-Arab and anti-Muslim sentiments and attitudes in Quebec schools.

7 As Renaud et al. remark, racial discrimination cannot alone account for these variations. There may be other factors coming into play such as, most importantly, group-differentiated access to social and professional networks (Renaud 2003, 179).

8 These data were kindly provided to me by Quebec's Human Rights Commission in August 2005.

CHAPTER FOUR

1 Readers who wish to know exactly how this global index was measured and then converted into an ordinal variable should take a look at appendix A, section 1.

2 In Quebec, ethnic minorities tend to mobilize the "Quebecois" and "Canadian" categories, either cumulatively or separately, for purposes

of building cultural identity (Helly and Van Schendel 2001). Consequently, it was necessary to provide respondents with a choice of answers that would reflect the dual character of majority group identities in Quebec. However, to keep the choice of answers as short as possible, the words "or Québécois" were put in brackets following the "Canadian" category. One limitation, then, is that it becomes impossible to compare the relative weight of "Quebecois" and "Canadian" categories in one's identity structure. However, this is not overly problematic since this section's primary concern is to shed light on the "language" through which respondents construct their ethnic selves, rather than their sense of belonging to majority groups.

3 Thus, as previously reported, a poll commissioned in March 2003 by the Association for Canadian Studies from the Environics Research Group revealed that 30 percent of the 2,002 Canadians surveyed felt that Arabs project a negative image, while 33 percent held the same opinion about aboriginals, 13 percent about blacks, and 11 percent about Jews.

4 Note that these patterns are once again fully consistent with the findings yielded by the 1993 Ontario survey (cited in Hayani 1999).

5 The preference of Egyptian-origin respondents for a hyphenated (Arab-Canadian) identity is probably attributable to the fact that this group comprises a majority of Copts, who are likely to have spent the longest period of time in Canada since their parents typically migrated in the 1960s and early 1970s.

6 It is not surprising that French prevails over English in conversations with siblings, since the majority of respondents making up this sample were recruited in French-speaking cegeps.

7 "Ethnic music and programs" refers, in the questionnaire, to music and programs pertaining to the respondents' ethnic background.

8 Readers who wish to know exactly how this global index was measured and then converted into an ordinal variable should take a look at appendix A, section 2.

9 Interestingly, this informant used the word "inflicted" to refer to the values that her parents transmitted to her. While probably a coincidence, this choice of word could also be seen as a revealing slip.

CHAPTER FIVE

1 Readers who wish to know exactly how this index was measured and then converted into an ordinal variable should take a look at appendix A, section 3.

2 However, it must be stressed that, since ethnic and religious identity's respective strengths were measured using in part different indicators, the above results should be interpreted with caution. Ideally, comparing ethnic and religious identities would have required greater similarities between the two sets of items making up each scale. But ethnic and religious identities had to be quantified by means of indicators suited for the specific nature of each type of process. That being said, there are sufficient overlaps between the two scales to allow for comparisons between ethnic and religious identity's respective strengths.

3 Note that the coefficient measuring the strength of religious identity's subjective/cultural dimension was computed based on a single question with four categories. Therefore, it is perhaps not as accurate a measurement tool as the three other subvariables.

4 Readers who wish to know exactly how the parental religious identity index was measured and then converted into an ordinal variable should take a look at appendix A, section 4.

5 Note that the expression "sharing the same mentality" was also commonly used by participants to justify their preference for marrying an ethnic peer.

6 For one thing, it should be stressed that the smaller number of Muslims in the sample (88 Muslims versus 162 Christians) makes it risky to generalize these prayer frequency results to the whole population of Muslim youth of Arab origin attending cegep.

7 Details on how ethnic residential segregation was measured are provided in appendix B (see variable 64).

8 Although fasting is also a Christian practice, it clearly takes on greater symbolic value in the Muslim faith nowadays.

9 A meat is said to be "Halal" (literally "permissible") when the animal has been slaughtered in conformity with Koranic regulations.

10 This pattern remains unchanged whether one is Christian or Muslim.

11 However, among Christian Arabs, feelings of belonging to the religious community is multi-layered since there are multiple Middle-Eastern Churches that each gives rise to different religious allegiances and rites. This aspect was not fully explored in the present research, and certainly calls for further investigation.

CHAPTER SIX

1 Readers who wish to know exactly how this index was measured and then converted into an ordinal variable should take a look at appendix A, section 5.

2 Indeed, it must be recalled that a majority of them oppose premarital sex for girls (at 66 percent), while a majority of them accept premarital sex for boys (at 55 percent).

CHAPTER SEVEN

1 As a reminder, it was shown in chapter 4 that both Muslim and Christian respondents identify more with the Arab label – taken alone or in a hyphenated form – than with their national community.

2 Note that this amalgamation is paradoxical in a Canadian context where 51 percent of the Arab-origin community are Christians (Statistics Canada 2001, *Census Data*).

3 Informant O, a Canadian-born Christian female of Lebanese origin, also endorses what she perceives to be an accurate stereotype of Arabs. She describes this stereotype as follows: "The image of the typical Lebanese girls and guys who speak on their cellphones, check out every girl from head to toe, with this blue necklace that every Lebanese guy wears."

4 Had these informants been interviewed after September 11, 2001, the Muslims among them would have probably emphasized even more the equation "terrorist=Arab=Muslim."

5 It should be noted that discriminatory actions can take either a direct, indirect, or systemic form, but it is beyond the scope of this analysis to expound on the differences between these types (for more details on these conceptual distinctions, see Chicha-Pontbriand 1989).

6 Note that, according to Hayani, the question used in the Minority Report to measure self-reported discrimination is the same as the one used in the Ontario study.

7 See chapter 3 for an overview of various nationwide surveys that have teased out some of the negative representations of Arabs and Muslims by Canadians.

CONCLUSION

1 Once again, ethnic tensions in France and Great Britain are also aggravated by the scars left by colonialism in the memories of a great many ethnic minorities.

2 It should be noted that we found partial evidence to support this hypothesis: only a small minority of respondents chose the "Canadian" or "Quebecois" categories – taken alone or in a hyphenated form – as a meaningful source of identification. But of course, more research is needed to address this question, which was beyond the scope of the present investigation.

Bibliography

Abraham, Nabeel. 1989. "Arab-American Marginality: Mythos and
Praxis." In *Arab-Americans: Continuity and Changes*, edited by B.
Abu-Laban and M.W. Suleiman, 17–45. Belmont: Association of Arab
American University Graduates.

Abraham, Sameer Y. 1983. "Detroit's Arab-American Community: A
Survey of Diversity and Commonality." In *Arabs in the New World.
Studies on Arab-American Communities*, edited by S.Y. Abraham and
N. Abraham, 84–109. Detroit, MI: Wayne State University, Center for
Urban Studies.

Abu-Laban, Baha. 1980. *An Olive Branch on the Family Tree. The Arabs
in Canada*. Toronto: McClelland and Stewart.

– 1983. "The Muslim Canadian Community: The Need for a New
Survival Strategy." In *The Muslim Community in North America*,
edited by E.H. Waugh, B. Abu-Laban, and R.B. Qureshi, 75–93.
Edmonton: University of Alberta Press.

– 1988. "Arab-Canadians and the Arab-Israeli Conflict." *Arab Studies
Quarterly*, no. 10: 104–26.

– (1995). "Arabs." In *Encyclopedia of Canada's Peoples*, edited by P.R.
Magocsi, 202–12. Toronto: University of Toronto Press, published for
the Multicultural History Society of Ontario.

Abu-Laban, Baha, and Sharon M. Abu-Laban. 1999. "Arab-Canadian
Youth in Immigrant Family Life." In *Arabs in America. Building a
New Future*, edited by M.W. Suleiman, 140–53. Philadelphia, Temple
University Press.

Abu-Laban, Sharon M. 1989. "The Existence of Cohorts: Identity and
Adaptation among Arab-American Muslims." In *Arab-Americans:*

Continuity and Changes, edited by B. Abu-Laban and M.W. Suleiman, 45–65. Belmont: Association of Arab-American University Graduates.

Abu-Laban, Sharon M., and Baha Abu-Laban. 1999. "Teens Between: The Public Spheres of Arab Canadian Adolescents." In *Arabs in America. Building a New Future*, edited by M.W. Suleiman, 113–28. Philadelphia: Temple University Press.

Abu Odeh, Lama. 1993. "Post-Colonial Feminism and the Veil: Thinking the Difference." *Feminist Review*, no. 43 (Spring): 26–37.

Afshar, Haleh. 1993. "Schools and Muslim Girls: Gateway to a Prosperous Future or Quagmire of Racism? Some Experiences from West Yorkshire." In *Religion, Ethnicity: Minorities and Social Change in the Metropolis*, edited by R. Barot, 56–67. Kampen: Kok Pharos.

Ahmed, Leila. 1992. *Women and Gender in Islam. Historical Roots of a Modern Debate*. New Haven, CT: Yale University Press.

Ajami, Fouad. 1987. "The End of Pan-Arabism." In *Pan-Arabism and Arab Nationalism. The Continuing Debate*, edited by T.E. Farah, 96–115. Boulder, CO: Westview Press.

Ajrouch, Kristine J. 1999. "Family and Ethnic Identity in an Arab-American Community." In *Arabs in America. Building a New Future*, edited by M.B. Suleiman, 129–39. Philadelphia: Temple University Press.

– 2004. "Gender, Race, and Symbolic Boundaries: Contested Spaces of Identity among Arab American Adolescents." *Sociological Perspectives* 47, no. 4: 371–91.

Alba, Richard. 1990. *Ethnic Identity: The Transformation of White America*. New Haven, CT: Yale University Press.

Anctil, Pierre. 1984. "Double majorité et multiplicité ethnique à Montréal." *Recherches sociographiques* 25, no. 3 (September): 441–56.

Antonius, Rachad. 2002. "Un racisme respectable." In *Les relations ethniques en question: ce qui a changé depuis le 11 septembre 2001*, edited by J. Renaud, L. Pietrantonio, and G. Bourgeault, 253–71. Montreal: Presses de l'Université de Montréal.

Antonius, Rachad, and Naima Bendris. 1998. "Des représentations sociales aux transactions interculturelles: l'image des femmes arabes et son impact dans les situations de conflit personnel." In *Champ multiculturel, transactions interculturelles : des analyses, des théories, des pratiques*, edited by K. Fall and L. Turgeon, 215–39. Paris: L'Harmattan.

Assad, Fouad. 1995. "Egyptians." In *Encyclopedia of Canada's Peoples*, edited by P.R. Magocsi, 453–62. Toronto: University of Toronto Press. Published for the Multicultural History Society of Ontario.

Baali, Fuad. 2004. *Arab Unity and Disunity. Past and Present.* Lanham, MD: University Press of America.

Bannerji, Himani. 2000. "The Paradox of Diversity: The Construction of a Multicultural Canada and Women of Colour." *Women's Studies International Forum,* 23, no. 5: 537–60.

Barazangi, Nimat Hafez. 1989. "Arab Muslim Identity Transmission: Parents and Youth." In *Arab-Americans: Continuity and Changes,* edited by B. Abu-Laban and M.W. Suleiman, 65–70. Belmont: Association of Arab-American University Graduates.

Barth, Fredrick. 1969. "Introduction." In *Ethnic Groups and Boundaries: The Social Organization of Cultural Differences,* edited by Frederick Barth, 9–39. Boston: Little Brown.

Bastenier, Albert. 1998. "L'incidence du facteur religieux dans la conscience ethnique des immigres marocains en Belgique." *Social Compass* 45, no. 2: 195–218.

Baumann, Gerd. 1996. *Contesting Culture. Discourses of Identity in Multi-Ethnic London.* Cambridge: Cambridge University Press.

– 1997. "Dominant and Demotic Discourses of Culture: Their Relevance to Multiethnic Alliances." In *Debating Cultural Hybridity. Multicultural Identities and the Politics of Anti-Racism,* edited by P. Werbner and T. Modood, 209–22. London: Zed Books.

Begag, Azouz. 1990. "The Beurs: Children of North African Immigrants in France – The Issue of Integration." *Journal of Ethnic Studies,* 18, no. 1: 1–13.

Berger, Peter. 1967. *The Sacred Canopy. Elements of a Sociological Theory of Religion.* Garden City, NY: Doubleday.

Bhabha, Homi. 1990. "The Third Space. Interview with Homi Bhabha." In *Community, Culture, Difference,* edited by J. Rutherford, 207–21. London: Lawrence and Wishart.

Bibby, Reginald. 1987. *Fragmented Gods: The Poverty and Potential of Religion in Canada.* Toronto: Stoddart.

– 2002. *Restless Gods. The Renaissance of Religion in Canada.* Toronto: Stoddart.

Blancel, Nicolas. 1997. "De l'indigène à l'immigré: images, messages et réalités." *Hommes et Migrations,* no. 1,207 (May-June): 6–30.

Bloul, Rachel. 1998. "From Moral Protest to Religious Politics: Ethical Demands and Beur Political Action in France." *The Australian Journal of Anthropology,* 9, no. 1: 11–20.

Bramadat, Paul. 2005. "Beyond Christian Canada: Religion and Ethnicity in a Multicultural Society." In *Religion and Ethnicity in*

Canada, edited by P. Bramadat and D. Seljak, 1–30. Toronto: Pearson Longman.

Brass, Paul R. 1991. *Ethnicity and Nationalism: Theory and Comparison*. New Delhi: Sage Publications.

Breton, Raymond. 1964. "Institutional Completeness of Ethnic Communities and the Personal Relations of Immigrants." *American Journal of Sociology*, 70, no. 2: 193–205.

– 1983. "West Indian, Chinese and European Ethnic Groups in Toronto: Perceptions of Problems and Resources." In *Two Nations, Many Cultures*, edited by J.L. Elliott, 425–43. 2nd ed. Scarborough: Prentice-Hall.

Breton, Raymond, Wsevolod W. Isajiw, et al. 1990. *Ethnic Identity and Equality. Varieties of Experience in a Canadian City*, Toronto: University of Toronto Press.

Brouwer, Lenie. 1998. "Good Girls, Bad Girls: Moroccan and Turkish Runaways in the Netherlands." In *Muslim European Youth. Reproducing Ethnicity, Religion, Culture*, edited by S. Vertovec and A. Rogers, 141–67. Aldershot: Ashgate.

Caglar, Ayse. 1997. "Hyphenated Identities and the Limits of Culture." In *The Politics of Multiculturalism in the New Europe*, edited by P. Werbner and T. Modood, 169–83. London: Zed Books.

Calhoun, Craig. 1997. *Nationalism*. Minneapolis: University of Minnesota Press.

Casanova, José. 1994. *Public Religions in the Modern World*. Chicago: University of Chicago Press.

– 2001. "Civil Society and Religion: Retrospective Reflections on Catholicism and Prospective Reflections on Islam." *Social Research*, 68, no. 4 (Winter): 1041–80.

Cesari, Jocelyne. 1998. "Islam in France: Social Challenge or Challenge to Secularism." In *Muslim European Youth. Reproducing Ethnicity, Religion, Culture*, edited by S. Vertovec and A. Rogers, 25–39. Aldershot: Ashgate.

– (2002). "Islam in France: The Shaping of a Religious Minority." In *Muslims in the West. From Sojourners to Citizens*, edited by Y.H. Haddad, 36–52. New York: Oxford University Press.

Chicha-Pontbriand, Marie-Thérèse. 1989. *Discrimination systémique, fondement et méthodologie des programmes d'accès à l'égalité*. Montreal: Les éditions Yvon Blais.

Cohen, Steven M. 2003. "Jewish Identity Research in the United States: Ruminations on Concepts and Findings." In *Continuity, Commitment*, *and Survival. Jewish Communities in the Diaspora*, edited by S. Encel and L. Stein, 1–23. Westport, CT: Praeger.

Das Gupta, Monisha. 1997. "What Is Indian about You? A Gendered, Transnational Approach to Ethnicity." *Gender and Society* 11, no. 5 (October): 572–96.

Dekmejian, R. Hrair. 1995. *Islam in Revolution. Fundamentalism in the Arab World*. 2d ed. Syracuse, NY: Syracuse University Press.

Dobbelaere, Karel. 1999. "Towards an Integrated Perspective of the Processes Related to the Descriptive Concept of Secularization." *Sociology of Religion* 60 no. 3 (Fall): 229–47.

Dubet, François, et Didier Lapeyronnie. 1992. *Les quartiers d'exil*. Paris: La Découverte.

Duprez, Dominique. 1997. "Entre discrimination et désaffiliation. L'expérience des jeunes issus de l'immigration maghrébine." *Les Annales de la Recherche Urbaine*, no. 76: 79–88.

Eid, Paul. 2002. "Postcolonial Identity and Gender in the Arab World: The Case of the Hijab." *Atlantis: A Women's Studies Journal* 26, no. 2 (Spring): 39–51.

Environics Research Group. 2006. *Canadians' Views on the Arab Muslim Community Are Positive: Trudeau Foundation Poll*. Media report on a poll commissioned by the Pierre Elliot Trudeau Foundation. Online: http://erg.environics.net/media_room/default.asp?aID=618. Accessed on December 22nd, 2006.

Espiritu, Yen Le. 1992. *Asian-American Panethnicity: Bridging Institutions and Identities*. Philadelphia: Temple University.

Esposito, John. 2001. *Women in Muslim Family Law*. 2d ed. Syracuse, NY: Syracuse University Press.

Esposito, John, and François Burgat, eds. 2003. *Modernizing Islam: Religion in the Public Sphere in the Middle-East and Europe*. New Brunswick, NJ: Rutgers University Press.

Farah, Tawfik, ed. 1987. *Pan-Arabism and Arab Nationalism. The Continuing Debate*. Boulder: Westview Press.

Gans, Herbert. 1994. "Symbolic Ethnicity and Symbolic Religiosity: Towards a Comparison of Ethnic and Religious Acculturation." *Ethnic and Racial Studies* 17, no. 4 (October): 577–92.

Gelvin, James. 1999. "Modernity and Its Discontents: On the Durability of Arab Nationalism in the Arab Middle-East." *Nations and Nationalism* 5, no. 1: 71–89.

Glazer, Nathan, and Daniel P. Moynihan. 1971. *Beyond the Melting Pot: The Negroes, Puerto Ricans, Jews, Italians, and Irish of New York City*, Cambridge, MA: MIT Press.

Glock, Charles Y. 1973. *Religion in Sociological Perspective*. Belmont: Wadsworth Publishing Company.

Gordon, Milton M. 1964. *Assimilation in American Life: The Role of Race, Religion and National Origins*. New York: Oxford University Press.

Gross, Joan, David McMurray, and Ted Swedenburg. 1997. "Rai, Rap, and Ramadan Nights: Franco-Maghribi Cultural Identities." In *Political Islam*, edited by J. Beinin and J. Stork, 259–69. Los Angeles: University of California Press.

Guillaumin, Colette. 1972. *L'idéologie raciste: génèse et langage actuel*. Paris: Mouton.

Haddad, Yvonne Y. 1983. "Arab Muslims and Islamic Institutions in America: Adaptation and Reform." In *Arabs in the New World. Studies on Arab-American Communities*, edited by S.Y. Abraham and N. Abraham, 64–81. Detroit: Wayne State University, Center for Urban Studies.

– 1994. "Maintaining the Faith of the Fathers: Dilemmas in the Religious Identity in the Christian, and Muslim Arab-American Communities." In *The Development of Arab-American Identity*, edited by E. McCarus, 63–82. Chicago: University of Michigan Press.

Hall, Stuart. 1990. "Cultural Identity and Diaspora." In *Identity: Community, Culture, Difference*, edited by J. Rutherford, 222–37. London: Lawrence and Wishart.

– 1991. "Old and New Identities, Old and New Ethnicities." In *Culture, Globalization and the World System. Contemporary Conditions for the Representations of Identity*, edited by Anthony King, 41–68. New York: SUNY.

Hayani, Ibrahim. 1999. "Arabs in Canada: Assimilation or Integration." In *Arabs in America. Building a New Future*, edited by M.W. Suleiman, 284–303. Philadelphia: Temple University Press.

Helly, Denise. 2004. "Are Muslims Discriminated against in Canada since September 2001?" *Canadian Ethnic Studies* 36, no. 1: 24–48.

Helly, Denise, and Nicolas Van Schendel. 2001. *Appartenir au Québec. Citoyenneté, nation et société civile. Enquête à Montréal, 1995*. Quebec: Les Éditions de l'IQRC.

Hobsbawm, Eric. 1983. "Introduction: Inventing Tradition." In *The Invention of Tradition*, edited by E. Hobsbawm and T. Ranger, 1–14. Cambridge: Cambridge University Press.

Hoodfar, Homa. 1993. "The Veil in Their Minds and on Our Heads: The Persistence of Colonial Images of Muslim Women." *Resources for Feminist Research (RFR)* 22, nos.3–4: 3–11.

Huntington, Samuel. 1996. *The Clash of Civilizations and the Remaking of World Order*. New York: Simon and Schuster.

Isajiw, Wsevolod W. 1974. "Definitions of Ethnicity." *Ethnicity* 1, no. 2: 111–24.

– 1977. "Olga in Wonderland: Ethnicity in Technological Society." *Canadian Ethnic Studies* 9: 77–85.

– 1990. "Ethnic Identity Retention." In *Ethnic Identity and Equality. Varieties of Experience in a Canadian City*, edited by R. Breton et al., 34–91. Toronto: University of Toronto Press.

– 1997. "On the Concept of Social Incorporation." In *Multiculturalism in North America and Europe: Comparative Perspectives on Interethnic Relations*, edited by W.W. Isajiw, 79–103. Toronto: Canadian Scholar's Press.

– 1999. *Understanding Diversity: Ethnicity and Race in the Canadian Context*. Toronto: Thompson Educational Publishing.

Isajiw, Wsevolod W., and Tomoke Makabe. 1982. *Socialization as a Factor in Ethnic Identity Retention*. Toronto: University of Toronto, Centre for Urban and Community Studies. Research paper no. 134.

Isajiw, Wsevolod W., Aysian Sev'er, and Leo Driedger. 1993. "Ethnic Identity and Social Mobility: A Test of the 'Drawback Model.'" *Canadian Journal of Sociology* 18, no. 2: 177–96.

Jabbra, Nancy W., and Joseph G. Jabbra. 1995. "Lebanese." In *Encyclopedia of Canada's Peoples*, edited by P.R. Magocsi, 919–29. Toronto: University of Toronto Press. Published for the Multicultural History Society of Ontario.

Jazouli, Adil. 1995. "Les jeunes 'Beurs' dans la société française." *Migrations et société* 7, no. 38: 6–24.

Jedwab, Jack. 1999. *L'appartenance ethnique et les langues patrimoniales au Canada*. Montreal: Centre de langues patrimoniales et Éditions Images.

– 2002. *The Impact of September 11th in Canada*. Analysis of a poll commissioned by the Association for Canadian Studies from Environics Research Group/Focus Canada. Online: http://www.acs-aec.ca/Polls/Poll13.pdf. Accessed on December 22nd, 2006.

– 2003. *The War and Concerns Over Tolerance in Canada: Is it a Problem?* Analysis of a poll commissioned by the Association for Canadian Studies from Environics Research Group/Focus Canada. Online: http://www.acs-aec.ca/Polls/Poll27.pdf. Checked on December 22nd, 2006.

Jenkins, Richard. 1997. *Rethinking Ethnicity: Arguments and Explorations*. London: Sage Publications.

Juteau, Danielle. 1997. "Ethnic Communalizations in the World System: Theorizing from the Margins." In *Multiculturalism in North America and Europe. Comparative Perspectives on Interethnic Relations and Social Incorporation*, edited by W.W. Isajiw, 187–210. Toronto: Canadian Scholars Press.

– 1999a. "L'ethnicité et la modernité." In D. Juteau. 1999. *L'ethnicité et ses frontières*, 185–97. Montreal: Presses de l'Université de Montréal.

– 1999b. "Les communalisations ethniques dans le système-monde." In D. Juteau. 1999. *L'ethnicité et ses frontières*, 151–76. Montreal: Presses de l'Université de Montréal.

Kalbach, Warren E. 1990. "Ethnic Residential Segregation and Its Significance for the Individual in an Urban Setting." In *Ethnic Identity and Equality: Varieties of Experience in a Canadian City*, edited by R. Breton et al., 34–91. Toronto: University of Toronto Press.

Karim, Karim H. 2003. *Islamic Peril. Media and Global Violence*. Montreal: Black Rose Books.

Kayal, Philip M. 1983. "Arab Christians in the United States." In *Arabs in the New World. Studies on Arab-American Communities*, edited by S.Y. Abraham and N. Abraham, 44–64. Detroit: Wayne State University, Center for Urban Studies.

Keck, Lois T. 1989. "Egyptian Americans in the Washington, DC Area." In *Arab-Americans: Continuity and Changes*, edited by B. Abu-Laban and M.W. Suleiman, 103–27. Belmont: Association of Arab-American University Graduates.

Khosrokhavar, Farhad. 2000. "L'Islam des jeunes Musulmans. Sur l'exclusion dans la société française contemporaine." In *Revue de philosophie et de sciences sociales*, no. 1, edited by W. Kymlicka and S. Mesure, 81–99.

Kucukcan, Talip. 1998. "Continuity and Change: Young Turks in London." In *Muslim European Youth. Reproducing Ethnicity, Religion, Culture*, edited by S. Vertovec and A. Rogers, 103–31. Aldershot: Ashgate.

Kuusela, K. 1993. "A Mosque of Our Own? Turkish Immigrants in Gothenburg Facing the Effects of a Changing World." In *Religion, Ethnicity: Minorities and Social Change in the Metropolis*, edited by R. Barot, 43–55. Kampen: Kok Pharos.

Kymlicka, Will. 1998. *Finding Our Way: Rethinking Ethnocultural Relations in Canada*. Toronto: Oxford University Press.

Labelle, Micheline. 2004. "The 'Language of Race.' Identity Options and 'Belonging' in the Quebec Context." In *Social Inequalities in Comparative Perspective*, edited by F. Devine and M. Waters, 39–65. Malden (MA): Blackwell Publishing.

Lacoste-Dujardin, C. 1994. "Transmission religieuse et migration: L'Islam identitaire des filles de Maghrebins immigrés en France." *Social Compass*, 41, no. 1: 163–70.

Lambert, Yves. 1999. "Secularization or New Religious Paradigms?" *Sociology of Religion* 60, no. 3: 303–33.

Lans, Jan, and Margo Rooijackers. 1994. "Attitudes of Second-Generation Immigrants towards Collective Religious Representations of Their Parental Culture." In *Belief and Unbelief. Psychological Perspectives*, edited by D. Hutsebaut and J. Corveleyn, 111–33. Amsterdam: Rodopi.

Laperrière, Anne, et al. 1994. "Mutual Perceptions and Interethnic Strategies among French, Italian, and Haitian Adolescents of a Multiethnic School in Montreal." *Journal of Adolescent Research* 9, no. 2 (April): 193–217.

Lapeyronnie, Didier. 1987. "Assimilation chez les jeunes de la seconde generation de l'immigration maghrébine." In *Revue française de sociologie* 28: 287–318.

Leveau, Rémi. 1997. "The Political Culture of the Beurs." In *Islam in Europe. The Politics of Religion and Community*, edited by S. Vertovec and C. Peach, 147–56. London: MacMillan Press.

Lian, Jason Z., and David Matthews. 1998. "Does the Vertical Mosaic Still Exist? Ethnicity and Income in Canada, 1991." *Canadian Review of Sociology and Anthropology* 35, no. 4 (November): 461–81.

Loomba, Ania. 1998. *Colonialism-Postcolonialism*. London: Routledge.

Lorcerie, Françoise. 1997. "La catégorisation sociale de l'immigration est-elle coloniale?" *Hommes et Migrations*, no. 1,207 (May-June):78–86.

Luckmann, Thomas. 1967. *The Invisible Religion. The Problem of Religion in Modern Society*. New York: Macmillan.

McAndrew, Marie. 1985. "Le traitement du monde arabe dans les manuels scolaires québécois: dernier racisme légitime?" *Near East Foundation of Canada, Newsletter* 1, no. 3 (November).

– (2002). "Le remplacement du marqueur linguistique par le marqueur religieux en milieu scolaire." In *Les relations ethniques en question: ce qui a changé depuis le 11 septembre 2001*, edited by J. Renaud, L. Pietrantonio, and G. Bourgeault, 131–48. Montreal: Presses de l'Université de Montréal.

McAndrew, Marie, Calvin Veltman, et al. 1999. *Concentration ethnique et usages linguistiques en milieu scolaire*. Montreal: Immigration et Métropoles.

McClintock, Anne. 1997. "No Longer in a Future Heaven: Gender, Race, and Nationalism." In *Dangerous Liaisons. Gender, Nation, and Postcolonial Perspectives*, edited by A. McClintock, A. Mufti, and E. Shohat, 89–113. Minneapolis: University of Minnesota Press.

McDonough, Sheila, and Homa Hoodfar. 2005. "Muslims in Canada: From Ethnic Groups to Religious Community." In *Religion and Ethnicity in Canada*, edited by P. Bramadat and D. Seljak, 133–53. Toronto: Pearson Longman.

Meintel, Deirdre. 1993. "Transnationalité et transethnicité chez des jeunes issus de milieux immigrés à Montréal." *Revue Européenne des Migrations internationales* 9, no. 3: 63–79.

– 1998. "Les comportements linguistiques et la nouvelle pluriethnicité montréalaise." *Études Canadiennes* 45: 83–93.

Mellah, Fawzi. 1985. *De l'unité arabe. Essai d'interprétation critique*. Paris: L'Harmattan.

Melluci, Alberto. 1997. "Identity and Difference in a Globalized World." In *Debating Cultural Hybridity. Multicultural Identities and the Politics of Anti-Racism*, edited by P. Werbner and T. Modood, 61–70. London: Zed Books.

Morck, Yvonne. 1998. "Gender and Generation: Young Muslims in Copenhagen." In *Muslim European Youth. Reproducing Ethnicity, Religion, Culture*, edited by S. Vertovec and A. Rogers, 133–45. Aldershot: Ashgate.

Naff, Alexa. 1983. "Arabs in America: A Historical Overview." In *Arabs in the New World. Studies on Arab-American Communities*, edited by S.Y. Abraham and N. Abraham, 8–30. Detroit, Wayne State University, Center for Urban Studies.

Nagel, Joane. 1994. "Constructing Ethnicity: Creating and Recreating Ethnic Identity and Culture." *Social Problems* 41, no. 1 (February): 152–76.

– (1998). "Masculinity and Nationalism: Gender and Sexuality in the Making of Nations." *Ethnic and Racial Studies* 21, no. 2 (March): 242–69.

Nijsten, Cécile. 1996. "Living as a Muslim in a Migration Country: Moroccan Youngsters in the Netherlands." In *Political Participation and Identities of Muslims in Non-Muslim States*, edited by W.A.R. Shadid and P.S. Van Koningsveld, 160–73. Kampen: Kok Pharos.

Okamura, Jonathan Y. 1981. "Situational Ethnicity." *Ethnic and Racial Studies* 4, no. 4 (October): 452–65.

Portes, Alejandro, and Min Zhou. 1993. "The New Second Generation: Segmented Assimilation and Its Variants." *Annals of the American Academy of Political and Social Science* 530 (November): 74–97.

Portes, Alejandro, and Dag MacLeod. 1996. "What Shall I Call Myself? Hispanic Identity Formation in the Second Generation." *Ethnic and Racial Studies* 19, no. 3 (July): 523–47.

Portes, Alejandro, and Ruben Rumbaut. 2001. *Legacies: The Story of the Immigrant Second Generation*. Berkeley and Los Angeles: University of California Press.

Quebec. Human Rights Commission. 1988. *Minorités visibles et ethniques. Bilan de recherche sur la situation des minorités visibles et ethniques dans le logement et pistes d'intervention*. Research conducted by Muriel Garon, Montreal.

Raissiguier, Catherine. 1995. "The Construction of Marginal Identities. Working-Class Girls of Algerian Descent in a French School." In *Feminism, Postmodernism, and Development*, edited by M.H. Marchand and J.L. Parpart, 79–91. London: Routledge.

Raouf, Wafik. 1984. *Nouveau regard sur le nationalisme arabe Bat'h et Nassérisme*. Paris: L'Harmattan.

Read, Jen'nan Ghazal. 2003. "The Sources of Gender Role Attitudes among Christian and Muslim Arab-American Women." *Sociology of Religion* 64: 207–23.

Reitz, Jeffrey G. 1988. "Less Racial Discrimination in Canada, or Simply Less Racial Conflict? Implications of Comparisons with Britain." *Canadian Public Policy* 14, no. 4: 424–41.

Reitz, Jeffrey G., and Raymond Breton. 1994. *The Illusion of Difference: Realities of Ethnicity in Canada and the United States*. Toronto: C.D. Howe Institute.

Renaud, Jean, Victor Piché, and Jean-François Godin. 2003. "L'origine nationale et l'insertion économique des immigrants au cours de leurs dix premières années." *Sociologie et sociétés* 35, no. 1: 165–84.

Rooijackers, Margo. 1992. "Religious Identity, Integration, and Subjective Well-being among Young Turkish Muslims." In *Islam in Dutch Society*, edited by W.A.R. Shadid and P.S. Van Koningsveld, 66–75. Kampen: Kok Pharos.

– (1994). "Ethnic Identity and Islam. The Results of an Empirical Study among Young Turkish Immigrants in the Netherlands." In *Belief and*

Unbelief. Psychological Perspectives, edited by D. Hutsebaut and
J. Corveleyn, 99–107. Amsterdam: Rodopi.

Rowatt, Wade C., Franklin M. Lewis, and Marla Cotton. 2005.
"Patterns and Personality Correlates of Implicit and Explicit Attitudes
toward Christians and Muslims." *Journal for the Scientific Study of
Religion* 44 no. 1: 29–43.

Roy, Olivier. 1994. "Islam in France: Religion, Ethnic Community, or
Social Ghetto?" In *Muslims in Europe*, edited by B. Lewis and
D. Schnapper, 54–66. London: Pinter Publishers.

Rutherford, Jonathan. 1990. "A Place Called Home: Identity and the
Politics of Cultural Differences." In *Identity: Community, Culture,
Difference*, edited by J. Rutherford, 9–27. London: Lawrence and
Wishart.

Said, Edward. 1979. *Orientalism*, New York: Vintage Books.

– 2000. "America's Last Taboo." *New Left Review* 11, no. 6
(November/December): 45–53.

Santelli, Emmanuelle. Forthcoming. "Modalités d'insertion socio-
professionnelle des jeunes Français d'origine maghrébine d'un quartier
de l'agglomération lyonnaise." In *L'expérience sociale des jeunes de
"deuxième génération". Une comparaison France Québec*, edited by
M. Potvin, P. Eid, and N. Venel. Montreal: Athéna Éditions.

Schnapper, Dominique. 1991. *La France de l'integration: sociologie de la
nation en 1990*. Paris: Gallimand.

Schoenfeld, Stuart. 2001. "The Religious Mosaic: A Study in Diversity."
In *From Immigration to Integration. The Canadian Jewish Experience:
A Millennium Edition*, edited by R. Klein and F. Dimant, 165–82.
Toronto: Institute for International Affairs, B'nai Brith Canada.

Shaheen, Jack. 2001. *Reel Bad Arabs: How Hollywood Vilifies a People*.
New York: Olive Branch Press.

– (2003). "Reel Bad Arabs: How Hollywood Vilifies a People." *Annals
of the American Academy* 588 (July): 171–93.

Sharot, Stephen (1997). "A Critical Comment on Gans' 'Symbolic
Ethnicity' and 'Symbolic Religiosity' and Other Formulations of
Ethnicity and Religion regarding American Jews." *Contemporary Jews*
18: 25–43.

Shukrallah, Hala. 1994. "The Impact of the Islamic Movement in
Egypt." *Feminist Review* 47 (Summer): 15–32.

Smith, Anthony D. 1994. "Gastronomy or Geology? The Role of
Nationalism in the Reconstruction of Nations." *Nations and
Nationalism* 1, no. 1 (1994): 3–23.

Spivak, G. Chakravorty. 1988. "Can the Subaltern Speak?" In *Marxism and the Interpretation of Culture*, edited by C. Nelson and L. Grossberg, 271–313. Chicago: University of Illinois Press.

Stark, Rodney. 1963. "On the Incompatibility of Religion and Science: A Survey of American Graduate Students." *Journal for the Scientific Study of Religion* 3: 3–20.

– 1999. "Secularization, R.I.P." *Sociology of Religion* 60, no. 3 (Fall): 249–73.

Statistics Canada. 1991. *Census Data*. Online: www.statcan.ca

– 2001. *Census Data*. Online: www.statcan.ca

– 2003. *Ethnic Diversity Survey: Portrait of a Multicultural Society*. Ottawa: Ministry of Industry.

Suleiman, Michael W. 1988. *The Arabs in the Mind of America*. Brattleboro: Amana Books.

– 1999. "Introduction: The Arab Immigrant Experience." In *Arabs in America. Building a New Future*, edited by M.W. Suleiman, 1–21. Philadelphia: Temple University Press.

Suleiman, Michael W., and Baha Abu-Laban. 1989. "Introduction." In *Arab-Americans: Continuity and Changes*, edited by M.W. Suleiman and B. Abu-Laban, 1–17. Belmont: Association of Arab-American University Graduates.

Swatos Jr, William H., and Kevin J. Christiano. 1999. "Introduction – Secularization Theory: The Course of a Concept." *Sociology of Religion* 60, no. 3 (Fall): 209–28.

Taguieff, Pierre-André. 1997. "Universalisme et racisme évolutionniste: le dilemme républicain de la France coloniale." *Hommes et Migrations*, no. 1,207 (May-June): 90–7.

Taylor, Charles. 1994. *Multiculturalism. Examining the Politics of Recognition*. Princeton: Princeton University Press.

Venel, Nancy. 2004. *Musulmans et citoyens*. Paris: Presses universitaires de France.

Vertovec, Steve. 1998. "Young Muslims in Keighley, West Yorkshire: Cultural Identity, Context, and Community." In *Muslim European Youth. Reproducing Ethnicity, Religion, Culture*, edited by S. Vertovec and A. Rogers, 87–103. Aldershot: Ashgate.

Vertovec, Steve, and Alisdair Rogers. 1998. "Introduction." In *Muslim European Youth. Reproducing Ethnicity, Religion, Culture*, edited by S. Vertovec and A. Rogers, 1–24. Aldershot: Ashgate.

Viprey, Mouna. 2002. *L'insertion des jeunes d'origine étrangère*. Paris, Conseil Économique et Social.

Voyé, Liliane. 1999. "Secularization in a Context of Advanced Modernity." *Sociology of Religion* 60, no. 3 (Fall): 275–88.

Wannas-Jones, Jenny. 2003. "Globalization and the Reconciliation of Dissonant Hybrid Identities: A Case Study of Arab-Canadian Youths." Thesis submitted to the Department of Educational Policy Studies, University of Alberta, Edmonton.

Waters, Mary C. 1990. *Ethnic Options. Choosing Identities in America.* Berkeley: University of California Press.

– 1996. "Ethnic Options: For Whites Only?" In *Origins and Destinies: Immigration, Race, and Ethnicity in America*, edited by S. Pedraza and R. Rumbaut, 444–54. Belmont: Wadsworth.

– 2004. "Race, Ethnicity and Immigration in the United States." In *Social Inequalities in Comparative Perspective*, edited by F. Devine and M. Waters, 20–39. Malden, MA: Blackwell Publishing.

Weinfeld, Morton. 2001. *Like Everyone Else ... But Different. The Paradoxical Success of Canadians Jews.* Toronto: McClelland and Stewart.

Werbner, Pina. 1997. "Introduction: The Dialectics of Cultural Hybridity." In *Debating Cultural Hybridity. Multicultural Identities and the Politics of Anti-Racism*, edited by P. Werbner and T. Modood, 1–26. London: Zed Books.

Wilpert, Czarina. 1989. "Ethnic and Cultural Identity. Ethnicity and the Second Generation in the Context of European Migration." In *New Identities in Europe. Immigrant Ancestry and the Identity of Youth*, edited by K. Liebkind, 6–24. Aldershot: Gower.

Yalcin-Heckmann, Lale. 1998. "Growing Up as a Muslim in Germany: Religious Socialization among Turkish Migrant Families." In *Muslim European Youth. Reproducing Ethnicity, Religion, Culture*, edited by S. Vertovec and A. Rogers, 167–93. Aldershot: Ashgate.

Yuval-Davis, Nira. 1997. *Gender and Nation.* London: Sage Publications.

Index